DREAMS
Night Language of the Soul

DREAMS

Night Language of the Soul

Phoebe McDonald

TOPAZ PRESS
Baton Rouge, Louisiana, and Laguna Beach, California

Designer: Joanna Hill
Typeface: Linotron Galliard
Typesetter: G&S Typesetters, Inc.
Printer and binder: Thomson-Shore

LIBRARY OF CONGRESS CATALOGING IN PUBLICATION DATA

McDonald, Phoebe
  Dreams: Night Language of the Soul

  Bibliography: p.
  Includes index.
  1. Dreams. I. Title.
BF1078.M367 1985   154.6′3   84-62137
ISBN 0-914255-01-0

Second printing, December 1985

For further information, please contact:
  Topaz Press
  3855 Partridge Lane
  Baton Rouge, LA 70809
  or
  Phoebe McDonald
  353 Aster
  Laguna Beach, California 92651

I wish to express my gratitude to

My dear friend *Frances Tolchin*, whose enthusiasm and encouragement helped me start this book, and to

My dear niece *Joanna Hill*, whose guidance and expertise helped me finish it.

Contents

1   Introduction   1

2   The Interpretation of Dreams   15

3   Examples of Dream Interpretation   26

4   Mechanisms of the Unconscious   38

5   Aspects of the Inner Self   49

6   People in Dreams   80

7   The Body in Dreams   95

8   Sexual Symbols, Male and Female   117

9   Birth and Death Symbols   144

10   Emotional Growth Dreams   154

11   Animals in Dreams   164

12   Structures, Places, and Natural Elements in Dreams   182

13   Children's Dreams   198

14   Archetypal and Guidance Dreams   205

15   Reincarnation   219

viii   Contents

16   *Conclusion*   225
       Bibliography   227
       Index   229

DREAMS
Night Language of the Soul

Introduction

In the last few decades we have been reaching out to explore our physical universe. The depths of the ocean, the surface of the moon, the mystery of the stars have all revealed their secrets to us, and the knowledge gained has been rewarding indeed. But more recently there has been a new urge to discovery that is more inward, the hunger to touch our own center. The credo "know thyself" is heard everywhere. Bookstores are filled with volumes about how to fulfill one's potential and gurus have ardent disciples sitting at their feet. In short, the desire for growth and understanding has almost become a national pastime. Along with this search for inner knowledge, there has been a growing interest in the meaning of dreams.

The word "dream" has a certain magic; drop the word in any social gathering ("I had the strangest dream last night") and immediately you have not only an audience but others anxious to follow suit. "Wait until you hear *my* nightmare; it scares the socks off of me every time I have it!" Perhaps by now someone who has read one of the many dream books (which may be all right if by Freud or Jung, but beware of fads) will venture an interpretation. The point is that in a group of intelligent people there may be several who have much knowledge about many things, such as physics, mathematics, science, geography, astronomy, and business, but who have very little knowledge of their own inner natures. That is understandable when one realizes how comparatively few have had the opportunity or interest to learn the language of the psyche as it reveals itself through dreams.

But, unaware as they have been of their true meaning, most people can remember, as far back as childhood, vivid dreams whose emotional impact they have never forgotten. Despite not having any key to a dream's meaning, they still felt it was somehow important. Whether we understand or not, however, the unconscious wishes to be heard and keeps tapping on the door of the conscious mind: sometimes it whispers in a gentle voice and shows us subtle pictures, often it confronts us with great dangers so that we awake in trembling fear. But always it is the self talking to the self. No matter how horrendous or how beautiful the pictures and the action, the dream is entirely about us, our yearnings, our problems, and, yes, our rages. And then occasionally, like an undiscovered jewel, the gleam of a message of consolation or guidance will shine through and we realize that there's more wisdom down there than we ever imagined. Again, it is the self talking to the self.

"But," you might say, "that doesn't make sense. If I dream of my friend, Bill Jones, or my little four-year-old daughter, how can the dream be about myself?" The answer to that very logical question will be found later in this book; meanwhile, suffice it to say that in your dream Bill Jones, if you are a man, may represent some aspect of your own nature, and should you be a woman, the little girl may personify the child within you. Or they could, in the dream, play the role you have projected on them, based on how you feel about them.

A dream has a purpose, it tells a story, shows you pictures, and creates emotion. The more important the message of the dream, the more intense will be the reaction of the dreamer. Vivid dreams have vivid meaning.

No matter how vivid or commonplace the dream, everyone is still intrigued, instinctively sensing its innate significance. This mystery is one of the fascinating aspects of our dreams; after all, most things in life of great meaning usually do have an element of mystery. The dream reveals and it conceals and always leads us on to a still deeper meaning. Everything about the unconscious side of our nature is subtle and to a degree veiled, and we never completely plumb its depth. Just when we think we have, we may find still another secret door yet to be unlocked.

The purpose of this book is to show how such doors may be opened and help the reader, student or layman, become familiar with the symbolic language of the psyche so that he can better understand the psyche's dream messages. It is true that dream interpretation with its symbolic language does not appeal to everyone. There are those whose interest goes no deeper than the outward appearance of people and experiences. To them, only the obvious is logical. Dream analysis is a metaphysical experience that explores the realm of our nature below conscious reality. Some might ask, "But if my unconscious wants to tell me something, why doesn't it come right out and say it? Why does it have to talk in symbols?" One reason is that the unconscious has no voice, no language; its only medium of expression is imagery, symbolic imagery, the universal language that speaks with the same meaning to everyone, from the native of darkest Africa to the educated sophisticate. Most of our dreams are concerned with moods and abstractions, so the unconscious uses an image or a symbol that *represents* that abstraction, and it has an uncanny ability to pull up some person, animal, or thing that graphically conveys the message or purpose of the dream. Once we learn its symbolic language (and we'll probably never know all of it) we can begin the exciting experience of knowing that Other Self within us that is often more intriguing than our conscious self and frequently much wiser. It has been said that dream interpretation belongs to poets and philosophers, those who can sense the ebb and flow of inner meanings and glimpse the essence behind the mask. Certainly it is a creative experience and most people find the journey of self-discovery a rich and fulfilling one. With this in mind, it becomes evident that this book is not for those who want a quick answer to an immediate problem or whose attitude toward dreams is so simplistic as to conclude that "if you dream of green that means you're going to come into some money" or that "a dream of a wedding is a portent of death."

In dream analysis one point must always be kept in mind: all of our dream imagery only *represents* something; the reality is in *what* is being represented, not *how* it is being symbolized or represented. Rage per se has no form, so we dream of a warrior; guilt is only an emotion, so it is represented in the dream as something dirty to be cleaned up; aggression itself is invisible, but the form of the man who threatens or the animal that snarls is very visible. The same holds true for beautiful images. When we dream of archetypes, spiritual or mystical, we should see in the image of the noble goddess or the wise old man an embodiment of principles and truth. The Bible, for instance, is an archetypal book. Its greatness is not in the binding, leather, or paper nor even in the print on its pages but in the message contained within. This is lost on those who hold the Bible so close to their face they cannot see God.

The Chinese philosopher Chiang Tzu once said, "Last night I dreamed I was a butterfly. I do not know whether I was then a man dreaming he was a butterfly or whether I am now a butterfly dreaming I am a man." That says it all. And, incidentally, a butterfly often represents the soul in the language of dreams.

The material given in this book is the result of many years of study, starting with the David Seabury School of Psychology in Los Angeles, continued by reading the books of the pioneers in the field—Freud, Jung, Adler, Stekel, Horney, Gutheil—and later books and magazines on the subject. Most helpful, however, has been the experience of interpreting literally thousands of dreams of clients over a period of some thirty years of counseling. Through this experience it has been possible to test the validity of the meaning of various symbols. As Dr. Jung once said, in interpreting a dream, once you have found the right answer there is an instinctive response from the dreamer that confirms it. Dr. Freud once said there can be no analysis without dream analysis, and while that is a little strong, there is no doubt that the relating and then interpretation of a dream are of inestimable help. In the field of counseling, whenever an individual brings in some dreams, the door to the unconscious is already ajar and communication is not hard to establish.

The history of dream interpretation goes far into antiquity. Everyone is familiar with many Old Testament examples in which warnings, predictions, or guidance came to God's children as they needed them; the Greek myths, with all their symbology, have been called "the dreams of a race." The American Indians and tribes of Africa have seen dream messages as guidance from a higher source. As early as the second century A.D. the philosopher Artemidorus Daldianus delved deeply into the meaning of dreams and laid down a set of rules as to the kinds and meaning of dreams that is respected to this day.

Then, for a long period humanity turned to other matters and interest in dreams lagged. In the early part of the nineteenth century there was a revival of interest in metaphysical subjects, dreams among them. Then, when Sigmund Freud delved into the unconscious, dream analysis was on its way. Carl Jung learned from Freud and then developed theories and concepts that, while they did not entirely refute Freud's, opened up new, more metaphysical horizons in dream analysis. And today, as never before, the search goes on for methods of plumbing the depths of our own inner nature, to satisfy an intense urge to "know thyself."

In the book of Hebrew philosophy, the Talmud, it is pointed out that "a dream not interpreted is like a letter to the self unread." But how, one might ask, is it possible to read a letter from the self to the self if it is in a language unknown to the dreamer?

This brings us to the key word: symbology. Webster's defines it: "That which stands for or suggests something; also by reason of relationship, association, convention or accidental but not intentional resemblance; especially a visible sign of something invisible as an idea, a quality or totality, such as a state or church; an emblem as the lion is the emblem of courage, the cross is the symbol of Christianity. A symbol is a representation which does not aim at being a reproduction."

One important reason the unconscious clothes its true meaning in symbology is the necessity to bypass the dreamer's "censor," that part of the dreamer's ego-consciousness that prefers to believe only good about the self. If a man feels rage but will not express it, then he may in his dream see the rage violently expressed by another person. He can feel satisfaction that the object of his wrath was punished and at the same time awake with his ego and sense of virtue intact—after all, "the other fellow did it!" Should he subsequently learn something about the language of dreams, he might have occasion to develop a little healthy humility.

It has been said that "a child learns to hide from his parents and the adult has learned to hide from himself." So many of the natural instincts of children are taboo in the eyes of their parents, teachers, and religious advisers that they learn to cover up, as they would hold a forbidden toy behind their back. Then that which is repressed may eventually result in such a deep inhibition that it can be completely forgotten by the conscious mind. Later, it can only intrude into the conscious, rational world through some imagery that masks the true meaning.

Also buried deep in the unconscious are old hurts, rejections, traumas, and guilts too painful to remember but nevertheless producing nervousness, supersensitivity, and often a persecution complex. Much inferiority, sexual inadequacy, and spells of depression, for which the dreamer can find no conscious explanation, are rooted in long-buried childhood experiences. Some people try to uncover the hidden problems through hypnosis, but this alternative is not available to everyone. There is one avenue open to all by which one may become acquainted with the inner self, and that is the dream. No matter if the individual says, "But I never dream"; everyone dreams, every night and often many times a night, a fact that has been proven through many scientific tests. Many people have so long ignored the inner voice that they don't believe it is there. It is, nevertheless, and when one is desirous of listening, one will find that one's unconscious is eager to communicate. Our conscious selves are generally unaware of the true source of our problems, and the other persons from whom we seek help certainly don't know. The unconscious, however, always has known and will send up some "unread letters" as soon as it is invited to.

When the unconscious has something serious to impart, even though the dreamer has no knowledge of symbology, he may experience the same dream over and over. It is as though his psyche were saying, "There is something down here you should know about; don't ignore it." Sometimes it is a cry for help, or the expression of an unfulfilled longing or wish. It may keep knocking on the door of the dreamer's conscious mind for a long time. However, once the dreamer is able to interpret his dream, the unconscious is satisfied and the dream never occurs again.

The relationship between the conscious and the unconscious mind is illustrated by a simple analogy. A person could be described as a large corporation, the rational mind at the top being the general manager. Below are impulses, instincts, moods, yearnings of the subconscious self that might be called his subordinates, at work in the basement. Should a problem arise and a certain worker feel the need to let the general manager know about it, he will write his boss a letter (the dream), stating the problem. Rarely does this message go straight to the top; instead it passes through the hands of his secretary (the censor), who screens the contents to evaluate their acceptability. This secretary, or censor, wishes to protect the ego's peace of mind and will generally handle the matter in one of two ways: throw the letter in the wastebasket of forgetfulness and pretend it never arrived in the first place, or, before transmitting the letter to the manager, change its language into something more acceptable to him, with the result that the original message never arrives.

Then the manager, the dreamer, awakens with a feeling of unease and wonders why he feels so disturbed, has a faint recall of a dream, shrugs it off as meaningless, and goes about his conscious life—but there will be another message. And maybe another.

This practice of the censor translating the unacceptable into the acceptable has been called "displacement." While it is a handy little tool and a comfort to the ego, unfortunately, unless the dreamer learns something about the language of the unconscious, he goes on unaware of something he really needs to know. Often an individual who has disagreeable personality traits that he refuses to recognize will have dreams about an unpleasant person with irritating characteristics and, unable to see beneath the surface of this image, will awaken puzzled about why he dreamed about that "bad guy" in the dream, but with self-satisfaction entirely intact.

In other words, the first step in dream analysis is to start with the premise that the dream content, good or bad, is totally related to the self, our feelings, concepts, neuroses, attachments, or attitudes. Any mother in a dream can represent our own mother; any animal our own instinctual nature. Any battle represents our warring instincts, and any policeman the side of our nature that is trying to see that we behave and do not break moral or spiritual laws.

Symbology can be divided into two general classifications: universal symbology and personal symbology. Universal symbology is cosmic; it draws on the collective memory of people of all countries, races, and beliefs. Such symbols (sun, moon, earth, ocean, lion, snake, bird, baby) are rooted in our archaic background and bear more or less the same connotation for all peoples, with some variation according to the dreamer's personal experience. An example is the dream of flying, a type of escape dream. This usually expresses a universal wish to escape from the pressures of earthly, practical problems. (Of course, if the dreamer were a former pilot, then the dream of flying could simply express a wish to return to his former occupation.)

The most common of the escape dreams seems to be the one in which the dreamer flies under his own power. With a great sense of freedom the dreamer soars over the ocean, mountains, and fields, not only sensing the thrill of free flight but the added pleasure of being able to look down on the poor earthbound creatures below. Most people who take flight in their dreams are at the time under heavy pressure in their physical or emotional life: the mother overburdened with household duties and responsibilities ("You children get on my nerves so bad some days I could just fly away!"); the man chained to his desk or other routine work from which he sees no possibility of escape; and of course the individual who is physically handicapped or confined. ("If I had the wings of an angel, o'er these prison walls I would fly.")

Because the universal symbols emerge from the unconscious of the human race they carry the same meaning for everyone—from the most primitive to the highly educated. Personal symbology, on the other hand, is much narrower in meaning because it emerges solely from the unconscious of one person, the dreamer, and its images and personifications almost always are emotionally related to some meaningful memory, wish, or experience that was important only to the dreamer; therefore, they can be approached in interpretation as uniquely his own. The use of free association will reveal the significance of such personal images and symbols.

While dream material is complex and varied, dreams in general may be divided into four basic groups: problem dreams, wish dreams, status quo dreams, and, in much smaller numbers, superconscious or guidance dreams. By far the most numerous are the dreams relating to problems, in which the dreamer is threatened, pursued, fighting, struggling, sometimes falling, but always unhappy or troubled. The nightmare is, of course, the most extreme example of a deep disturbance in the psyche of an individual. Not only is the nightmare the most intense and the hardest to forget, it is also the most demanding of attention and revealing in interpretation. A panic button is being pushed deep within the unconscious of the dreamer; nightmares are an SOS from the unconscious to the conscious mind.

Sometimes, however, the source of the nightmare may be of a different kind. If the dreamer had, sometime in the past, even in early childhood, experienced a severe trauma, the memory of which has been suppressed through the years, he may relive the full impact of the original shock and suffering in his dream. Such nightmares are not at all uncommon to men who have suffered great pain and shocks in battle. It is almost as though the psyche of the soldier, during his sleep, were trying, by reliving the experience, to work through it and come to terms with it. Traumatic experiences in infancy and early childhood can manifest themselves in adulthood, not only through phobias and obsessions, but in what might seem like inexplicable nightmares.

The danger with which the dreamer is confronted in a nightmare may take the form of a threatening situation or force, the approach of a tremendous tidal wave, or perhaps the sensation of falling from a high place, but in most nightmares the frightening image takes the form of a dangerous person or vicious animal. Because so many people (and nice, good people, too) have voracious animals prowling through their dreams, it might be helpful to explain the meaning of the jungle whence these animals emerge in dreams. There is a term in psychology that applies to the most primitive area of our subconscious nature: the id. (This primary source of our elemental energy is described later.) We all have an id and to become acquainted with it is to no longer fear it or its emanations.

Now we come to wish fulfillment dreams—fantasies, trips, romances, luxurious experiences, and satisfaction of appetites—from which we are reluctant to awaken. Very frequently they take the form of escape; the worker who can barely scrape up enough money for carfare home may dream of boarding a luxurious liner headed for distant ports; the workaholic may in his dream be stretched out on the warm sands of a tropical isle, gentle waves lapping at his feet; the frustrated clerk may find herself the head of a large organization with everyone under her command—all of these to escape the pressure of a mundane existence.

Another wish dream that occurs primarily to lonely people is one in which their need for love, romance, and/or sexual satisfaction is fulfilled. The plain girl becomes the belle of the ball, pursued by the handsome hero or even a movie star, the timid youth wins the football game for his school or rescues a lovely maiden from some dire threat, while the downtrodden son in his sleep drives his father's sports car, very fast of course, to the admiration of all his classmates, particularly the girls. Then there is the compensation dream for the man disturbed by sexual inadequacy or inferiority, in which he is master of a very large machine, producing wonderful music from a huge pipe organ, for example, or at the launch controls of a rocket.

We cannot leave wish dreams without considering negative wish dreams. In these some long-buried resentment or wish for revenge expresses itself but almost always without the dreamer bringing it about. He is generally relieved on awakening to realize he didn't have a thing to do with it! Perhaps in his dream he received word of the demise of someone—usually someone who has been an irritant or a burden—but on coming back to consciousness feels a sense of relief that he didn't kill them off in his sleep after all!

To be included in the wish dreams also are those that are really catharsis dreams, in which the dreamer, having been too timid or inhibited to express his rage and frustration, finally turns loose and tells an adversary exactly what he's been wanting to tell him for a long time. If the dreamer has a pretty healthy id, he may punch the other fellow in the nose or do worse harm. From such dreams the dreamer rarely awakens with regret. He feels instead a sense of relief—"I finally did it!"

Then there are the dreams that express fulfillment of some taboo or immoral desire, something the dreamer would never think of doing in his waking moments. Plato advanced the opinion that "the virtuous man contents himself with dreaming of that which the wicked man does in actual life." And Freud made a statement that might soften somewhat the guilt of such a dreamer: ". . . I am therefore of the opinion that dreams should be acquitted of evil. Whether my *reality* is to be attributed to the unconscious wishes I cannot say . . . We would still do well to remember that *psychic reality* is a special form of existence which must not be confused with *material reality*" (quoted in Jastrow, *Freud, His Dream and Sex Theories*). In other words, a man cannot be condemned for what he might want to do, just so long as he doesn't really do it!

Less titillating but just as important is the next kind of dream, which for lack of a better term we shall call the status quo dream. It is a more practical type of dream, usually relating to what is taking place in the dreamer's life at the time. Sometimes these dreams seem to be almost a continuation of the work and problems of the day into the hours of sleep. The dreamer's psyche is so enmeshed in the activities of the day that it carries on where the conscious mind leaves off—and sometimes comes up with a long-sought solution to a problem. We are all familiar with stories of Thomas Edison and other inventors and scientists who, after exhausting all conscious effort to reach a solution to some major project, awakened with the answer arrived at through a dream. Sometimes, with less immediately practical results, the dreamer finds himself studying something under a magnifying glass or microscope, and the object of his observation represents an aspect of his life to which he should give more attention. The dreams of an individual undergoing analysis or experiencing a period of introspection and growth will often contain what might be called "progress reports," and because they keep pace with what is transpiring in the unconscious realm they are of great help to both the dreamer and the counselor.

The most meaningful dreams of all might be called the superconscious or guidance dreams. Whether these dreams arise from the psyche of the dreamer or from a source beyond himself, they can never be called simple statements from the unconscious. Their wisdom is ancient and they speak in archetypal symbology; the essence of their messages is always guidance or reassurance. They come to the dreamer only when he is deeply troubled and has asked to be shown the way. They are spiritual dreams.

For centuries such dreams or visions have been recorded in Greek myths, Jewish literature, the Old and New Testaments, ancient stories, and fables in which a voice spoke or an image appeared to the chosen one with warnings or divine instruction. While in our "practical," more materialistic society of today the occurrence of such dreams is less frequent, they still do come to the troubled soul seeking answers. The psyche or soul appears to wait, before offering guidance, until we have exhausted our conscious powers of thought.

Often people who experience what they feel is a prophetic dream are inclined to label it as evidence of spiritual guidance. These dreams usually seem to forecast some event, usually dire, such as an earthquake or, most frequently, the death of a loved one. While it cannot be denied that certain people have had, at times, truly prophetic dreams, one should be cautious of reading such a dream too literally. When subjected to symbolic interpretation, along with the free association of the dreamer, it will often be found that the message is entirely different from what it first appeared to be. Death in a dream almost never means death per se; that is, the demise of a living person. Instead it symbolizes the end or "death" of an attachment, an experience, or a stage of life, the closing of a chapter in the dreamer's life. It may be the ending of a neurosis that needs to die. Frequently a person under analysis will be alarmed by a dream in which a parent has expired, and it is usually the parent to whom he or she was most bound, either by resentment or devotion. This dream is usually a signal that the dreamer, willingly or not, is being freed from an overattachment. In other words, "momism" or "daddyism" is fading out of the picture.

Do we ever dream of impending death? The answer would have to be, very rarely, and then in symbology so subtle it is almost indecipherable. In fact, it does not seem wise to describe or search for symbols of death: not only would such symbols be anxiety-provoking, they might also be completely wrong. This is not to deny that there may be dream omens of that last journey, but they are usually more recognizable in retrospect than in preconception, which is perhaps as it should be.

Let us turn now from the various kinds of dreams to dream analysis. No discussion of dreams can be complete without reference to Freud and Jung. While much progress has developed in the study of the unconscious since the lifetimes of these two men, it all goes back to their work.

Freud, the father of psychoanalysis, was the first to explore deeply the concept of the unconscious and how it expresses itself in our dreams. He based his theories primarily on the concept that we are all a product of our original inherited racial instincts, on top of which we have an accumulated store of buried or forgotten memories of infantile impulses and attachments that are strongly conditioned and shaped by our parents. This conditioning, which starts at birth, continues on through the oral stage, then the anal period, and on into what Freud called the Oedipal period, at which time the child has developed a strong emotional attachment to the parent of the opposite sex.

Because he recognized that the Greek myths are essentially symbol stories, Freud borrowed from them many of the psychological terms used today. From Psyche, sometimes called the soul, we have psychology, while the term Oedipus complex was derived from the story of the troubled youth who unwittingly slew his father and married his own mother. Sometimes the name Electra, from another Greek myth, is applied to the girl's attachment to her father. Then there is the story of Narcissus, the handsome youth who, fascinated with his own image in the water, fell in and drowned, giving us the term narcissism.

Carl Jung, Freud's pupil, soon developed theories of his own—sometimes to the consternation of his mentor. In contrast to Freud's belief that we are the sum total of our past, Jung was more hopeful, maintaining, in effect, that only a dead man is known by his past, that a living person has a soul and dreams of the future. Jung broadened and deepened the field of psychology and of dream analysis with a more metaphysical approach. He gave us the concepts of the animus and the anima, the male and female polarities within each of us, through the understanding of which we can find balance within ourselves and harmony with the opposite sex (often compared to the yin and yang of eastern philosophy). In addition, he developed the concept of the two facets of our personality that he called the persona, the lighter, more personable side, and the shadow, or darker, unrecognized, or untransmuted part of our nature. All of these aspects of the self appear symbolically in our dreams, and the dreamer's recognition of them contributes greatly to self-understanding and growth.

Another difference in their approach to dream analysis was that Freud believed that the latent content of the dream was always different from the manifest content and that the hidden meaning could be reached only by free association. Jung, on the other hand, while agreeing that sometimes the true meaning of the dream could be obscure, held that the dream really means what it seems to be saying even though it is necessary to elaborate and reveal its meaning through interpretation.

Their disagreement also related to the different levels of the unconscious. While they both believed that the first level of the unconscious contained early memories and impressions, the greatest difference was in their ideas of what made up the deeper or lower level from which dream material emerged. As mentioned before, Freud spoke of that area of the subconscious as a reservoir of inherited, primordial racial memories and instincts; Jung, on the other hand, believed that the "collective unconscious" in each of us contains the same basic emotional and behavioral content. To this he added a powerful coda: from and through this collective unconscious we may have contact with the archetypes in symbols and images of wisdom and beauty beyond our mortal knowing. With the idea of the archetypes, Jung opened a door to understanding a much deeper center of the psyche, or soul.

One of Freud's strongest beliefs was that every dream expressed some suppressed wish, positive or negative. Granted that this may sometimes be the case, Jung maintained that the inner self, whether called unconscious, psyche, or whatever, may also have deeper and more meaningful purposes than mere wish-fulfillment. Freud's view did not allow for growth, and Jung believed that we are here for growth, to attain wholeness.

The difference between the ideas of the two men reaches its center at this one point, which applied not only to their ideas of dream but of psychology itself: Dr. Freud, when discussing a dream (or a problem), would raise the question of "Why?" Where did the dream come from and why did the person dream it? Jung, on the other hand, felt it was far more important for the dreamer to ask the self, "What for?" In other words, what was the purpose of the dream, what was it trying to tell the dreamer that he needed to know for self-understanding? His view of the dream was comparable to his view of life's experiences: "Why am I having this experience and what do I learn from it?"

Regardless of which approach may be most acceptable to a dreamer, both are useful in understanding ourselves through our dreams. And as one goes further into the countless symbols and various techniques of interpretation, it can only become apparent that this is a serious but exciting procedure, one that should not be approached quickly or lightly.

Our unconscious is never an enemy, but is always a friend, and one that has an almost magical ability to choose exactly the right symbol to express a very specific idea in a dream. It becomes an increasingly intriguing experience to search, through symbol and free association, and find the meaning hidden in our dreams, a discovery that no one else can make for us.

Whenever we question why the dream never shows us plainly what the problem or inner enemy is, why in a nightmare we are forced to face it obliquely, we should remember that our ego and/or our courage are not equal to a direct confrontation. So, using what Jung often referred to as our "active imagination," let us look to the example of Perseus. When he set about to slay the dreaded Medusa, knowing that he would be turned to stone if he looked directly at her, he asked for a shield. By using the shield as a mirror, he was able by *reflection* to cut off her evil head.

While few of us have to overcome a problem as dreadful as the Medusa, none of us would want to be "turned to stone" by the shock of confronting our darker sides too abruptly. Nature has provided us with a shield—our dream—in which we can see our enemy symbolically and cut off its head. The strength with which we wield the sword of courage can be drawn from the greatest of all archetypes, the God within.

2

The Interpretation of Dreams

2 4 1

The interpretation of dreams is a subtle and exacting step toward opening the door to the inner self. It is not to be taken lightly, as a parlor game, or to find quick, superficial meanings. To do it properly requires empathy, intuition, an awareness of mythology and religions, and a knowledge of symbology, both ancient and modern. (Carl Jung emphasized that the person who undertakes this important task needs to be knowledgeable about people and their problems and have a secure philosophical and even religious foundation.)

We start with the premise (proven both psychologically and scientifically) that we all have dreams, remembered or not. Those who do not believe they dream or cannot remember them have developed the ability to inhibit and repress their hidden emotions, and by relating only to the conscious mind and its logical concept of the outer world have unknowingly closed what Sigmund Freud called "the royal road to the unconscious." Dream analysis will help those who hunger to know and understand themselves better not only to seek answers to their recurring emotional disturbances but frequently to experience a spiritual awakening as well.

The first step then is to learn to capture and record one's dreams. One should, on retiring, place a pen and a notebook beside the bed, with this self-admonition: "I know I do dream and I want to wake up and record my dreams." It may take a night or two, but with this attitude the "censor" usually recedes and the dreams come through. The dream must be immediately written down, fragmentary or foolish as it may seem at the moment.

If one says to oneself, "I don't need to write it down; I'm sure I'll remember it," the dream will fade like mist before the sun, and there will be nothing left to interpret. Once the dream has been recorded, as soon as possible it should be read over and reconstructed, and any overlooked details that come to mind should be added. Then it would be helpful to follow a valuable suggestion outlined by Dr. Stephen A. Hoeller in his lecture on the nature of dreams at the Philosophical Research Society: he recommends that as soon as possible after you have a dream, you should relate it to someone else, whether they are knowledgeable about dream symbology or just a good friend. The sharing of the dream is very beneficial.

Later in the day when you have a quiet moment, review the dream. Read it over as though you were reading a short story. What is the mood of the dream? What emotion do you feel after reading it? If it were a true story, what would be its theme? Does it convey a feeling of rejection, sadness, despair, fear, rage? Or is it the happy expression of the fulfillment of a wish, a yearning for escape, recognition, or romance? Keep in mind that no matter what the content, the dream is totally your own, that everyone and everything in the dream relates to some aspect of your own feelings about yourself or others or life itself. Don't be too literal, just let the mood and the message of the dream speak to you, remaining completely open to anything that may be coming through. Then ask yourself, "What is my inner self trying to tell me?"

In the interpretation and evaluation of one's own dreams, a certain degree of humility is essential. It is necessary to put aside the ego, to be as objective as possible, and to accept whatever comes up, positive or negative. And because much of the dream content can be unpleasant and disturbing (after all, the unconscious may be trying to tell the dreamer something about himself that even his best friend won't tell him), in self-defense the dreamer will often declare, "I can't believe that is really about me" and will want to lay the dream aside. At this sensitive point it is helpful to the ego to recognize that the unconscious, in its desire to make certain that the dreamer gets the point, often exaggerates shamelessly and that the symbology is usually much worse than the true meaning of the dream!

When learning to interpret one's own dreams, it is often helpful to keep a written chronological record, a "dream diary." Upon reading the dreams over later, as one would a serial or story, it is possible to pick up a theme or emotional thread. From this one can deduce an underlying emotional or psychological pattern.

Whenever Sigmund Freud had dreams he could not interpret at the time of dreaming, he would put them aside and then a year or so later find that he was able to successfully interpret them. He reasoned that it was because he had, by that time, overcome whatever internal resistance he had earlier that had blocked his ability to understand them.

Interpreting the Dreams of Others

After you have learned how to interpret your own dreams, then you are ready to help someone else understand the meaning of his dreams. Because most people understand very little of dreams and symbology and are frequently a little fearful of what their own dreams might reveal, it can be helpful at first to spend a little time discussing the idea of the unconscious and symbology in general, establishing that the latent content is quite different from the manifest content and that there is nothing to be nervous about—no one can dream of any problem that everybody doesn't have to some degree.

In listening to the recital of the dream, it is best to show no reaction at all. Sometimes it helps, as Freud suggested, to ask the dreamer to relate the dream a second time, from the beginning. In doing so, he will almost invariably add, "Oh, yes, there was something I forgot" and then fill in material that is not only pertinent but often of major importance. The omitted portions often supply the key to interpretation.

It is not always advisable on the occasion of the first session of analysis to start dream interpretation, for several reasons. One is that nervous or insecure persons, when confronted too early with the meaning of their dream, may be confused or discouraged. They may become fearful that the counselor is about to discover secrets within them that they are not yet ready to reveal. When this happens an individual may unwittingly block all dream material and say, quite honestly, "I just don't know what is the matter with me, but I can't remember my dreams anymore." One other and very important reason not to start dream analysis prematurely is that the analyst cannot, so soon, be confident of the true meaning of the dream. It is absolutely essential to first become acquainted not only with the dreamer but with his problems, history, and inner longings of the present. Superficial dream analysis may not only be incorrect, but sometimes psychologically injurious. (Occasionally, the symbology and meaning of a dream are so clearly stated that it is possible to understand the general message of the dream without knowing much about the dreamer. This is a rare occurrence, however. It can be not only ineffective but somewhat risky to attempt to grasp the true meaning of a dream before learning of the person's life, problems, and emotional state.)

Later, assuming that the counselor or dreamer has kept a record of the first dream or dreams, the counselor should review them and ask the dreamer what he *thinks* the dreams mean. While the person may know nothing of symbology, it is, after all, his dream, and what it means to him is of primary importance and often quite valid. Often, when reviewing a dream, the dreamer will suddenly remark, "Now I remember another dream I had some time ago," and that recollected dream will reveal something relating to the present one.

Frequently a person coming for counseling, when asked about dreams, will say, "I had one last night (or before) and I thought I'd remember it, but now I can't remember any of it." At that point it is better not to push for remembrance. Generally, the gentler approach is more effective, such as telling the person not to worry about it, and reassuring him that the dream will come back to memory in time. A gentle nudging might help: "Would you say it was a happy or a troubled dream?" and "Have you any idea who was in it?" If there is still no recall, it might be better to let the subject rest for the moment. Emotional waters have been stirred, and often while talking of other matters the dreamer will suddenly say, "Now I remember my dream!"

When anyone is under analysis, it is essential that the "first dream of analysis" be carefully recorded because, as both Freud and Jung recognized, it is almost always very meaningful. It is as though the psyche of the individual, knowing he was going for help, was saying, "Here, take this in; this is the main problem to be worked on." Within this dialogue between the dreamer and his unconscious, the role of the analyst is that of an arbitrator, for instance when, in some dreams, the dreamer plays two roles, observing and being observed, both good guy and bad guy, felon and policeman, robber and victim. To accept the analysis of such a dream, it is necessary that the dreamer be made to understand that they are each aspects of two sides of his nature, his conscious, moral side and his repressed, negative drives. It is very significant for him to recognize which individual in the dream he identifies with. Does he play the role of the "bad guy" running from justice; that is, his own moral judgment? Or is his higher self in control, so that he is the "good guy" trying to restrain, even incarcerate, his "neurotic" self? This recognition helps the dreamer become aware of which side of his nature is dominant at the time.

We must remember, in analyzing our own and other people's dreams, not to be too literal; even if the dream is vivid in its content, we cannot rely on this as the voice of infallible wisdom. We are all full of contradictory elements; while accepting that the dream is telling us something, we need to know it is not always absolute authority. We must take into consideration our attitudes and experiences prior to the dream. The next night it may be a little different.

Dream Stimulus

An important step in dream interpretation is to find, if possible, the dream stimulus. Freud believed that our dreams always relate to the experiences of the previous day. In other words, the stimulus might be found among those experiences on which one has not yet slept. He even went so far as to say that all experiences more than two days in the past might be considered remote; that while the dream might select its material from any period of life, it would do so only provided that the emotional chain leads back from the day before the dream. Jung also put much emphasis on the stimulus of the dream, but he did not limit it to the previous twenty-four hours.

There are a number of ways of helping the dreamer locate the stimulus of his dream. After the dreamer has related his dream and perhaps repeated it with additions, the analyst may quietly ask, "Why do you think you had this dream?" "What do you think your dream is really saying?" If the dream happens to be a disturbing one, then the question would be, "It would seem that something really upset you yesterday. What were you worried about when you went to bed?"

A common dream stimulus is the book the dreamer was reading the night before, or the movie or play he had been watching. In such cases the person is sometimes convinced that his dream is actually a continuation of that book or play. At this point it is necessary to ask the dreamer what character or episode moved him the most. In this way, the stimulus of the dream may become apparent. Once the stimulus is identified, it becomes easier to approach the dream's meaning.

For clarification, dream stimuli can be divided into four main classifications: outside physical and inside physical and outside emotional and inside emotional. Outside physical stimulus can be noise such as a knock on the door or the telephone ringing, or a change in the temperature of the room. Any of these can be woven into the dream material. Inside physical stimulus could be hunger, thirst, or perhaps a need to go to the bathroom. Even an upset stomach can produce a vividly disturbing dream. Then there are the occurrences that fall in the category of emotional stimuli: something on the outside that arouses a feeling or mood in the dreamer such as a baby crying, wind blowing, rain pouring down, or music—any sound or touch that arouses buried memories, particularly sad or troubled ones. Inside emotional stimuli may comprise any number of conscious or unconscious moods or concerns with which the dreamer went to bed, such as worry, sadness, frustration, anger, longing, or sexual urges. Any of these may be so integral to the dream that it is difficult to separate the stimulus from the dream's more meaningful content. There have been instances in which an encroaching illness has manifested itself in a dream before the dreamer became consciously aware of it. But in most cases, illness in a dream is symbolic of emotional discomfort, not physical disease. Either way, proper understanding of the dream hinges on distinguishing stimulus from content.

Free Association

Of all the techniques used in dream interpretation none is as helpful as free association. This is the free flow of ideas, memories, images, concepts, and emotions brought to the dreamer's mind by a symbol, a person, a place, or a situation in the dream. To start the flow it helps to ask the dreamer: "What does that remind you of? And what else?" Has the dreamer ever been in that place and, if so, what experience did he have there? What does the person in the dream mean to him and what qualities does he find attractive or unattractive? If by some chance the dreamer becomes blocked and seems unable to arrive at any associated ideas, he has probably hit an emotional "snag," a sensitive point in the unconscious from which he retreats. In such a case it is best to drop that train of thought and start over from another symbol or angle of the dream. As the memories and associated ideas come forth, like a long chain drawn up from a well one link at a time, something may emerge that the dreamer had long forgotten or wanted to forget and that is the key to the dream. A dream has been compared to a capsule; once opened it can spread, by free association, in all directions. Sometimes it can be a Pandora's box, too, except that the "evils" that emerge when the lid is taken off the dream (the unconscious) can, when brought into the light, be transmuted into good. Remember, the one thing that remained in Pandora's box was Hope.

We can do no better than to quote Freud's recommendation for inducing free association:

> It is advantageous that the patient should take a restful position and close his eyes; he must be explicitly instructed to renounce all criticism of the thought-formations which he may perceive. He must also be told the success of the psychoanalysis depends upon his noting and communicating everything that passes through his mind, and that he must not allow himself to suppress one idea because it seems to him unimportant or irrelevant to the subject, or another because it seems nonsensical. He must preserve an absolute impartiality in respect to his ideas; for if he is unsuccessful in finding the desired solution of the dream, the obsessional idea, or the like, it will be because he permits himself to be critical of them. (Freud, *His Life and His Mind*)

Here is an example of free association. The dreamer is a young mother of three sons, divorced, ambitiously working toward a college degree.

> I went into my kitchen and was amazed to find it almost empty of both food and cooking utensils. Everywhere there was dust. I opened the door under the sink. A lot of trash was there—and then a whole bunch of bugs crawled out. They were just crawling everywhere. I was terribly upset because I normally keep a very clean kitchen.
>
> Then I opened the pantry, and all these shelves were empty, but there was a swarm of wasps that had built their nest there. They came flying out all over the place. I tried to shut them in but couldn't; there were too many of them.
>
> I said to myself, "This is terrible, and I have a lot of work to do to clean

all this up." But somehow I wasn't discouraged; I felt that no matter how bad it was I would be able to get it cleaned up. It would be work, but I could do it.

Her free association, word for word, was as follows:

> Kitchen . . . what does it stand for? Cooking for my family or even friends . . . Warmth, center of the home, nurturing, a mother's role. An empty kitchen . . . Well, of course I've fed my boys but I've been too busy with my studies to pay them much attention or do anything special for them. Guess I haven't been very warm to them lately. . . . Dust . . . means it hasn't been used for a long time. . . . Under the sink . . . usually keep soap and cleansers there to get rid of dirt. Trash . . . stuff that is no good . . . things in my life I really should be throwing out. . . . Bugs . . . Ugh! I hate them . . . dirty, crawly things . . . Somehow dirty creepy things remind me of guilt, feeling dirty about something . . . Wasps! They sting, bad . . . mean, sharp, frightening . . . Attack you . . . They are in the place where good food should be . . . Now I know what those wasps mean. I have been sharp and irritable lately, particularly with the children, too impatient . . . waspish. Now I know what my dream was telling me about myself.

By allowing her mind to lead her where it would, she discovered much that she could not have recognized in any other way: that her emotional center, the kitchen, had become empty of love and nurturing, that in her unconscious, "under the sink," she had accumulated emotional trash (a part of which proved to be a romantic affair that she deeply regretted), that she felt little creeping guilts that appeared as bugs, and, finally and perhaps most usefully, that she recognized a growing tendency to be irritable and critical, to have a "waspish" tongue.

How much more acceptable and meaningful it was to the dreamer to be able to discover these things through her own free association—much more acceptable to the ego, and to her psyche, than it would have been to hear the analyst tell her, "This is what your dream means, these are your problems, and it is time you did something about them." After her rather painful self-discovery, it was pleasant to be able to point out to her how honest and courageous she was at the end of her dream, when she assured herself that no matter how bad it was she knew she would be able to "clean it up."

Below is another dream that illustrates how a dreamer, by his own free association, became aware of a basic truth about himself and his life.

We will call him Dan, a healthy and attractive man in his early forties, intelligent, interested in psychology and so open to analysis. He carefully recorded his dreams and was fascinated with their meaning.

Dan was one of two sons of dominating and opinionated (quarrelsome) parents from the "old country." His mother had always used emotional blackmail skillfully, deeply implanting in her sons a sense of responsibility for her own unhappiness and discontent. The father, who had managed to become financially quite secure, had never doubted his own wisdom. For his growing sons he had two admonitions: "Work hard and save your money" and "Never get married; all a woman wants from you is your money." In view of the role models with which the boys grew up, the latter advice was not hard to follow and as time went on the single life became increasingly attractive.

Quite soon after attaining physical maturity, both boys chose to undergo vasectomies. In discussing it Dan remarked, "I don't know exactly why I did it but it just seemed the thing to do. And I have never regretted it or felt guilty for it."

For the last twenty years or so Dan, who had become financially secure through real estate dealings, had lived alone in a big house with a garden he tended, playing tennis, visiting friends, and enjoying life. He had no cause to be lonely in the evenings, with all the attractive single women not only willing but eager to spend time with him. When they became too eager, he graciously backed out, feeling no need for a permanent relationship or commitment of any kind.

But Dan did have one obligation: to his parents, to their every demand on his time and attention. By nature kind and sensitive, he was always hurt by their implication that somehow he had failed them, hadn't called them often enough or didn't do what they requested of him as well as he should have. He was constantly at their beck and call, inevitably returning home with a sense of inadequacy, feeling that again he had failed to please them. His failure as a peacemaker to bring harmony into their lives troubled him as well.

What brought this man to counseling? An increasing restlessness and dissatisfaction with his life, a sense of depression and nameless emptiness he had never had before. His ideal life was no longer ideal. "I used to enjoy everything? What is wrong with me?" Then came this dream:

> I was inside this huge empty building like a warehouse or storage place, and the wind was blowing very strongly. I dreamed there were trees inside the building. And underneath these trees my van was parked. It seems I had trimmed these trees to my satisfaction; I had trimmed them all in a sort of umbrella shape. Then when I looked them over I could see I had missed one long branch. It was a big strong branch sticking out all by itself. It didn't fit the umbrella shape of the trees, so I got my ladder and sawed the limb off.

Here is Dan's free association:

> Q. You mentioned several times that you wanted the trees to be in the shape of an umbrella. What do you think an umbrella stands for?
>
> A. Actually, I never have trimmed a tree like that. . . . Well, I suppose an umbrella stands for protection, something that covers and protects me. But when you stop and think about it, the roof of that big building was already a protection.
>
> Q. So you had two roofs, the building and you made a roof out of the trees.
>
> A. Yes, and my van had a roof, too; guess I had three roofs to get under. Sounds like I need a lot of shelter, doesn't it? I sure am protecting myself.
>
> Q. And that strong straight limb that stuck out—it didn't quite fit the picture, did it? [At this point an explanation was given of the rather obvious phallic symbology of the branch, his "branch," which he had felt needed to be lopped off (castrated) because it didn't fit the picture.] Why, do you suppose?
>
> A. Well, I guess my unconscious is telling me in this dream that I had felt that a vasectomy was my protection—though I really didn't think of it at the time—because that way I could never get a woman pregnant and have to marry her, and honestly I never have had any desire to bring children into the world. Certainly my and my brother's lives were miserable enough.
>
> Q. By the way, what kind of trees were they that you were trimming so neatly?
>
> A. Somehow I think they were pear trees; they are a kind of tree you don't see very often. While they are called pear trees, they never bear any fruit.

Dan recognized, through the message of his own dream, that his goal in life until now had been first to seek approval from his parents, second to provide for his own comfort and security, and third to avoid responsibility for any living soul. Those were his three roofs or umbrellas. Of course, even the kind of tree was symbolic: a pear can be interpreted as a genital (testicle) symbol, and his unconscious further completed the message by making it a tree that could never bear fruit. The most important result of Dan's understanding of his dream, however, was the possibility that his depression and sense of emptiness was due to his "fruitlessness" and that this sterility had been entirely of his own choosing. Since then, this basically kind and generous man has become involved in a fulfilling humanitarian activity.

Before leaving the subject of free association, it is necessary to mention the phenomenon of blockage. Occasionally, when free associating, the dreamer will find it impossible to continue. When this occurs, a blockage is indicated and no pressure should be put on the dreamer. Instead it is best to advise him to relax and start again. On returning to the original word or image, the dreamer then can be asked simply to describe logically what the person, place, or thing might be, often opening up a new train of thought.

When you are seriously involved in the techniques of making contact with the unconscious through dreams, you may find the following practice quite helpful. After you have experienced an important dream and you seek to know more, find a quiet spot to be alone, relax, and with your eyes closed drop back into your dream. With no desire to shape or direct the development of the dream, allow it to unfold and finish itself. Keep your conscious wishes out of it, and follow the dream wherever it leads. It may have more to tell you. As Jung once said, "I know that if we meditate on a dream sufficiently long and thoroughly, if we take it about with us and turn it over and over, something always comes of it. . . . it shows the individual in what direction his unconscious is leading him."

3

Examples of Dream Interpretation

Often people say, "I've read all the dream books I can, and studied what the symbols mean, but when I try to interpret a dream I don't know how to start, or put it all together." It might be helpful to take some dreams and, step by step, attempt to unravel their symbolic meaning.

The first dream is that of a sixteen-year-old male, introverted, with a feeling of unworthiness and lacking masculine identity. He had few friends and had never dated a girl. His parents were divorced, after much quarreling, when he was six, and his mother took him and his younger sister to another part of the country to live. As a result, he had seen his father only once or twice since. His father was a dynamic, aggressively masculine man whom the boy greatly admired but also feared, because when he was small his father had been so imperative and critical and had, at one time when the child was four, given him a beating. The mother not only favored the daughter but projected her dislike of her ex-husband by frequently telling the boy, "You're just like your father," in her case the most disparaging remark possible. Here is his dream:

> There was this real pretty girl I liked. She was a little younger than I, and I wanted to go up to her and talk to her. I thought she was a real sweet girl, and I liked her. That is why I got in trouble; because I wanted to approach her. She was beautiful and blonde. Somehow I felt she was a singer. She seemed to be a very important person, and she had power. And she had all these men, sort of guardians, around her. They did exactly what she wanted them to do. And they kept coming after me. I

hadn't done anything wrong, but they were after me. I did not want to fight or hurt anybody; I just acted in self-defense.

This was outdoors and there was a well there. They thought I had fallen in it, but I hadn't. Another man had fallen in it before, and he had died.

It seemed like the guilt they put on me built up and built up.

Sometimes I was watching what was happening; sometimes I was doing it. While they were searching for me in the well I was really hiding in the bushes. People everywhere. I was pretty close to a cliff. Someone heard me in the bushes and as they were searching there I ran quietly and hid in another bush. They were coming closer. As I was creeping through the branches a guy spotted me. There were no more bushes, no place to hide, and I went down into a little ditch. But now this fellow, a very huge man, like a gorilla, could see me and was running toward me. I didn't think I had much chance if I had to fight him, he was so big, so I thought I would have to shoot him. I took my pistol out. It just clicked. I had used my last shot. So I just walked out of the ditch. No use putting up a fight. And that was the end of the dream. I woke up feeling awful.

At this point the counselor used a simple technique by which the unconscious of the individual was invited to spontaneously send up other material relative to the dream content:

Q. Would you please say the first person's name that comes to your mind?

A. Marilyn.

Q. What emotion do you feel when you think of Marilyn?

A. Anger . . . at her attitude. It used to be constant. She just didn't care. Didn't bother about me. She didn't have to. I didn't count. That was what her mother always showed toward me—why shouldn't she show the same thing? Of course I was angry. Why shouldn't I be? I wonder what connection this has to the dream . . .

Q. Describe Marilyn.

A. Really a pretty simple person. If the situation or somebody feels happy, she feels happy; if the situation is sad, she becomes sad; if somebody is sorry for somebody, then she is sorry for them. But she can be nice. She hasn't had the opportunity to learn to be considerate. She's a beautiful girl, a very sweet-looking girl when she smiles.

Q. Does she sing?

A. Oh, she has a beautiful voice, sings in school and church.

Q. Who is Marilyn?

A. My sister.

After this much had been accomplished, Freud's next step was used:

Q. Now tell me the first number that comes to your mind.

A. Five.

Q. And what pops into your mind in connection with that number?

A. Masculinity. I don't know why I said that, but that is what I thought.

Q. Also, when you think of five years of age, what do you associate with that time in your life?

A. That was my age when my little sister was born.

Then the next step:

Q. Please tell me now the first song that comes to your mind, spontaneously.

A. "Rock-a-Bye Baby."

Q. Since all songs create a feeling, a mood, what would you associate with that song?

A. Comfort. A feeling of being loved and cared for.

Q. Now what mood do you feel?

A. Sad . . .

Going back to the dream itself:

Q. What do you think the well in the dream signified?

A. My unconscious. Depression. But now I can see that even if they expected me to drown in it, I didn't!

Q. Who do you think the big man in the dream represents, the one who finally chased you down?

A. I guess that was my father, the way he seemed to me when I was little. The time he was after me, when I was five, and he chased me into the closet he seemed so big. I felt helpless. I couldn't remember what happened after that, but Mother later told me he caught me and gave me a beating.

Q. Why do you think "Rock-a-Bye Baby" came to your mind?

A. I know why. I never felt loved after my little sister was born. I can remember once when I was little my mother was mad at me and jerked my hair and I asked her, "Mommy, don't you want to have a boy?" But I knew she didn't. I always wanted to love my little sister, but Mother always told her not to pay any attention to me.

Without the free association of the dreamer, the obvious and more shallow interpretation might have been that this lonely young man simply wished to know some pretty girl. How much deeper the meaning becomes when we learn that she is the little sister to whom he could never get close.

The "power" Marilyn wielded in the dream symbolized the authority given her as the favorite of both parents. Then the "men guardians" may be read as personifications of rejection and criticism from which the dreamer could not escape and that imbued him with a sense of guilt, without knowing what crime he was supposed to have committed. The "bushes" in which he attempted to hide probably symbolize the various interests into which he withdrew. By nature nonaggressive, his defense against his aloneness became reading and studying music, at which he became very proficient. Eventually, forced into the open, he feels helpless because he has "fired his last shot"; he has no more emotional ammunition with which to fight. And finally, it is to his respect and/or fear of his father that he finally surrenders.

His response to the number five is, of course, very revealing: it is significant that his dethronement at the birth of his sister brings to his mind the word "masculinity," the quality in which he feels most deficient. If he perceived his young maleness to be rejected upon the arrival of a little female, then he, too, might reject it within himself.

The young man said that, as a result of understanding his dream, he could see much more clearly how intensely he had always wanted and needed to be close to his only sister, and that she herself had not truly rejected him but only reflected the attitude of her mother. Also, he could now see how he had assumed a role untrue to his masculine identity, a manner quieter and softer than he really was. The dream helped him learn what of the past he needed to correct and how to develop his true self.

The next dream is another problem dream that contains some interesting symbology.

The dreamer is a young college boy who came from a cultured, fairly well-to-do family. He was the middle child, with an older brother and younger sister. He was by nature something of a peacemaker in a family composed of strong personalities. Here is the dream.

> It was like Des Moines, where we once lived. I am with two other people, maybe a brother and sister. All of a sudden there is like a cloud coming over, getting dark, something evil going on. I know it is something to do with a situation.

All of a sudden all these crows are coming through the air, coming after us. I start running, was afraid we couldn't make it home in time.

Then I get sort of like a magician, waving my arms, calling on the powers to drive them back. We get inside the house.

Then two of our cats are there, female cats we used to have, dead now. It is like somehow a witch gets into them. The evil got into the two of them somehow. I take them and wrap them up in towels and decide to put them in storage so they can't get out. It seemed like I put them in the refrigerator. But at the same time I am really worried that they will be able to get out. And one got out of its towel, and it just stood and looked at me.

Free association:

Q. When did you have this dream?
A. When I went home for a visit over the weekend. All of my troubled dreams lately seem to be when I go home.
Q. What does Des Moines bring to mind?
A. Where we used to live several years ago. Everything went wrong. The unhappiest time of my life.
Q. Did anything upset you when you were home on the weekend?
A. The constant quarreling, especially between my mother and sister.

As was explained in an earlier chapter, the setting of a dream usually relates to some place in the dreamer's life as a symbol to bring up the emotions or memories associated with that place. In this boy's dream, Des Moines was an indication that he was reliving the turmoil and unhappiness that he had experienced at an earlier time.

The dark cloud symbolized depression. Crows represented dark thoughts flying through his mind. Cats are female symbols. The witch, a negative female image, might represent the mother. "Trying to be a magician": the boy wishes he could magically wave his arms and bring peace in the family. He tries to "put the cats on ice" to cool off their tempers, but his natural kindness causes him to wrap them in towels before he does. The dream ends with a confrontation still to be met.

After discussing the dream, the young man said he felt much relieved. He had feared that the dream meant something much more sinister and he added, "I can see the whole thing now and I feel better."

The next dream is particularly interesting because it is related to the preceding one. It occurred at approximately the same time and the dreamer is the young man's sister. She was a pretty young girl who had just finished her first year of college. She was quite caught up in the free-thinking, anti-establishment, free-love attitudes of her peers, attitudes that her parents were attempting if not to accept, at least to tolerate.

> In my dream I dreamed I was dreaming. It was telling me something, like a warning. I finally woke up, but I was still in the dream. It was so vivid, each detail so clear.
>
> It was just like my home. I heard something outside and saw something go by the window and knew I was supposed to wake up, like it was a warning.
>
> Then there was this chanting sound. Across the hill all of these members of a cult were coming out, streaming out. All had hoods on and some torches and were chanting. Kind of invading the neighborhood. I ran up to Mom and Dad's room and told them what was going on. I remember screaming once. Then outside one of the cult started laughing and screamed back, like an answer. They made me think of coyotes. I told Dad to go call the police. He and I walked out in the hall, then we glimpsed a dark form go by in the dining room. Now they were in the house.
>
> So Mom and I ran into the bathroom, because it is the only door that locks. As I was closing the door, two came in, pushing on the door. They ran in, horrible little creatures, dwarfish. I bit one of them in a rage, and he laughed. They grabbed Mom and kept me back. Walked her down the hill. I became ill like I had a fever. The next thing I knew they were leaving the house, and as they went out they warned me that Dad was going to die within a week. I woke up so scared.

Before we attempt to analyze this dream we should remember that almost always the enemy in the dream is an enemy within the dreamer, in this case threatening not so much the dreamer herself as the well-being of her parents.

Q. Since this dream takes place in your home, has there been any problem there?

A. Mom and I have been arguing a lot. I do wish I could get through to her that she needs to change, especially her old-fashioned way of thinking. Of course she thinks I need to change, too. But she's too sensitive, gets hurt over everything I do and say.

Q. Your dream has a cult in it. Do some free association on cults.

A. It wasn't like the Ku Klux Klan or anything, it was different. But on thinking about it—maybe this is it: In college a bunch of us have been doing a lot of talking, sometimes sitting up past midnight, about a new way of looking at life. The boys say they don't want to just think about business as their dads do. We all want to find another meaning to life, enjoy life and be free. Get rid of the taboos on sex, smoke pot if we feel like it. And one boy said he'd like to sit and talk to his dad about the things that are important to him, not just sit and watch television. I guess in a way that is a cult; it certainly is different from our parents' way of life.

Q. You said in the dream the members of the cult approached from "over the hill." What do you relate to that direction?

A. That is where in reality some unpleasant neighbors live. And they have a mean dog we are all afraid of. He's really vicious, attacked our dog once. That is the direction the cult members were coming from.

Q. In the dream your reaction to the cult was one of fear. Why?

A. Now that I think about it, what I was talking about at school does kind of scare me, because I don't really see what the future holds. But maybe the worst part of it is that that way of thinking is breaking up my relationship with my family.

Q. In the dream you remember that, when the cultists separated you and your mother, you tried to attack them, bit one of them. With your understanding now, what do you think that meant?

A. I know that while I have been going along with the cult talk, one part of me doesn't like it. And I am really afraid of what it might do to Mom and me. After we argued the last time we both cried and hugged each other. I know I really do love her.

Q. Then what about the part in the dream where they warned you that your dad would die within a week? Are you really worried about his health?

A. That really scared me, when they said that. He is really in good health but works awfully hard and we all worry he will overdo. Maybe in my dream it is a warning to me, that down inside I'm afraid if I cause him a lot of worry it might cause him to have a heart attack or something. Maybe it is my own guilt for worrying him. I remember at the beginning I felt the dream was a warning.

The girl's free association and self-analysis are so clear that the dream needs little further elaboration. She said at the beginning of the dream, "In my dream I dreamed I was dreaming." This is an indication that her conscious mind was close enough to her subconscious to be aware of what was going on. This occasionally happens to dreamers, particularly when the person is under analysis and open to the communication of the sleeping self.

It is significant in this girl's dream—as it is in most of our dreams—that despite her desperate efforts to lock out the ugly creatures, she still finds them inside her home, within her emotional self. She discovered, as we all must, that there is no lock or key that will keep out the enemy within!

It is, of course, apparent from the girl's own remarks how meaningful the message of the dream was to her. After discussing it, she remarked, "Oh, I feel so much better now that I understand it. I know myself better and I know what is best for me to do."

It takes no extensive knowledge of dream analysis to interpret the following dream, particularly in light of the free association following it. The dreamer was a thirty-year-old, rather passive man whose wife was threatening divorce because of his ineffectiveness in and out of bed. She complained that she felt like his mother.

> It was a short dream. There was a little calf on the outside of a tall chain-link fence. On the other side of the fence was its mother. The calf was bawling and bawling for its mother, and I felt real sorry for it.

In lieu of free association, he was given a simple test:

Q. Tell me the first name that comes to your mind.
A. Mary Lou.
Q. Number?
A. Two.
Q. Song?
A. It sounds silly, but all I can think of is "Rock-a-Bye Baby in the Tree Top."

It turned out that Mary Lou was his mother's name. The number he gave reminded him of when he was two years of age and when asked how he felt when he thought about the song, his reply was: "Safe and warm and loved." And when we remind ourselves that it was milk the calf was crying for . . . Need we say more?

After these examples, the question arises of whether every dream lends itself to interpretation. Not always. Sometimes they are like wandering thoughts and vagaries of the imagination, fleeting impressions without much apparent meaning or emotion. The importance of a dream is almost always commensurate with the intensity of its emotional impact. On the other hand, the dream content might be important but difficult to interpret because of the defenses of the ego. Freud explains it:

> The question whether every dream can be interpreted is to be answered in the negative . . . One is opposed by the psychic forces that are responsible for the distortion of the dream. Whether one can master the inner resistances by one's intellectual interest, one's capacity for self-control, one's psychological knowledge, and one's experience in dream-interpretation depends on the relative strength of the opposing forces. It is always possible to make some progress; one can at all events go far enough to become convinced that a dream has meaning and generally go far enough to become convinced of some idea of its meaning. (In Jastrow, *Freud, His Dream and Sex Theories*)

When such resistance is encountered, it may be best to await a later dream, one less marked by the ego's censor. In general, it is not always essential to pin down the meaning of every dream or every symbol, or to reproach the dreamer for not remembering every dream. It is safe to assume that if the unconscious has something important to tell the dreamer, it will send it up again in another dream.

An intense dream life need not stem from emotional trauma. Because nature always seeks a balance, dreams are frequently a compensation for an unfulfilled life. It is interesting to note that when an individual is living a full life physically and emotionally, his dreams may be so bland and dull he can scarcely remember them, while the person enduring an uninteresting and inhibited existence with unexpressed love and creativity may toss all night with intense, exciting, even lurid dreams. In other words, rich life, poor dreams; meager existence, rich dream content.

But when one hears the remark that dreams have no meaning, are foolish, and should be ignored (usually from someone who has had no knowledge of or exposure to valid dream interpretation), it is well to remember what Jung once said: "No amount of skepticism or critical reserve has ever enabled me to regard dreams as negligible occurrences. Often enough they appear senseless, but it is obviously we who lack the sense and the ingenuity to read the enigmatical message from the nocturnal realm of the psyche . . . No one doubts the importance of conscious experiences; why then should we question the importance of unconscious happenings?"

While daydreams have not been discussed, they have been thought by Jung and others to be as important as night dreams because they emanate from the same level of the psyche as fantasy and wish fulfillment. A repetitive daydream may be interpreted in the same way as a repetitive night dream.

Here are some further ideas that I have found helpful in dream analysis. Some are direct quotations from Freud and Jung, others are somewhat paraphrased. I have also included theories and concepts that my own practice has validated.

In dream analysis, one should never become dogmatic about method and symbols, but remember that dream symbols have different meanings to different people in different situations—a further reason why the practice of free association is essential. Jung said: "The analyst doesn't always know what the nature of the problem is, the client doesn't know or he would have gotten over it, but the unconscious does know and tries its best to tell us through our dreams what is the subjective cause of our physical and emotional distress."

In approaching any dream, we would do well to remember these words of Dr. Frederick cam Elden, neurologist, poet, and hypnotherapist, quoted in *The New World of Dreams*, edited by Ralph L. Woods: "I simply wish to point out what so many men of science seem to forget. We hear Freud's triumphant assertion that *all* dream-life is now explained . . . no concrete reality can be attached to such an explanation. It is against this scientific arrogance that I utter a warning. No theory has as yet explained *all* about dreams; no! not even more than the tiniest part; we have not as yet crossed the threshold of that world, which for us is still 'occult.'" Confirming this, Dr. Stephen Hoeller, professor of comparative religions and well-known lecturer and author, agrees with Jung that no one interpretation of a dream can be final, that there is layer after layer of meaning to be revealed.

Another student of dream psychology makes this comforting observation in Wood's book—comforting, that is, to people who are shocked by the "immoral" symbols in their dreams: "If immoral dreams—in which we include all dreams which deviate from the sense of righteousness which is present when awake—are to be considered indicative of one's inner character, then everyone is immoral at times, for these dreams occur to all persons irrespective of their conduct in waking life. Unless habitual, they are far from being indices of the true character. Such dreams really tell what the dreamer knows, even though the knowledge is theoretical. As Kant has re-marked, they give us an idea of what we might have been were it not for education." It also helps to remind ourselves that the unconscious always exaggerates for emphasis—apparently so that we cannot fail to take note of the coded message.

Our dreams ought never to shock us or make us afraid. Indeed, Dr. Ste-phen Hoeller suggests that, since we are all so confined by our consciences in our waking moments, at night we should relax and enjoy our dreams, take advantage of the temptations offered while nobody is there to criticize or stop us. The thought arises: how many of us, enticed in a dream by some appealing temptation, halt just before yielding (that superego never seems to sleep!) and on waking feel virtuous but quite frustrated!

Whether a dream to be analyzed is simple, like the examples cited above, or complex, we must remember that dream analysis is a fairly complicated process, requiring training and experience, a knowledge of symbols, my-thology, and various religious concepts, plus a sensitivity to human nature and to the emotional state of the particular person whose dream you are attempting to understand. Even if the dream is a long one, first help the dreamer identify its major outline and theme. Then, using free association and any other means at hand, proceed step by step through each aspect of the dream.

What about the new theory propounded today that it is not necessary to undergo analysis or learn to interpret the meaning of a dream, that all one need do, when troubled by a nightmare or violent dream, is to treat it as a conscious experience, to confront and "face down" the threat, and that once that is done, the problem is solved! How simple and, unfortunately, how ineffective. This approach ignores the way dreams express meaning through the language of symbols. It might be likened to a man in a jungle who, fearing tigers, tears up a picture of one and then believes he has nothing to fear. Again, as the Talmud puts it, a dream uninterpreted is like a letter un-read. If one receives a threatening letter from an unknown antagonist, the problem is not resolved, harmony is not established, by tearing up the letter and throwing the scraps away, even if this is followed by the most positive thinking. What about the next letter, or an urgent telegram that repeats the original threat? If one does not look beyond the message, the symptom, then the cause is never discovered.

If one happens to look into a mirror and is confronted by an unattractive image, would it be purposeful or logical to want to smash the mirror? (In a dream the mirror has the magical ability to show to the dreamer by reflection the state of his unconscious.) Wouldn't it be more logical instead to be grateful for having a mirror in which we can get a picture of what is unattractive about us, what needs correction, and go to work on that instead of attempting by willpower and positive thinking to erase the original image in the mirror? And, by correcting the cause, hope for a happier image? The efficacy of this approach is that once the problem itself is recognized and worked on the nightmare and its prowlers do not return—the shadow projection no longer exists because the emotional energy behind it is dissipated.

4

Mechanisms of the Unconscious

With the realization that our unconscious, in delivering a dream to us, both reveals and conceals at once, it is helpful to become acquainted with some of the methods the unconscious uses in dreams to satisfy both ends. All of these mechanisms of the self, it must be remembered, are overlapping and interwoven and no one can be isolated in practice.

Projection

The process of projection is one of the most effective of all ego-protective devices. The small child learns to say, "I didn't do it, Mamma, *he* did," and the adult finds it easy to blame others for what he has not faced within himself.

The unconscious uses this mechanism very cleverly in dreams. Almost always, when two people are involved in a dream, the "other guy" or the "other woman" plays the negative role. If the dreamer is a woman she may have an irritating experience in the dream with "that catty woman in the office"; if a man, he may relate a dream about some fellow whom "I just don't like or trust, but don't know why." From such dreams the dreamer will naturally awaken with a feeling of self-satisfaction, that he is all right while that other person is no good. From such superficial interpretation of the dream, with its resultant ego superiority, he will learn nothing. How much more fortunate is the person who can discover that this unpleasant "other person" is really some aspect of himself and that by removing the mask it is possible to see an inner problem clearly and realize an opportunity to grow.

Such projection, though common to all of us, is found most frequently in the individual who is constantly critical of others. As the Bible puts it, "And why beholdest thou the mote that is in thy brother's eye, but considerest not the beam that is in thine own eye?" (Luke 7.3). To find our own mote, dream interpretation is often the truest (and subtlest) way.

The purpose of this book is not, of course, to moralize. But in interpreting one's own dreams, and in helping others to understand theirs, we must admit that "this is *my* dream; every aspect of it is related to *me* and *my* feelings about someone or something. My dream is a mirror and the shadows I find there belong to my own shadow self."

Compensation

Just as our body in waking moments uses compensation to maintain equilibrium, so does the psyche. Anything polarized or extreme in nature calls for compensation to bring about balance, so we find that the relation between the conscious and the unconscious is often compensatory. It is fairly well recognized, for example, that men who boast constantly are attempting to compensate for some hidden sense of inferiority. In interpreting certain dreams, particularly when there is some extreme emotion or attitude and the dreamer says, "I don't see how this could really apply to me," one should always ask: For what *opposite* conscious attitude might this be a compensation? If the dreamer is by nature a quiet, inhibited individual, calm and collected during his waking moments, how can compensation operate? The dreams of such a person may involve outbursts of rage or tears, or, more frequently, through projection, the dreamer will witness explosions or eruptions of nature, earthquakes or volcanic eruptions. The person who suffers from inferiority of stature or accomplishment may in his dream loom large in one or the other respect. The brow-beaten little boy gets the best of Daddy (Jack and the beanstalk); the plain little girl outshines her mother. Here is a simple illustration:

The dreamer was a tall, thin, shy boy of high school age. He had a dynamic and successful father who constantly urged him into athletics, for which he was totally unsuited. Retiring with girls, he had never dated.

> I have had this dream several times and it always makes me feel good. In the dream I have a big powerful red sports car, a Jaguar I think it is, and I'm going full tilt around the school in it. All the kids are watching me; I'm the only one of the guys that has such a car.

The compensation in this dream is too obvious for interpretation. It might be recognized, however, that in addition to an expression of power and superiority, the "big red sports car" has phallic resonance; there is yet another way he'd like to outshine the other guys.

Inversion

When a repressed emotion is too intense to be faced consciously or released, then a dream, through the process of inversion, can transpose it into an opposite but equally intense emotion. When inversion occurs in a dream, it would seem to be more frequently related to emotion than to people or objects. One is naturally reminded of the adage of the sad man behind the comic face of the clown. We do know that one is prone, under great stress, to break into laughter and often when one is very happy it is not unusual to find oneself weeping. For example, a young woman related, with great self-reproach, that when she attended the funeral of an aunt who had reared her and whom she loved deeply, she burst into hysterical laughter as she stood beside the coffin.

For whatever reason, dreams sometimes hide the dreamer's anxiety or grief behind humor. When in relating a dream the dreamer says, "It was all so funny, I found myself laughing so hard I woke up," frequently, free association will reveal that the dreamer has been in a mood of deep depression or hopelessness. The uncontrollable laughter replaces the unshed tears.

The following dream is an example of how a dream may show someone how he is practicing *conscious* inversion.

The dreamer was a young married woman. She was a very conscientious wife and homemaker who had been attempting, through positive thinking, to overcome or "clean up" the problems in her life.

> It seemed that I was housecleaning in my dream, but the strange thing was that the rug was not on the floor but on the ceiling and I was having a hard time trying to get my vacuum cleaner up there to clean it. I woke up wondering why it was upside down.

Not understanding that the problems that needed "cleaning up" were really underfoot, she had been trying to approach them only through her logical mind. Her dream illustrated, through the language she understood, that her approach was upside down.

Condensation

A dream has been compared to a capsule, or a Pandora's box, out of which something small can be opened and expanded into very large significance. The unconscious may compress characteristics of several people or experiences into one person, place, or object. For example, this dreamer was a married man under analysis. At the time of the dream he was reviewing his childhood, his maternal attachment, and the conflicts of his marriage.

> There wasn't much going on in the dream; I was just talking to this rather attractive young woman. But somehow I felt disturbed and confused and didn't know whether I didn't like her or what she was talking about. It doesn't really mean much, does it?

His free association:

> Q. What did she look like, blonde, brunette, tall or short? Remind you of anyone?
>
> A. She was built like my wife, but my wife is blonde and this girl had black hair.
>
> Q. Anybody important in your life with black hair?
>
> A. The girl I was dating—I was crazy about her—before I married my wife had very black hair.
>
> Q. How was she dressed? What did she have on?
>
> A. I remember clearly, it was a cotton print dress, white with little blue flowers all over it. Come to think of it, that was my mother's favorite dress; I remember her wearing it a lot. In fact, I have a picture of her in it.

There were a few more details, but it became plain that, through the process of condensation, his unconscious had presented him with a composite of the three most important women in his life, a composite anima image, one might say, a condensed representation of what he relates to and expects from all women—at this time from his wife in particular.

Another example of condensation in dreams, as Freud pointed out, is the case of words replacing things, and things, words. "Six" can be a symbol of "sex" and everything related; "ate" can replace "eight"—or they can be reversed.

Transference and Displacement

While the process of projection is almost always involved with human personalities, the mechanism of transference replaces one object, or one organ of the body, with another. In dreams involving a problem of a sexual nature, the transposing of an organ or object often takes place. For instance, a woman who has experienced the trauma of rape may dream of a hole torn in her skirt, or of a broken window in her bedroom, even of the threat of a gun or knife that she cannot escape. Frequently transference involves different organs of the body. A man's nose may symbolize his penis displaced upward, and, if he has a castration complex, instead of dreaming of his genitals he may dream of the loss of a finger, an arm, or a leg. Displacement can be more subtle, too, as in the case of a woman guilty about an abortion who dreamed that everywhere she went she had to carry a little white box, the size, she said, to hold flowers—or a baby. What did it mean when a man dreamed that his wife had given him a dictionary as a wedding gift? Through the process of displacement he was being told by his unconscious that she had brought to the marriage more intellect than romance.

A significant form of transposing, and more difficult to detect, is one in which the dreamer subtly "gets even" with someone for whom he feels anger by having that person in the dream do to him, the dreamer, what he in reality would like to do to the other person. An example was a little boy who felt suppressed anger at his mother after he learned she was secretly unfaithful to his father. The boy, of course, could not and would not threaten his mother. So what did he do? He had a very vivid dream in which his mother was chasing *him* all over the house with a butcher knife in her hand! The mother, of course, after his recital of the dream was puzzled and shocked that her son could picture her in such a vicious role. By the process of transference he had put his rage into his mother and had her do to him what he unconsciously would have liked to do to her.

Transference onto the Analyst

In all counseling or analysis some transference onto the analyst takes place, positive or negative—fortunately, it is generally positive. Freud felt that such transference was essential, that it created the battleground on which the neurosis was conquered. The analyst becomes a substitute figure for important people in the person's life. He transfers to the analyst the feelings of fantasy or emotional conflicts that he previously felt for his mother, father, or another to whom he was either greatly attached or toward whom he felt much resentment. It is essential for the analyst to recognize this, handle it carefully, and use it to help the client to recognize and come to terms with his own emotional conflicts. The mechanism of transference is often quite apparent in dreams; such dreams often reveal to the analyst the intensity of the transference. It behooves the analyst to handle the interpretation of these dreams very carefully in order that the dreamer can understand and accept them.

Jung did not entirely disagree with Freud's belief in the necessity of transference. He considered the relationship between analyst and client important, suggesting that it is best for the dreamer, instead of "reliving" alone, in dream, the traumatic emotions of life, to do so together with an active partner. It may even be helpful for the analyst to step out of his anonymity and share his own experiences, even his own dreams.

One young woman, who doubtless felt the counseling was getting uncomfortably close to a problem, surprised her analyst with an anxious call quite early one morning to inquire, "Are you all right?" On being assured that the analyst was in good health, the young woman explained, "I had the most dreadful dream about you last night. You were in bed very ill, and in such pain I almost got up in the middle of the night to call and see how you were." This is a clear example of transference, in which she imposed on her counselor an exaggeration of the "pain" she was feeling in analysis.

Here is another dream example of negative transference and distortion.

(Lest the reader from these examples get the impression that the experience of analysis and dream interpretation is fraught with resistance on the part of the individual undergoing analysis, let me hasten to explain that such reaction is the exception; usually the experience is friendly on the part of both the client and the counselor.) The dreamer was a teenage girl who had been reared by a somewhat shrewish mother. She had reached a delicate point in her analysis at the time she brought in her dream.

> I dreamed I came for my appointment with you. But when I got here, you weren't in the chair where you always sit; instead there was a witch woman sitting there in your place. She looked mean, had stringy black hair, and wore black clothes. I just saw her, and then I woke up. Why in the world would I have such a dream?

Her free association:

Q. Tell me anything else you can remember about her.
A. Well, she was dark-skinned and had a crooked nose.
Q. Anything else?
A. Come to think about it, her hair was cut in bangs across her forehead.
Q. Who's the first person you can think of who wears bangs, or ever did wear bangs?
A. (Pause) I can't think of anybody but myself. I always wore bangs until a short while ago.

Because it was her dream, her free association, and her hairstyle, it was not too difficult for her to understand that the witch was "hers"; that through the process of transference and distortion her unconscious had projected her negative image of her mother, and a touch of her own "witchiness," into the place of the counselor.

Exaggeration and Diminution

In their attempt to convey messages to the conscious mind, dreams often use size symbolically. To an infant all things and people are huge, so that later on, when a dream represents people and animals as oversized, buried memories and emotions of infancy are involved. When a thirty-year-old man dreamed of sitting next to huge thighs that belonged to a large woman who had her arm around him, it wasn't difficult to tell that he was in a regressive mood and missed his mother. In "Jack and the Beanstalk" (fairy stories are like dreams in many respects), Jack was afraid of the Giant father figure. He managed not only to elude the Giant but to take the Golden Egg of love and security back to his mother. A large person or animal may symbolize a childhood trauma, a shock or fear of such magnitude that the child's psyche buried it in the unconscious. In the wake of such dreams, free association is the only way to recover the original source of the trauma. Sometimes exaggeration of size does not connote any threat, but rather power or rank.

At the other end of the scale is diminution. Smallness in a dream (and sometimes out of one) generally means insignificance or inferiority. Insecure and rejected children sometimes dream they are so tiny nobody sees them (and if they are surrounded by threatening adults this may be a refuge). Diminishing someone's stature may represent a wish to "knock them down to size." The woman who dreams of men as "runty little creatures" is attempting in her dream to gain power over those whom she considers her enemies.

When dealing with exaggeration in dreams, we must remind ourselves that the unconscious emphasizes by exaggeration. On awakening it is reassuring to remember that no matter how high the cliff from which we fell, we rarely hit bottom and are never hurt; that the tremendous tidal wave towering over us did not drown us; and that after all the knives and guns there is no blood.

Distortion

Distortion in dreams occurs because of two primary forces at work within the dreamer: the unconscious "content" of the dream, and a censorship imposed on that content, resulting in distortion. In a dream one may admire and disparage at the same time, making someone appear ugly who is in reality attractive. Here is an illustration. The dreamer was an attractive young woman who had been the "baby of the family" and who, because of her natural charm, was usually the center of attention. She related to the analyst that the night before her dream she had double-dated with a girlfriend of hers and her boyfriend. During the evening both young men were more attentive to the other girl than to the dreamer. This proved to be the stimulus of the dream. The dreamer mentioned that her girlfriend bore a strong resemblance to the actress Joan Crawford, which turned out to be significant.

> In my dream I was talking to Joan Crawford and I was impressed with how beautiful she was. But then when she turned to walk away from me I was surprised to see what big fat legs she had and I couldn't help but think what a pity it was. Also I wondered how she could ever be a star with such awful legs.

Her wish fulfillment, which produced the distortion, is apparent in the dream. Her ego was restored by the knowledge that her own legs were lovely, allowing her to feel pity for the unfortunate actress.

Another form of distortion found in dreams is called "doubling" or "twinning," in which a person, object, or thing appears in duplicate, expressing two facets of the dreamer's self.

The next form of distortion and displacement is a very subtle one. In this case the dreamer, with the secret wish that another person be humiliated, projects himself into the other's place and is *himself* embarrassed. Such a dream serves two purposes: by displacement it downgrades the other person and yet also conceals from the dreamer's conscious mind his jealousy and malice—a sort of atonement in reverse.

Here is another interesting example of a negative wish resulting in distortion in the dream content. The dreamer was a rather submissive middle-aged woman, not too happily married. By nature peace-loving, she had attempted for years to live without friction with a critical, supersensitive husband. Prior to the following two dreams her frustration had been compounded by the selfishness of her adult son and his spoiled wife. It is not difficult to recognize the latent import of her dream, that of an overtly devoted wife and mother:

> Three nights in a row I dreamed my son had died. I went out and bought the casket, and then after that I went to his funeral. When I woke up I was surprised at how philosophical I had felt about the whole thing.

Here is her second dream.

> It seemed it was Easter vacation when everybody is out of school [her son is a medical student]. I am not going but in the dream my son and his wife are flying to Palm Springs. Oh, yes, and my husband is going too. It seems they were flying in an old two-seater, rather rickety plane. My

daughter-in-law was wearing the old-fashioned clothes for flying, and was wearing goggles. I was helping them go.

Here again a latent wish is expressed through distortion. Her prosperous, successful husband who always traveled first class is reduced to a more humble mode of transportation, while she places her self-indulgent, well-dressed daughter-in-law in a costume she wouldn't be caught dead in. If that rickety plane doesn't make it to Palm Springs, nobody can hold the dreamer responsible!

It should be made clear that an apparent wish for the death of a relative (or for that matter, anyone important) in a dream cannot be interpreted or translated literally. It is rather a wish to be rid of the *problem* that that person poses to the dreamer, a wish that the problem would "die."

There is another kind of dream that is baffling to interpret if taken at face value. It occurs most frequently to a son or daughter who has had a parent of superior attainments. Compared to this parent, the son or daughter always feels inferior. The superior mother or father may have chided their offspring for various shortcomings. Here is an example.

The dreamer was a young man in his thirties, self-effacing, shy in social situations, and going through a period of frustration and low self-esteem. He was the only son of well-to-do parents. His father, who had died several years before, had been a successful businessman who started his own business and developed it into a large organization. His mother was alternately over-protective and scolding. The son had worked for his father and still worked for the company under other management. He constantly said that he was poor at business, that "when I was the boss's son, as long as he was around I could fall back on that. But I never felt I measured up. He was always a kind of giant."

> In the dream I was at home talking to my mother about something when my dad walked in. It looked like him in the face but in no other way. He had been drinking, I guess he was plain drunk, and he looked sloppy and sort of fat. I was disgusted with him and sorry for him at the same time, and my mother was shocked.

This is his free association:

> I never saw my father drunk once; in fact, I don't think he ever took more than one drink at a time. And he loved nice clothes and was always

well-groomed. I always looked up to him. But in the dream I was sorry for him and ashamed of him at the same time.

A clear example of distortion. Never in his waking moments had the young man ever had an opportunity to feel anything but inferior to his dynamic, successful father; in the dream he not only "gets even" with him, but pities his father. In addition, he has his mother on his side. The dreamer said he could easily recognize the expression of his hidden wish.

Transposing to Opposites

Sometimes, an element in a dream may symbolize its opposite. Freud pointed out that such symbols can only be recognized by paying careful attention to the context of the dream. For instance, when someone dreams of diving into a pool of water or crawling into a hole, Freud points out that this may refer to the memory of emerging from the womb, as well as the wish to return to it.

The dream given below contains a clear example of transposition. The dreamer was a middle-aged married man who was sexually impotent, and, as is often the case, extremely suspicious of the faithfulness of his wife. They had a very pretty teenage daughter.

> I was in the bedroom of our neighbors next door. Their young daughter was in bed and she was exposing her breasts to me. I must admit that I was shocked that she would be so bold.

The meaning of this dream emerged soon after when the man's daughter came for analysis. With much embarrassment she related that her father had for some time been stealing into her bedroom at night and sexually stimulating her, always with the admonition that "it's all right, I'm your father." His dream had protected his ego by transposing the guilt from himself to the girl—even to the point of "being shocked."

5

Aspects of the Inner Self

In the attempt to understand dream content and its source, different aspects or areas of the unconscious come under consideration, all of which can be classified only subjectively. There are no psychological, physical, or even mental boundaries by which they can be measured. But they are there. We recognize that our thoughts, images, and impulses originate somewhere, and these sources have been given names. The descriptions and examples given are far from explicit; countless lengthier and more elaborate definitions are to be found in scholarly books on psychology and dreams, but it is hoped that the following discussion of these different areas of the inner self will be helpful and provide some signposts as we travel the road of self-understanding through dream analysis. We must bear in mind that almost nothing emerging from the psyche through dreams (or in any other way) is clear cut or definite. Instead, everything is relative and interconnecting, always with some mystery and always with the possibility of other meanings.

The Id

First to be considered is the id, that primary source of all instincts and energies. Webster's International Dictionary gives us a definition of the id that is both brief and succinct: "The fundamental mass of the tendencies out of which the ego and libido develop."

The id of some people would seem to be much stronger and more dynamic than that of others. They are people whose actions and desires seem to spring from elemental or basic urges rather than motivations on a higher level of consciousness. But because the id is the source of our energy, the stirring of the life force itself, it must be recognized as innately good, though it often needs refining.

Very simply, the id might be compared to the engine in the deep dark hold of a ship, strongly and mindlessly churning away, turning the wheels and furnishing the power that enable the ship with its cargo of passengers to move through the sea. In this same way the id powers our passage through life. In dreams, the id can appear as a primitive jungle (whence emerge the animal instincts), a powerful motor, even a smoldering volcano.

Libido

Next we come to the energy emerging from the id, and we find two definitions, one from Freud and the other from Jung. Both considered libido as basic energy but arising from different sources. The dictionary defines libido as "sexual desire, lust, energy, motive force, desire, or striving, either as derived from the sex instinct (according to Freud), or as derived from the primal and all-inclusive instinct or urge to live, according to Jung. Loosely, desire or motive force in general."

Accepting the concept of both Freud and Jung that libido starts as basic energy, we might say it expresses four primary urges: first, to survive; second, the hunger to eat or devour; third, the wish to satisfy love or sexual appetite; and finally, to overcome or destroy that which stands in its way— or, when transmuted, to flow into channels of creativity and growth.

When blocked or frustrated in the fulfillment of any of these primary impulses, the resulting fear may be turned into aggression. However, libido itself can be considered neither evil nor good. Energy itself is neutral and flows as directed; it is only the direction that can be labeled evil or good. Dr. David Seabury once remarked that the same force that could destroy a building when transmuted and redirected could build a far more beautiful building. And we would do well to remember that the object of libido, whether love or hate, takes on importance as a result of the focus of the libido. Once the libidinal attention is withdrawn or turned to another object or person, the first object fades in importance.

When considering the id and its force and energy (libido), both very potent aspects of the unconscious, we need to remember what Carl Jung had to say in *Modern Man in Search of a Soul.*

> The unconscious is not a demonic monster, but a thing of nature that is perfectly neutral as far as moral sense, aesthetic taste and intellectual judgement go. It is dangerous only when our conscious attitude towards it becomes hopelessly false, and this danger grows in the measure that we practice regression . . . That which is feared—I mean the overwhelming of consciousness by the unconscious—is most likely to occur when the unconscious is excluded from life by repression or is misunderstood and depreciated.

Once brought into the light of consciousness, the "demonic monster" can be "de-clawed" and "de-fanged."

In dreams libido can express itself in the form of fire (either rage or lust, depending on the connotation), powerful animals such as horses, or as an automobile or locomotive. The sexual aspect of the dreamer's libido occurs in the act of making love, producing the emission dream of the male and the orgasm dream of the female, or the libido in the dream can take a regressive turn and produce an incestuous experience with the dreamer's parent, frequently the mother. And because the expression of our first libidinal urge was to nurse at our mother's breast, when in a regressive emotional state the dreamer may re-experience in dream the pleasure of eating or drinking the warm, sweet foods associated with the mother and her care.

From the jungle of the id some pretty fearsome animals emerge in the dreams of most of us. In contemplating this next dream, however, one gets the feeling that the dreamer's unconscious had to reach far back into the primordial instincts to come up with the creatures that beset her poor husband. The dreamer? A small, soft-spoken, quiet young woman who at the time was undergoing much frustration, depression, and even rage over the apparent neglect and emotional withdrawal of her husband. One might say the pot was boiling over when she had this dream:

> My husband and I and my two little daughters were in our garage. Suddenly Bob was attacked. There were a jaguar, a monkey, and two

snakes, one a black one with green eyes, about two feet long, and a red one with a distorted huge head and giant jaws. The mouth looked like a shark. Bob was attacked by all of these animals. My daughter Janette and I chased off the monkey and the jaguar, and then we captured the black snake.

By this time we were in the back of an old beat-up station wagon and I started driving like crazy. One of Bob's legs was slashed, big gashes, and it was bleeding badly. We had captured the black snake in a gunnysack, and the red snake we were holding at bay so it wouldn't attack him. It didn't seem to be going after anybody but Bob.

Then it was night and I pulled up in a parking lot that I thought was a hospital, and it was a school. I jumped out of the car and the girls went to find help. We couldn't find the emergency entrance, and I thought the hospital was supposed to be there and instead I had found a school building. The red snake started after Bob again, and I remember grabbing the snake again and I woke up screaming.

As happens in so many dreams of revenge, at the last moment the dreamer attempts to rescue the victim from her rage. When asked what the red snake might have done to Bob if she hadn't held him, she replied, "I was afraid it would kill him!"

A very significant part of the dream is her disappointment at finding only a school when she knew she needed to find a hospital. Meaning, of course, that she was symbolically calling for help and couldn't find the "emergency entrance." The dream was stating that at this crisis in her life she didn't want to learn something, which was all the help a school could give her—she and Bob needed more immediate action. Fortunately she was able to secure help before the red snake got to Bob.

Regardless of the shape or direction libido takes, no one should feel guilty about such dreams. Instead they should be interpreted as an indication of some emotional incompleteness and/or immaturity.

The Ego

This aspect of the self partakes more of the conscious mind than of the unconscious, since it is formed largely from what the individual thinks of himself, his sense of worthiness or unworthiness. Sigmund Freud recognized, and the theory has been accepted ever since in the field of psychoanalysis (and therefore in dream analysis), that the formation of ego identity starts in very early childhood. It is the self-protective aspect of a person, the part that feels it must shield itself from criticism but also establish and prove its sense of worth and importance in the eyes of others. It expresses itself through the will to power and the wish for recognition. It is that part, and the only part of the individual, that is supersensitive and emotionally defensive. It is by nature self-centered and can be selfish. It cannot by any means be considered bad; it is an essential part of the developing personality, the outer shell formed to protect the deeper and more vulnerable inner nature, the sensitive soul, or psyche. The soul *yearns* for protection; while the ego *demands* and enacts it.

Again, here is the dictionary definition: "Ego: The entire man considered as union of soul and body. The conscious and permanent subject of all experience. The consciousness of the individual's distinction from other selves. The self-assertive and self-preserving tendency."

The flow of the libido and its fulfillment or frustration play a large part in the quality and maturity of the developing ego. Fortunate indeed is the person who has reached adulthood with a healthy ego, neither demanding nor defensive; this person can be said to be in good emotional health. The less fortunate one who has what might be called a sick or weak ego, resulting from neglect or rejection in childhood, often follows a pattern in life whereby he or she will attract or even create more failure and rejection. In contrast to the weak or deflated ego, there is also the person with an "inflated" ego, the boaster, constantly demanding attention and compelled to prove superiority. The swollen ego is an irritant to all of his associates and generally a burden to the individual himself. In fact, an over-developed ego, by placing emphasis on false values, might prevent the individual from developing the humility necessary for mental and spiritual growth.

Because it is instinctive for the ego to demand protection, in dreams it generally hides behind or beneath some form of symbolic cover or mask. Rarely, in other words, does the ego per se appear in a dream in such a way that the dreamer can say, "Oh, that must be my ego." It is only after dream interpretation that the true face of the clown or tragedian appears.

Many people consider the ego in an unfavorable light, believing that to be highly evolved it is essential to dissolve the ego. Dr. Stephen Hoeller has said that "the ego is the carrier of the light of consciousness; if you destroy that light you have naught but darkness. You should not confuse the light bulb with the electricity that gives it the light. The light bulb is the ego, the electricity however is generated in the unconscious and it is brought to the consciousness through various conduits, and one is the dream. The two together bring the individual illumination. But the ego must lose its arrogance which it exercises over our lives. That occurs in the dream . . ."

And how is the ego symbolized in the dream? By people with the same characteristics as the dreamer's own ego identity: feelings of pride and superiority will appear in the dream as a boastful individual, while feelings of inferiority will be represented as small, weak, and self-effacing figures. In such dreams, the mechanism of exaggeration is always at work—no doubt to make sure that the dreamer gets a clear picture of what is going on in his ego.

The following dream illustrates how the ego appeared in the dream of an accomplished professional woman.

> It took place in a drugstore. As I watched a man came into the store, walking with a rather rolling swagger. But what was fascinating about him was his general shape: he was very round all over, sort of puffed up as a balloon or tire when inflated. He was a pleasant enough fellow, you felt he would bother no one, but he sort of swaggered as he walked through, giving the impression that he was extremely pleased with himself.

The dreamer had a few days before been given a little praise, but in response she had brushed it aside with what she believed was true modesty. Instead the dream held up the mirror of self-recognition and she was shown how "puffed up" she had really been over a modest accomplishment.

The Superego

"Super" means greatest, best, superior, above. In dream analysis it is always represented by a figure of critical authority, or the person who is superior to the dreamer's own ego-consciousness or attainments. In a way the superego should be considered before the ego, because it is that which forms the child's ego in the first place.

It is well recognized that the infant starts life as a little bundle of vulnerable, impressionable responses, with no conscious identity of any kind. It slowly builds a self-image out of the approval and disapproval of its parents, the superego figures. Its first feelings of worth or worthlessness are formed by the attitude of its parents, love and praise or criticism and rejection. Naturally, with no innate understanding or guidance, the child starts molding himself into what is expected of or projected onto him to gain the protection and security parents can bestow. The child develops an ego, healthy or unhealthy, according to the mold presented by the parents, now the child's superego figures. And what they have projected, good or bad, in a few years of conditioning are introjected by the child, becoming his own concept of himself. Out of their expectations and projections he has built his own superego, which through his life sits in judgment on him.

Too frequently people live bedeviled by a superego that inhibits the expression of their natural instincts, as though a tape recording had been implanted in the mind that continues, long after separation from the parents, even after their death, to pass judgment on the individual's actions and motivations. It is from this source that most of us get what Dr. David Seabury called the "Thou shalts" and the "Thou shalt nots" that strongly channel our emotional life.

After the superego images of the parents come the teachers, the religious figures, and others of authority whose guidance is sometimes positive and sometimes not. Then there is the opposite example, the over-indulgent superego parents who rob a child of reality: "You are so smart, darling, I just know you're going to be famous. Here, let mother do that for you. I'll have a talk with that teacher unless she gives you better grades. Did that mean old table hurt your head; I'll have to spank it," etc., etc. The grandparents often get into this act, too.

While the criticized child never knows his good qualities, the over-praised child believes that he is beyond criticism. This child, in contrast with the rejected child, is almost totally unprepared for the vicissitudes of life; it will be almost unthinkable to find later that he is only human.

Because we all have an active superego, good, bad, or indifferent, it is essential in dream interpretation to learn how to recognize it. Our superego usually appears in dreams as a figure of authority, watching what we do, often either speaking or implying criticism. Whenever the dreamer feels nervous, guilty, or embarrassed in a dream, look for the superego figure somewhere in the background. Many people, in relating a dream, will remark, "It seems like in nearly all my dreams my mother is somewhere in the background. And yet she lives in another part of the country" or "I wonder why I keep dreaming about my grandmother. She's been dead for years. I was always afraid of her; she was constantly preaching at me." Then there is the sad, reproachful figure of the minister or the school teacher of long ago. These must not be interpreted as images of the real person but as the embodiment of their influence on the dreamer, their praise or criticism, which have become the dreamer's own superego. And, because the purpose of dream analysis is to achieve self-understanding, it is of great importance that we learn to recognize whether we are being guided by our own inner sense of what is right and best or are still living in subservience to our superego. It has been said that the harder the parent is on the child, then the harder that child, when an adult, will be on himself. Objectivity about one's superego is the first step toward freedom.

Superconscious

We now come to another aspect of the inner self, a far subtler but at the same time a far nobler voice from within, that of the dreamer's superconscious. It dwells at the opposite end of the emotional spectrum from our starting point, the id, for the superconscious is that part of the dreamer's higher self that waits upon our need and then comes through in the sleep state as the voice of wisdom or guidance, the part of which the philosopher Manley Hall spoke when he said, "We are all wiser than we know." Symbolically, this aspect of the inner self appears in dreams as the wise and loving parent, the kind teacher, or the inspiring spiritual leader. One might say that the superconscious waits quietly in the wings of the dreamer's unconscious while he plays out the drama of life's experiences. Only when the dreamer is ready to listen does this quiet voice of wisdom, which has been there all the time, begin to speak.

Borrowing from Greek myths and biblical parables, in which ideas are personified, let us create an imaginary experience by which we can become acquainted with the different aspects of our human nature as they might appear in human form.

As we, in imagination, look down the road before us, we see four people approaching. At first there seems to be only one man, and then he shifts and divides and we see four men again. The one we recognize first we know to be Mr. Id; we couldn't fail to recognize him because he pushes himself forward in a very brash manner. He wears a bright red shirt and has a mop of thick dark hair over a rather low brow. He impresses us as a rather coarse fellow, not one we would willingly invite to a party of well-bred people. But what he lacks in quality and intelligence he makes up for in muscle and energy. He would be a handy man to have in a fight—on our side. A rather simple fellow, uncomplicated by logic, ethics, or philosophy, he appears interested only in what he wants, the satisfaction of his appetites, either food or sex, and is troubled not at all by conscience or morals. You wouldn't want to cross him. He's not really mean, just a simple creature following his primitive instincts. But strong! Look at those muscles!

Walking beside and a little behind him is Mr. Ego. And what a character he is! Now you see him, now you don't, for he's always changing. Sometimes he appears very tall and proud with a head that is distinctly oversized, but then after he glances around nervously as though looking for attention and approval, he appears to shrink. He seems to lack substance or a sense of inner strength; he is living on the outside of himself. His clothing changes, too; sometimes it appears flamboyantly colorful and dashing and then, when the man within shrinks, his clothes, too, become nondescript and gray. Not a bad fellow, really; he just seems to be obsessed by his own importance, or lack of it, and what others may be thinking of him—when it appears that nobody is noticing him at all.

Now our gaze turns to the third character, easily recognized as Mr. Superego. Holding himself stiffly erect, a frown between his brows and with pursed disapproving lips, it is obvious that he is judging and criticizing his companions. He is on the right side, of course—he would never be any place else. Much older, and in his old-fashioned clothes with his superior manner, it is quite apparent that he is inhibiting his companions. At first he seems like an older man, but occasionally his countenance shifts, and he looks like a stern grandmother. He—or she—is definitely of the "old school," with no intention of ever changing.

Following quietly a little behind these three is a dignified, reserved fellow who with his serene, detached bearing commands respect. We recognize him as Mr. Superconscious, the gentleman who is aware of ideas and philosophies that his companions never dreamed of. He is quite a bit taller and carries himself with a gentle dignity. As he accompanies them, he makes no comment and seems to feel no need to give direction or advice, leaving his companions to find their own way. Yet we sense that if they get themselves in a tight spot, if Mr. Ego becomes confused and tries to bluff his way through, if Mr. Id, in his bullheaded manner, attempts to ram his way through a problem, if after worse comes to worst and in desperation they finally turn to Mr. Superconscious for help, he will gently and calmly guide them back to the right path. But first they have to ask him. He might chide them a little, but he is not one to criticize. He will not become too emotionally involved and his thoughts are in another realm entirely. He has compassion, but he waits for the stumbling individuals to make their mistakes and to learn that he is there when they need him.

But these are not the only personages coming down the same road. In the distance we can glimpse another group of four people: a man and woman, arms coupled, so much alike they look like brother and sister. They are Animus and Anima. With them is a couple strikingly different; we recognize Persona because of his air of self-satisfaction to the point of smugness. He is quite personable and attractive, but one senses it is all superficial, that other qualities might lie beneath that pleasant exterior. Perhaps there is a subtle relationship with his companion who seems to be his exact opposite, a shadowy, furtive fellow, keeping always in the background, dodging the light, so that "now you see him, now you don't." Of course, he is the Shadow; in himself he has no substance, but he carries the symbology of all that is dark and troubled, that is unknown and not yet brought to light.

What a strange lot, what odd characters! To know them better, we need only look at the face in our mirror—and learn to understand our dreams.

Animus and Anima

Dr. Jung made a great contribution to self-understanding as well as to dream analysis when he developed the concepts of the animus and anima. The animus, or masculine aspect of the self, is dominant in men. The animus is bigger, physically stronger, more rational than emotional, and by nature more aggressive and competitive. But every male has within himself an anima, or "soul within." This inner self is his gentler side, his spiritual nature. If well-adjusted, his animus is naturally uppermost in his life; if "inverted," he may find himself too dependent, receptive, and over-sensitive.

The essence of the female is called the anima, expressing itself as being physically and emotionally softer, more dependent, and nurturing. She, too, has her inner, other aspect called the animus, which enables her to fulfill herself intellectually and in a career. This inner strength gives her great courage in a crisis. If, however, the roles are confused and she becomes "inverted," she may take on too many masculine characteristics and become aggressive, competitive, and opinionated.

According to Dr. Jung, "We each have . . . contra-sexual traits in ourselves. The man, those of the woman, the woman, those of the man. Adaptation to the world naturally requires the development of the traits corresponding to one's own sex. The others fall into the unconscious, but reappear in the function that establishes relations with the inner world. . . . These functions, particularly the anima, are well suited to projection. Many men can tell even what their soul image looks like, and this can often guide a man in his choice of a love-partner, for he may seek the anima in a real woman" (quoted in Schaer, *Religion and the Cure of Souls in Jung's Psychology*). Because a boy generally bases his anima image on his mother, through the process of projection he will often marry a woman with the same qualities and temperament, even the same appearance, as his mother. The same principle is at work in the woman's projection of her animus image, whether positive or negative, upon the men who are important in her life. If her animus is negative, she is in trouble with the opposite sex.

These concepts did not begin with Jung. Emanuel Swedenborg in *The Principia* said that he considered the mind in two parts: rational mind, the animus, and above this the "soul of anima." The soul, he believed, "is a faculty distinct from the intellectual mind, prior and superior to, and more universal than the latter . . . and that it flows into the intellectual mind after the manner of light" (Toksvig, *Emanuel Swedenborg, Scientist and Mystic*). In eastern philosophy this male and female polarity in each of us is called yin and yang. And the concept is deeply embedded in popular belief as, for instance, in the widely held idea that "man is strong on the outside and weak inside, while woman is weak on the outside and strong within."

The polarity of the animus and anima runs through all of nature and all of history and was frequently beautifully enacted in the Greek myths. As a little exercise in the Jungian "creative imagination," let us take the story of Pygmalian and Galatea and attempt to interpret it as we would a dream. As we recall this myth, let us keep in mind the modern theory of the animus and anima but also the ancient truth that man relates to woman through the projection of his inner soul, his anima.

Pygmalian, it will be remembered, was a sculptor and out of cold marble created the statue of a beautiful woman. So lovely was she that he fell in love with the creature he had made, and, longing to wed, he then turned to the goddess Aphrodite in prayer for a wife similar to the statue he had made. Aphrodite took pity on him and gave life to his creation by turning the statue into a beautiful woman, called Galatea. In joy Pygmalian was now able to clasp to his heart the beauty of the image he had created from within the depths of his own nature.

The images of this myth are all archetypal. From the depths of his own creativity the sculptor projected and carved his anima image of beauty. Once it had taken form outside of himself, his masculine (animus) nature yearned to join again with this loveliness and, by "marrying" it, make himself whole. He could not do this alone, so he called upon the goddess of love, beauty, and the ocean (the great universal unconscious, mother of all life), Aphrodite, for help. It would seem that only she could turn his dream into life. Indeed, it was believed by some at the time that he created his statue first in the image of Aphrodite, who as the goddess of the ocean would also be the personification of the cosmic mother. We have learned from both Freud and Jung that the male models his first love object after the image of his mother.

When approaching the interpretation of a dream in which someone of the opposite sex plays an important role, the dreamer must ask himself: Is this really true of this person or only my concept of them? Are all men (or women) like this, or can I be projecting onto the person in the dream my own animus or anima image?

Because all dreams can come only from the dreamer's own psyche, then for simplification one might say that the woman in a man's dream typifies his own anima, or the feminine side of his nature, which he either likes or dislikes. By the same token the woman must recognize that the man she repetitively dreams of is a projection of her own animus, or of the masculine side of herself, which she may like or not.

The following dreams illustrate both negative and positive aspects of the animus and anima. They are the dreams of an "animus woman." In early life she had been hurt and rejected by her father. She was subsequently hurt and disappointed by men she knew. Finally, her marriage failed. To compensate she had become overly independent, successful in running her own business but insecure in human relations. In the first dream she is confronted by her negative animus; in the second she is yielding to her own true nature and attracting (through change in herself) a much finer animus.

> I was in this nice big spacious house, modern, huge rock fireplace, all comfortable and nice. My two daughters and maid were there. Then this man came in, no one I really knew, but I had the feeling something was not right and I told the girls and the maid to get out. He was really a nice-looking, rather handsome man, but I still felt somehow he was a threat to the girls. Nothing sexual, just mean. I sat down with this man on the couch and as I looked at him he started changing into something evil and horrible, a sort of Dracula. Before he made the complete transition I said, "Will you excuse me; there's something I have to take care of" and I went into the bedroom, locking the door behind me. Then I tried to go out the other door and found it was locked.
>
> I turned around and there he was! I was locked in both ways, there was no way I could escape. By now he had made the complete transition to Dracula. I looked around for something to defend myself, a stick, or a cross, or a crucifix. I couldn't find anything—and then he came at me, at my neck.
>
> I expected to die, that he would draw the blood out of me. When I looked at him last he had blood dripping from his teeth. I woke up shaking.

Her nightmare proves that no matter how comfortable her physical life (financial success reflected in a large expensive home) she still has to face her own ugly animus. She has a wish to protect her daughters and maid from what she already knows to be her problem, a tendency to domination and sarcasm. The sequence of the dream indicates that only when she has faced what she first considered attractive does the ugliness beneath start to emerge. Then she discovers she cannot lock it out, since it is really within herself. Ideas of self-protection, methods of attack, and even religious symbols prove of no avail and she awakens in a panic that her own ugly, powerful animus is about to draw the very lifeblood from her anima nature, her true self. Since all vivid dreams have different levels of meaning, one aspect of this dream is that she has not outgrown her fixation at the childish orally aggressive stage, vividly illustrated by the image of Dracula with blood on his teeth.

After becoming aware of how her feminine nature had been inverted and even warped by her mistreatment by her father, resulting in the formation of her own vindictive animus, this dreamer began to be able to love and identify with the anima side of her nature. She brought up another dream that reflects this inner change.

> This is the best dream that I have had in years. I was going through an open park, beautiful green grass and trees. It seems I was going to a club-house to attend some function there. I remember feeling good walking through the garden, everything natural and pleasant. When I got to the clubhouse people were lined up to fill their plates at the buffet.
>
> As I walked by there was this handsome hunk of a man who tried to flirt with me. I was embarrassed because I wasn't expecting that kind of attention and didn't quite know what to do. We talked for a while and then I went on to fill my plate and was almost through. The man then came up and spoke to me again but again I told him, "Let me finish filling my plate; people are waiting behind me," and he replied, "This is the second time you have ignored me" and started turning away. For fear of losing him I quickly said, "Wait just a minute until I put my plate down," which I did, although I hadn't finished filling it. Then he took me in his arms and we started dancing, just beautifully. He swirled and lifted me off my feet in a beautiful waltz; we were turning and turning. I just let him sweep me off my feet, a wonderful feeling. I felt love and happiness coming from him, warmth, protection, and safety.

Much of this dream is self-explanatory. It starts with a good feeling about nature, grass, and flowers. She is headed toward the clubhouse—social companionship. The dreamer is considerably overweight and has often re-marked that she knew she'd have to lose weight to be attractive to men. Her ambivalence appears when she keeps telling romance to wait until she has filled her plate once more. The climax of the dream comes when she finally puts her plate down and turns to the man. The message the attractive man gives her, that this is the second time she is turning her back on love and romance (for food: the oral problem again!), is highly significant.

Her euphoric sense of joy at the end of the dream is almost that of a little girl receiving the love and protection she never had from her father. But the message of the dream is that, regardless of her past, she still has the choice of making a change within herself. She said she awoke with a calm feeling that there are good men after all and that it was possible for her true self (anima) to attract love and contentment.

Here is another dream of a young woman emotionally and sexually frustrated:

> It seemed I was in my bed and I became aware that a big strong man was holding me down. It wasn't sexual or frightening; he wasn't mean, it was just that he was bigger and stronger than I was and I felt helpless under his control.

This is a simple illustration of how her love nature or anima was being "held down" and thwarted by her animus, which in the dream was stronger and dominating her feminine self. This is a clear example of inversion.

If a woman has an ambivalent image of her father, as partly kind and partly unkind, her animus image may be split into "black and white" or "good and bad." The following woman's dream illustrates this point:

> I was watching a struggle going on between a coarse mean man and a fine cultured man. As I watched I was very worried over which one would win.

The thief in a dream usually symbolizes some neurotic aspect of the dreamer's nature that threatens to rob his better self of some quality (not material thing) of value. Keeping this in mind, let us consider this next dream. The dreamer was a strongly opinionated woman with a mild, receptive husband whom she didn't particularly respect. They were sleeping in separate bedrooms.

> Before I relate the dream I want to explain that in my bedroom, in a shadow box over my bed, I have something which is very precious to me, a lovely treasure handed down from my grandmother to my mother and then on to me. It is a delicate hand-painted fan. Well, the other night I had a vivid dream in which I sensed that there was a man in my bedroom and I just knew he was a robber. It seemed like I woke up just as he was closing the door behind him. My first thought was what could he have stolen? In looking around I discovered the space over my bed was empty; he had robbed me of my beautiful fan! When I woke up I was so relieved to find it was still there, that it was only a dream. But that dream stayed with me all day.

Because the dreamer had delved into psychology it wasn't difficult for her to understand and accept what her unconscious was pointing out to her, that unless she softened her aggressive animus aspect, it could rob her of the "lovely treasure" of femininity handed down from her grandmother to her mother and in turn to her.

The next graphic dream illustrates what happened in a young woman's psyche when she not only faced her negative animus but gave it a scolding! A little of her background will explain how her problem came about. She was the fourth and last daughter of parents who craved a son, something of which she was made aware at a tender age. She did all she could to become the boy her father never had—difficult in her case, in view of the fact that she was naturally quite feminine in build and nature. At the time of the dream, she was filling the male role as best she could, although unhappily. It might be added that her romantic experiences with men had proved to be extremely disappointing. Here is her dream:

> I was in a shadowy kind of a room. Over to one side was a coffin and in it was a lovely young blonde girl, pale and apparently dead. My heart ached for her; it seemed so sad that such a beautiful girl had to die. Then I became aware of a young man standing to one side, a young man whom I didn't like at all. I knew somehow that he was responsible for the girl's death. Anger swept over me that this was so and I turned to him and scolded and shamed him as hard as I could for what he had done to this lovely girl. He just stood there. After I had scolded him I walked over to look at the girl in the coffin again and was amazed and thrilled to see a faint blush of color on her face, and while I stood watching her eyelids fluttered. A wave of joy swept over me and I said to myself, "Oh, she isn't dead after all; I just know she's alive and going to get well!" I woke up feeling happier than I have felt in a long time.

The girl stirring to life was not only her anima, but her love nature itself, which had been badly inhibited by her animus identity, symbolized by the man beside the coffin whom she instinctively disliked. Her dream states clearly that the turning point came when her true self turned in rage against the destructive force of her false animus identity. Only after that recognition did her lovely femininity have a chance to awaken and bloom.

One of the fascinating aspects of dream interpretation is to observe how the images and personalities change in the dream material as a result of changes taking place in the psyche of the dreamer. The two dreams given below illustrate a striking metamorphosis in a young man's anima image.

He had been conditioned by a domineering, negative mother and as a result his relations with women had been frustrating both socially and sexually. Here is his dream:

> I was walking along with a very ugly young woman, so ugly I didn't even want to look at her and I didn't anyone to see me with her. She had dark monkey-like skin and hair that was stringy and coarse. [In reality his mother is a handsome woman; this creature is an exaggeration of his negative anima.] I wanted to get away from her as fast as I could.

After undergoing counseling so that he could understand and begin to resolve his negative conditioning, he developed a much finer emotional and even spiritual outlook on life. Then, his unconscious sent him the following dream:

> I had a date with the loveliest young girl. She was sort of like the princess in a fairy story, delicate and sweet. I could hardly believe she was with me. I felt a strong urge, because she was so lovely and precious, to take care of her and protect her.

It is scarcely necessary to add that his relations with women improved, resulting sometime later in a fulfilling marriage.

Now let us consider the other side of the picture, how a man in his dream can be threatened by a negative anima. As a woman in her dream fears rape or other injury from an aggressive animus, the man dreams of being robbed, injured, or in some way trapped by a female figure (bitten, perhaps, by a black widow spider). Rarely is such a threat taking place in his conscious life. Instead his dream contains a warning that some part of his nature, his anima or feminine side, is emasculating him. This problem is illustrated in the following dream. The dreamer was a young man, a musician, troubled with sexual impotence and at the time separated from his wife.

> I was lying prone on the floor. A young woman whom I occasionally date—whom I suspect has a touch of lesbianism—was sitting on top of me. In reality she is not a large girl but in the dream she was larger than I was. She wasn't hurting me, just holding me down. I felt helpless because I couldn't get up.

Not only does the dream indicate inversion, that his anima had outgrown his animus or true masculine nature, but it also explains his sexual inability to "get up."

This next dream contains an interesting example of how a man can undergo frustration in competition with the masculine side of his overly ambitious wife. Her own animus becomes the "other man" with whom he has to compete for the love and attention he craves from her. For quite some time he had felt neglected, that his wife scarcely noticed him in her almost total absorption in studying and trying to develop a career for herself. His dream:

> In this dream I was the observer, and I felt out of it. It all took place at our home. My wife was entertaining some guy; he was good-looking, sort of the "ideal" business type. They were taking some sort of class and studying together, being very expressive with each other, holding hands. They walked out arm-in-arm and she gave him a little tender kiss. As he went to his car she waved and said, "I'll see you tomorrow," very loving and tender. As I watched I was thinking in the dream that this was going too far; she doesn't give me that kind of affection. . . . In reality I know that my wife is not unfaithful to me, and there really isn't another man.

But there really was "another man" in the image of his wife's ambitious animus in the dream. Once he understood the symbology of his dream he accepted it, and while it did not promise that his wife's libido would be withdrawn from her ambition and be redirected to him, at least he understood more clearly who and what his real competitor was.

There is one aspect of the animus/anima image in dreams that is perhaps not recognized enough, and that is the importance of the age level of the dreamer's image. Does the contrasexual aspect appear in the dream as a child, an adolescent, at the same level of maturity as the dreamer, or even older? Here is a dream that illustrates this point. The dreamer was an intelligent middle-aged man whose attention in life had been focused almost wholly on work, sports, hunting, fishing, prize-fighting, and other extrovertedly masculine activities. The sensitive, idealistic side of his nature rarely became apparent; in fact, there had been little enough in his life to stimulate or inspire its growth. Congruent with his emotional immaturity was the fact that his relationships with mature women had proved frustrating.

Before relating his dream he remarked: "I have had this dream or others like it for a long time. It doesn't make any sense to me because I can't associate the child in the dream with anybody I have ever known."

> There is always a little girl, about five or six I would guess; she's a cute little girl and while I don't know who she is I always feel that somehow

she belongs to me and I must take care of her. The strange part is she isn't like my sisters or any child I have ever known.

When asked to describe her clothes he replied: "That is another strange thing; she always has a kind of old-fashioned dress or coat on, and a little bonnet, the kind little girls wore years ago when I was a kid." Her clothing doubtless dated back to the time in his life when his anima self, his gentler, idealistic, spiritual side, stopped developing.

The next dream reads almost like a story, that of a man in search of his youthful love nature. The dreamer is an intelligent and good man, faithful to his work, his family, and his church. For a period of more than a year he had had to accept a sexless marriage, which he did apparently without complaint, meanwhile turning more and more to his religion as compensation. It was after a discussion of the inhibition of his love nature that he had this dream. It is important to know that, of his two daughters, the one in his dream was the one most like him in looks and personality.

> It involved my little girl Becky. We were in a church and there were tunnels underneath the church. Becky was playing with another little girl, playing around the entrance to one of these tunnels and they wanted to go in and explore it. They had a rope tied around themselves; going in with the rope behind them they figured when they wanted to come out they would follow the rope back out.
>
> They got in too far and came to a place where they made a turn and got lost in there. I realized they were lost and this friend of mine [his alter ego] was helping me try to find them. It was difficult for us to run, the ground was all slippery. When I got to the entrance they were not there.
>
> I hollered in, didn't hear anything back. I was really worried. I thought maybe there was still another entrance, so I went around to the right and got back into the church again and was looking for the entrance to the tunnel from the other side—and all of a sudden she showed up, came through the door, had found her way out.

Consider the symbols: the church (his religion), the tunnels underneath the church (areas of his own unconscious, underneath his religion), where his love nature or young anima took the wrong turn and became lost (inhibited). She emerged, on her own, from the last place he would have looked for her. The rope she took with her could symbolize the tie to the logical world to which we cling when exploring the labyrinth of the unconscious. Best of all, his young soul image returned exactly where it had disappeared, in this case no older or wiser but healthy and safe. The dreamer, however, was wiser for having understood and responded to the meaning of his dream.

While this final example did not appear in a dream, it still emerged from a man's psyche and, although sad, it is such a beautiful example it seems worthwhile to include it. The man was past middle age, a kind, loving, and courteous gentleman who had tragically lost his way in life through alcohol. Like all alcoholics, he felt he was a failure and was very lonely. When he wasn't reading, he sat silently in deep thought for long periods of time. It was at those times that he said, and I quote: "The most beautiful young woman comes to me. She really appears. She is pure and fine and lovely, and we talk. I see her and I hear her. I will not tell you what she says, it is between us, but she helps me and it is wonderful to know she is there." Sick though his animus was, how beautiful his anima, his soul!

Persona and Shadow

Carl Jung is also responsible for the concepts of the persona and the shadow. Simply stated, these are names or identifications of two opposite facets of everyone's nature. The persona is the more positive and attractive face that we present to the world, while the shadow represents the negative, darker, usually unrecognized and less developed side. The important point to remember is that neither is the real or total self, only an *aspect* of the personality. We might say the persona is what we want to be and hope we are, while the shadow is what we don't want to be and hope we are not!

First, the persona. Webster gives a concise definition: "A type of personality conceived as the full realization of the self." Not the full realization of the self, but *conceived* as such. We must keep this in mind when the interplay between the persona and shadow appears in a dream. This interplay, not only in each individual's personality but in life itself, is a form of polarity that creates action, reaction, and in many ways the drama of life itself. We are all to some degree both Jekyll and Hyde.

The shadow self appears more frequently in dreams because of the fact that most of our dreams are related to problems yet to be brought to the light and worked through. After all, what is a real shadow? It is cast by something that obstructs light. A shadow of itself has no substance. It is only that on which light has not yet been shed. It is important to remember this. In addition, the dictionary reminds us that a shadow may be "a reflected image as in a mirror or water" and "having form without substance."

The shadow may appear in a nightmare or other problem dream in the form of a lurking animal, an unattractive person, a repulsive or threatening form, a nameless mass or force. Any or all of these may be personifications of some negative side of the dreamer's personality not confronted before. Here are some examples.

This is the dream of a young man who appears outwardly gentle and kind (in his persona). He was disturbed by this recurring dream:

> I am walking along with my girlfriend, whom I really like and hope she likes me. But each time I am aware that a black panther is slipping silently along on one side and a little behind me. I am always very nervous in the dream for I fear the girl I am with will see it.

His girlfriend had previously mentioned in confidence that while she liked this man and he was very nice to her, she "felt there was something there that somehow I am always a little afraid of."

Later, after understanding that his panther-shadow symbolized his latent sadism and attempting to grow into a truly kinder man, he had another very significant, if somewhat ludicrous, dream that showed his progress. In this dream he was struggling with a gorilla (again the shadow) for possession of the Hope diamond. The diamond symbolized his identity and worth, in fact his very soul, which he was struggling to rescue from his animal nature.

The next dreamer was a young man who at the time had been suffering from a severe chronic headache. Nothing the doctor had done alleviated the pain. His dream:

> I dreamed I was walking along attending to my own business when wham! I was hit on the head from behind. I turned around and faced the dark figure of the man who had hit me. I woke up with the back of my head pounding.

This is a rare example of the shadow actually attacking the dreamer. In analysis it emerged that for years he had attempted to turn his back on a strong latent homosexuality. Once brought out, faced, discussed, and no longer feared, the pain in his head completely disappeared. He reported later that it did not return.

In the next dream the shadow appeared as mean and old, this time to a very precise, ladylike person, someone who very much identified with her persona. She happened to be the wife of a successful merchant and was starting a small boutique, located in one wing of her husband's store. To understand the dream it is helpful to know that she was at the time quite competitive with her husband's success. Her dream:

> I was driving along in my own car when a big express delivery truck came alongside and nearly crowded me off the road. I became very angry because I felt he was taking up more than his share of the road, so I blew my horn at him. All of a sudden I felt a sort of cold chill on the back of my neck. With a feeling of foreboding I glanced back over my shoulder and saw an ugly looking man in the back seat, grinning maliciously at me. I was very scared and woke right up.

Through free association it became clear that the express truck was used by her husband to ship his merchandise, and further that she did feel he was "crowding her" with his bigger and more successful business. But, she said, she simply could not imagine what the man in the back seat stood for; she didn't know anybody like that. At that point it was necessary to introduce to this very nice lady her own shadow self, in this case a strongly competitive aspect of her nature (her animus) that in the dream took on the form of an ugly man.

Most people are willing to accept the idea that whatever emerges in their dreams must originate from something within their own subconscious. It proved too difficult, however, for this persona-identified lady to acknowledge that such an unattractive shadow could be possibly lurking beneath and behind her very proper concept of herself. No pressure was put upon her to accept the idea, but as proof that her psyche was touched and even shaken by the possibility that this might be the case, in the middle of the night following the interpretation of her dream she was awakened by a violent psychosomatic reaction, including vomiting and a simultaneous attack of diarrhea. She was doubtless trying to "discharge" her problem and her rage at her dream analyst both orally and anally! Her husband called for the doctor but by the time he arrived that morning her malaise had completely cleared up. His examination uncovered no physical symptom. The doctor "wondered if she hadn't had some sort of emotional disturbance the day before." This woman survived analysis very nicely, retaining, undisturbed, her pleasant persona. Fortunately, the recognition by most people of their shadow self rarely causes such strong reactions, either mental, emotional, or physical.

Next is a dream in which the shadow is reflected back to the dreamer by the symbol of the mirror. The dreamer is an unhappily married and very attractive young woman.

> This dream really jolted me. I dreamed I looked in the mirror to see if I had my make-up on right, and instead of my own face in the mirror there was a man's face looking back at me. That was startling enough—but what really shook me up, he was such a mean-looking man, looking straight at me!

In considering this dream we must remind ourselves that a mirror cannot reflect anything that is not projected into it. And since this was not her outwardly attractive appearance (her persona), the unattractive man could be no other than the personification of her shadow self. In discussing the dream she admitted that she knew she did have an unpleasant tendency to dominate, and now, facing it, she wished to outgrow it.

In a dream what is in front of us represents something we are now confronting or will later have to face, while what is behind us relates to either the past or something on which we have turned our backs. This is why the shadow in the dream is almost always lurking behind us. It might also be hiding behind something, like a curtain. For growth to occur, painful as it sometimes is, we must bring that undeveloped and unrecognized side into the light of consciousness. Once we have done so, we are usually surprised at how our fear subsides. "So *that* is what I was afraid of all the time!"

We generally discover that it is almost impossible to escape our shadow, as the next dream illustrates. The dreamer was a rather strong, dominating middle-aged woman, with a husband, son, and daughter who respected her but also greatly feared her disapproval. This was her dream:

> It was night and I was on a bus going home. When I stood up to get off the bus I became aware that a man was standing right behind me, a dark and rather threatening character. My first thought was, "I do hope he's not getting off where I do," because I was afraid of him. But he did get off right behind me. I started walking fast, and he walked fast. I broke into a run and I could hear him behind me running. When I finally got to my front door I dashed in and with a feeling of relief quickly closed the

door behind me. But when I turned around—there he was inside standing right behind me!

This dream and the previous one in which the lady was frightened by the ugly man in the back seat of her car show how frequently in dreams we encounter the shadow/anima or the shadow/animus that has developed generally because of bad childhood conditioning. As a result of this conditioning the child has "introjected" a negative image of the opposite sex. Through the mechanism of projection, then, the dreamer often does not truly see his or her mate as he or she is, but rather through the lens of his or her own shadow concept. As a result the individual's relationship with the spouse is clouded. For example, the husbands of both of the above-mentioned unhappy ladies were quite agreeable individuals.

As one becomes aware of one's own shadow images and projections, the "scales drop from one's eyes" and others can be seen more clearly. This process of growth, almost transmutation, manifests itself in dream content. The example of the young man who in one dream found himself walking beside a very ugly girl and then in a later dream found himself with a lovely and charming female companion illustrates such growth. It is not necessary to mention that there had been no actual change in his associates; he simply no longer viewed the opposite sex through the dark lens of a shadow.

The next dream illustrates how a woman's animus/shadow interfered with her life. She is an attractive, intelligent young woman, intensely ambitious, who has just finished a master's degree. Her second marriage has recently ended with her husband complaining that he couldn't keep up with her ambition. Just before the first dream she had been invited to go on a hayride with a group of friends but was too busy to go.

> I am on a hayride, we are in the country, a group of people, a beautiful day. There were two men, whom I know very very well, best friends from high school days, now grown up and two very strong men. I know I have previously had relations with them.
>
> They were talking with each other and looking at each other and talking about me, making fun of me and judging me, reinforcing what I felt were their negative opinions of me. It hurt but it wasn't destructive. I felt it was okay but it stung.
>
> It was time for the hayride to go back to town where we had started. A lot of people get on the wagon. I am the only one not in the wagon. It's very crowded but there is some room by these two men and they sit there

and snicker at me and won't move over and make room for me. I am standing there . . . and the wagon moves away—and it is all right with me because I know that I will get where I want to go.

The next night she had another dream:

> I am standing at the bottom of a long staircase-to-heaven type of thing. At the top of this staircase is a symbol: a married couple, symbolizing a solidly good marriage. I am at the bottom of this ladder and I know this is where I want to go, but the ladder is steep, more like a staircase. It's a good road to go. I am climbing and getting about three rungs up the stairs and I turn around to a man behind me and want him to come with me. He had no features—I shouldn't say shadow, but a dark person. I want him to come with me and he jerks me back down. Then I am climbing again—this is where I want to go—but I am jerked back down again. I keep reaching and climbing but never make it beyond the fourth step before I am jerked back down again. I know this is where I want to go; this is what I really want for me, for us.

The dreamer is a very intelligent woman, and after relating her dream she said, "I know there is something about me that causes my relations with men to always go wrong, but I don't know what it is." After an explanation of the animus and anima, and in her case of the animus/shadow, the meaning of her dreams became clear to her. She is an attractive woman but, as her dreams show, because of her confused polarity she either imagines or experiences rejection from men—the shadow pulls her back from her desires.

My last example is especially interesting. This man wore his piety like armor, announcing to all and sundry that he was "born again" and that he knew the Lord was with him at all times and in all he did—a statement that raised many quizzical eyebrows among his close associates (behind his back, of course). After trying in vain to straighten out his family (his wife and two sons) and still convinced that the family discord was the result of their turning a deaf ear to his wisdom, he turned in desperation to the last resort, counseling, not for himself but to learn how he could bring his family into the "light." He was an entirely persona-identified person.

A large man, he was, beneath his bluster, kind and generous, but he lived within his convictions and had no awareness of his inner self. After he became intrigued despite himself with the idea that there was another self inside his opinionated superiority, he began to remember his dreams. Here again is an illustration of the great value of dream analysis. This persona man became aware of his own shadow self by means of his dream in a way he might never have accepted had the idea been presented to him by the counselor.

The occasion was his fourth or fifth hour of counseling, and when asked if he had brought in a dream he replied that he couldn't remember any. Half an hour or so later he suddenly "remembered" one he had had the night before, saying he hadn't thought it worthwhile to mention. The dream was unpleasant, he said, and he was sure it didn't mean anything:

> This one guy showed up, black hat, black coat and pants. Just standing there looking at me. I thought, "That is a weird-looking guy staring at me." Then I thought, "No problem." But the dream went on. All of a sudden here comes this guy standing there again looking at me, black hat, black coat and pants, even black glasses. Then I thought I'd just take a poke at him to make him turn around. I wanted him to turn around to show me what was behind him. It was like he was holding something in his hand behind his back, hiding something. But I woke up before I could see it. All I can say is that he was sure a negative kind of fellow.

Fortunately he was open to Jung's concept of the shadow self and could accept that, because the dream was his, all the symbols in it had to be his, including the "negative kind of fellow" in the dark clothes. It made sense to him that through further analysis he might discover not only what the unpleasant character meant and what was behind him, but at the same time become acquainted with the darker side of his own nature that had been ostracizing his family. Another example of the message, the "letter from the unconscious."

But what about the person who is shadow-identified? Most people are naturally persona-identified, because it is easier and more pleasant to think of ourselves as likeable and well-adjusted people. Our ego is more comfortable with this concept. But there are some unfortunate souls who are shadow-identified. And while the ego of the persona-identified person is impressed with how nice he is, often the ego of a shadow-identified individual is impressed with how very bad he is. It is as though as a result of rejection by others in early life, in an attempt to find some ego-importance, some sense of worth, this person boasts of how terrible he really is, about what horrendous things he has done. He may say, "I'll bet you've never known anybody before who has been in jail," and perhaps add, "And I'm an alcoholic, too." For someone to shrug off the magnitude of their sins is to minimize the size of the shadow with which their ego is identified, so it may be kinder to be impressed and somewhat shocked at the recital of their misdoings. And then what? Carefully introduce them to their persona, their innate good qualities. Sometimes the shadow-identified person is embarrassed and resistant when confronted with his persona, just as the persona-identified individual is shocked and irritated at having his shadow presented to him.

To recognize which facet of the personality is dominant, it is helpful in interpreting dreams to recognize which side the dreamer identifies with: is he the criminal on the run or a member of the posse? Is he the jailor or the jailed? The good guy or the bad guy? That would be where his identity was at the time of the dream.

The Oedipus Complex

The various aspects of the inner self often appear in mythical configurations. No Greek myth has provided more psychological terminology than the Oedipus legend. "Oedipus complex" is the name given to a child's attachment to the parent of the opposite sex. It is natural in early childhood and becomes a "complex" only when it is too strong and lives on into maturity.

According to the myth, the king of Thebes, Laius, and his queen, Jacosta, were warned that a son would be born to them and that in time the son would take his father's life. Later, when a son was born, Laius lost no time in smuggling him into another kingdom and leaving him to die. He was tied with thongs around his ankles: "Oedipus" translates as "bound feet." The infant did not die, however, and, unbeknown to the king and queen, was found, adopted, and reared to manhood. Oedipus, a young man now, decided to travel to Thebes. On the way he met King Laius, they fell into a quarrel, and Oedipus struck the king a fatal blow. Unaware of what the Fates held in store for him, he continued his journey. Before he was allowed to enter the gates of Thebes, he had to solve a riddle, one that held great portent for the citizens. His success in solving the riddle brought such joy to the Thebans that he was offered the granting of any wish. He chose to wed Jacosta, the beautiful widow of the man he had killed. For years he and Jacosta lived a happy life. After a blight came over the kingdom an old man told Oedipus the whole unhappy history. Striken with remorse at the knowledge of having committed both patricide and incest, Oedipus turned his rage against himself. One version has it that, in a gesture of atonement, he blinded himself.

Even today there are instances when a man even unconsciously suspects his incestuous desire for his mother he will be found to have an otherwise inexplicable compulsion to injure himself or to deny himself normal sexual expression—usually without being aware of his hidden wish for atonement. The Oedipal instinct in itself is not bad; the mother is naturally the boy's first love object and her tenderness—or lack of it—forms the boy's image of women and conditions what he will expect later on from the opposite sex. A girl, on the other hand, at an early age withdraws her devotion from her mother and "falls in love" with the first man in her life, her father. Concurrent with this phase of emotional development a subtle resentment often develops in the child: the boy is jealous of his father or brother, and the girl frequently would like to eliminate her mother and sisters, who may seem to rob her of her father's attention. During this period, thousands of little boys have said to their mother, "Mommy, when I grow up I want to marry you." These are the same boys who, after reaching manhood, awaken shocked at their dream of intercourse with their mother. Freud observed that the men who dream of making love to their mother had usually been Mother's favorite.

A woman's Oedipal attachment usually does not express itself in dreams so sexually (although one of the dreams to follow is an exception); instead, she dreams of being held or cuddled by this strongly protective, masculine figure, always with a delightful sense of security. She feels loved and protected. This dream can reflect a longing to sit on Dad's lap as she used to do, or, sadly, it may express a yearning to experience something of which she was deprived in childhood.

Below are a number of dreams, of both men and women, in which one can discern the wish to either hold onto, or get rid of, a strong attachment to the mother or father. These dreams are not necessarily incestuous in nature; the bond has more to do with affection than with sex per se. Occasionally the Oedipal image is masked, as in the first dream.

Before relating the first dream, it is necessary to explain that the dreamer was a serious, religious young man whose marriage had come to an end largely because of his sexual incapacity. For several years since his divorce he had lived with his devoted mother. This was his recurring dream:

> I am always on a train, looking forward eagerly to my destination and the woman who is always waiting there for me. When I get off the train I always run to meet her and I'm so glad to see her I take her in my arms and hold her close. And she always hugs me back. But the strange part of the dream is that I can never see her face, and after I wake up I still don't know who she is.

This dream is a classic example of how a dream can both reveal and conceal. When the dreamer cannot (or will not) recognize the object of his devotion, the identity is hidden so that the incestuous attachment does not have to be confronted directly. Simply stated, when we cannot see a face in a dream it generally means we cannot face what it means.

Here is the gentle dream of a pretty young woman and mother who, for some time, for whatever reason, had denied her husband (a healthy, attractive young man) any physical contact, in bed or out.

> These are dreams I have had lots of times. I love to have them. Nice cuddly dreams. Really not sexual; I just feel warm and loved. This man is holding me and I feel wonderful, but I never can see his face. I always awaken from this dream with a great sense of loss.

Her revelation that she had always been "the apple of Daddy's eye" was scarcely necessary. One can only wonder what might be taking place in *his* dreams.

The following Oedipal dream, that of a young man, clearly states the dreamer's ambivalent feelings toward his mother, a rift between his deeply buried resentment of her cruelty to him as a child and his more mature wish not to hurt her.

> I have dreamed this many times over the years. Every time I am somewhere with my mother and I know there is going to be a terrible explosion [his rage], like an atomic bomb. I am worried about my mother and feel I should hide her somewhere where she will be safe. And I feel that I have to hide from her at the same time.

He unconsciously realizes that if his bomb of repressed rage ever explodes, his mother would suffer great emotional hurt, which he does not want. Neither, however, does he want her to know of his feelings about her. He learned how to discharge his pent-up emotion through catharsis so that he did not need to hide so much from his mother.

Freudian psychology makes a great deal of the son's attachment to his mother. Occasionally a dream comes along that reveals an equally strong attachment on the part of the mother.

> My son and I were living in a lovely house, half above ground and half below. I remember on the dining room table there were bowls all heaped up with ripe juicy fruit, peaches, pears, apples, etc., and I was glad, because my son loves fruit.

It is easy to recognize the significance of "half above and half below"; her attachment is both conscious and unconscious. Round fruits usually symbolize the breast; in this case, of course, they would represent her nurturing love.

It might be interesting, for purposes of comparison, to consider two completely dissimilar approaches to the interpretation of a dream that has to do with a man's attitude toward women. The dream is one of Emanuel Swedenborg's, and we can compare his interpretation with a speculation as to how Freud might have handled it. Swedenborg dreamed of two women, one young and the other older. He cared for them both and kissed the hand of both, but was in doubt about which of them he would make love to. His interpretation was that both women represented aspects of his work: the older woman representing his older, intellectual work (science), and the younger woman symbolizing his newer and more spiritual endeavor, which often preoccupied him; the dream, he believed, enacted the ambivalence he felt regarding these two life interests. Sigmund Freud might have replied, "Work, indeed! Mr. Swedenborg was doubtless torn between his devotion to his mother and his attraction to a new woman in his life! His solution is to cling to both until a decision can be reached." Of course this is pure speculation and we cannot know which would have been the more valid interpretation. Swedenborg was in any case a brilliant and deeply moral man. After all, it was *his* dream and *his* free association. But we must remember that intellectual work would be symbolized by a masculine, or animus, figure.

The following Oedipal dream is so graphic in symbolic meaning that it scarcely needs interpretation. As is often true of such dreams, through the process of displacement the mother appears in the image of another mature woman, in this case "a friend of my mother's." Given the emotional web from which the dreamer, a young man, is trying to escape, it is easy to understand why the symbol of the spider so often represents a too possessive mother. (On a deeper level it must be recognized that the son or daughter is entrapped as much by his or her own need for the mother's affection or fear of her disapproval—after all, the umbilical cord is fastened at both ends.)

The dreamer under discussion was a quiet, placid young man who had been living with his mother for a long time, much too long, as the dream shows:

> I was kidnapped with two or three other men [other masculine aspects of the dreamer's self] and taken to a home. We were being held hostage. The only person I knew in the dream was a middle-aged woman, a friend of my mother's. She was the gang leader.
>
> The other guys trying to escape were killed, knifed in the stomach. It was obvious that my turn would come. The woman was trying to be nice to me. I wasn't panicked, but I still knew my time was coming, although she was trying to say things to make me feel I wasn't on her list.
>
> She left the room. Nobody was holding me. I ran out the door. I couldn't run so I flew about thirty feet off the ground. I flew by paddle-swimming motions, the way I first learned to swim as a kid.
>
> It was early in the morning now and I could hear them shouting, trying to catch me. I ran into some people who didn't or couldn't help me. Finally I got to a phone booth and called the police [the counselor]. Then those pursuing me were arrested, taken away, and it was a happy ending.

It is interesting to note that when he flew to escape the reality of his problems, he regressed to the swimming motions of his childhood. This is often the case with people caught in an all-enveloping mother attachment. One might well wonder whether this is not a primordial memory of life within the womb. When the dreamer says, "Those pursuing me were arrested," we might understand him to mean that he was freed from the neurotic attachments binding him.

6

People in Dreams

The people in a dream can symbolize several things. They may represent just who they seem to be, particularly if this is someone of strong personal importance in the dreamer's life; they may represent not the real person but the dreamer's image or concept of that person; or, if in the dream they are of no particular importance or even strangers to the dreamer, then their significance is much more subtle. Free association is essential to learn what that significance might be. Often an individual will remark, "I had a strange dream about someone I don't even know, or someone I haven't seen in ages. I can't imagine why I'd be dreaming about them." Starting with the premise that everyone and everything in a dream have some meaning, the dreamer must learn to ask, "What does that person mean to me; what do they represent?" And, very important, "How do I feel about them?"

A very significant role in most people's dreams is played by older individuals; if not the actual parents of the dreamer they generally appear in some parental or authoritarian role. Aunts, uncles, and even the parents of our friends generally embody images and memories of our own parents. If the dreamer feels disturbance, a sense of guilt or anxiety, rage or rebellion, he may be reliving buried childhood hurts inflicted by his parents.

The mother is the greatest external force in early life, whether of love and tenderness or coldness and rejection. The maternal image in dreams represents conception and nurturing. Other mother images (in addition to the actual mother) include other people's mothers, a queen, the wife of the president or other prominent figure, a nurse, a landlady, a cook or waitress, or a female teacher. A ship, a cow, a kitchen, or a fireplace can also represent the mother. Her archetypal forms include the moon, a witch (negatively), or, in a positive sense, the madonna and other biblical images or figures from Greek mythology.

Below are two dreams in which mother attachments appear, even though the mother images take widely different roles. The first dream is that of a young man, his mother's first-born, who strongly resented the mother's favoritism toward his sister:

> I was sitting in a restaurant waiting to be served. A young girl came in after me and placed an order with the waitress behind the counter, who was very cordial and proceeded to serve her immediately, despite the fact that I had placed my order first. It hurt my feelings and made me mad.

Not only does his mother appear as the waitress but she is also "behind the counter." Frequently the Oedipal or incestuous object is in some physically unattainable position; she can serve, but she cannot be reached.

In the next dream the mother image appears in an entirely different form. The dreamer, again a young man, was the only son in a family of girls and the apple of his mother's eye. He had recently gotten married, and this dream occurred soon afterward:

> I was standing on a seashore. Moving away from me toward the horizon was a beautiful white ship. Across the side of it in big black letters was the word "Nevermore." As it moved away from me toward the horizon I had a great feeling of sadness.

We need only recall the term "mother ship" to understand his dream. It was fortunate that his charming bride did not count dream analysis among her talents!

Then there is the figure of the female not as mother but as giver of guidance and wisdom. She is the archetypal woman. Beautiful, majestic, profoundly wise, generally larger than life, this is a figure that appears rarely in dreams. When she does, the dreamer is both guided and blessed. She is considered the embodiment of spiritual direction and seems to appear only when the dreamer is deeply troubled. From such a dream the dreamer, male or female, awakens refreshed and enlightened, having had a glimpse of ancient knowledge personified, the eternal wisdom of the soul.

Symbology of the father in a dream may also be personal or universal. Either way it is generally colored by the dreamer's memory of his own father as a benevolent protector or a dispenser of judgment and punishment. Father images (in addition to the dreamer's own father) can take the following forms: other people's fathers, the king or a president, a judge, an employer, a landlord, or an uncle. Other forms include an oak tree, a bull, the devil or a giant (negatively), or heros of Greek mythology, saints, or other biblical figures (positively).

The dream given below represents the father as president. The dreamer was a young girl, at the time irritated with her father because, she said, "He lets Mom wear the pants." Her dream:

> I was talking to President Kennedy and I told him I thought he was too weak to be president; that he wasn't doing a good job and it was high time he took charge and started running things better.

The symbol of the oak, a strong, "patriarchal" tree, spreading protective limbs and dropping acorns from which new trees sprout, appeared in the dream of a girl who had been recognizing and attempting to outgrow her strong father attachments, albeit reluctantly.

> It was a kind of awesome dream. I saw a great majestic oak tree slowly topple to the ground. While I knew somehow it was old and had to fall, I felt an overwhelming heartache that it had to be so.

Perhaps the most significant emotion in the dream of a girl or woman about her father image is the almost euphoric sensation of warmth and protection she feels when held by him. This can be remembered or express a yearning for something never had. The dream below is that of a young woman who had been separated from her father at such an early age she scarcely remembered him:

> I had been having a lot of trouble in my dream and felt very disturbed. Then I dreamed Clark Gable was holding me in his arms. This big strong man. I felt he was really the man I had been looking for; it was a deep love, wonderful feeling. And he wanted to hold me. It was like I was very small, like I was a baby nestled to someone's breast. The things he said to me were what I dream of. Things my father or a boy friend never said.

The actor in a dream, as in real life, always plays the role of somebody else.

Another archetypal figure, always described with flowing gray hair and a long beard, is the wise old man. We must not forget that when the wise old man and the archetypal woman appear in a dream, it is not the images themselves we should respond to but the spiritual guidance that they embody, the soul message they express.

Having dealt with mother and father images from several perspectives, it might be helpful to become more specific about men and women in dreams, either of the same or the opposite sex of the dreamer and of different ages.

Persons of real importance to the dreamer may retain their true identity in the dream. However, almost always a person of the same age and sex as the dreamer embodies some aspect of the dreamer's own nature. The dreamer must be willing to accept the possibility, even the probability, that, unattractive though the image may be, his unconscious is holding up a mirror. All such reflections are not negative; when we are growing in a positive direction our dreams can be peopled with charming individuals whom everybody likes. Quite frequently people who have been attempting through analysis to overcome irritable and unpleasant personality traits will have delightful dreams in which they welcome the return of a kind friend whom they had not seen for a long time or even feared was dead. The friend would personify their own long-lost patience and charm. A short dream of a young married woman is a case in point. She was trying to overcome some very unpleasant attitudes and habits that had put a strain on her relations with her husband. Then she had this dream:

> It seemed that a girl friend of mine, a girl I hadn't seen since college days, came to visit and stayed in our home for a while. She was such a pleasant person my husband and I were both glad to have her. I can't imagine why I would have a dream about her. I thought I had forgotten her.

The dreamer recognized that the welcome guest symbolized the return of her former pleasant disposition.

The person of the same age but opposite sex in a dream may be just who they seem to be—brother, sister, husband, wife. But if they are simply someone of the opposite sex and of no particular importance, they represent something else that must be discovered through interpretation. They

could be the dreamer's concept or image of the opposite sex or a personification of the dreamer's own animus or anima.

In a woman's dream, her sister may represent her true sister or her feelings toward her sister; however, more frequently the sister appears as the
dreamer's unconscious or "sister self," often called the alter ego.

If a daughter appears in a woman's dream and the dreamer is going
through a time of emotional stress or conflict with her daughter, then her
feelings about that stress should be examined. Otherwise, a daughter usually represents the dreamer herself at a younger age and embodies her immaturity. The "child within" may be demanding recognition. This short
dream is a good illustration. The dreamer, a young married woman, was
sitting in the front row at a lecture on dream analysis and raised her hand to
share this with the group:

> This is a dream I have had several times and it bothers me. In reality
> I don't have a child, but in the dream there is a little girl, about two I
> would say, in a highchair, and she's always fussing and demanding atten-
> tion and everybody in the family is always trying to fix her up and make
> her happy but she never seems to be happy.

When the lecturer cautiously suggested that we often dream of some side of
our own nature, the look that crossed the face of the woman's husband beside her was all the "free association" necessary.

If a brother or other man near the dreamer's age appears in a woman's
dream, one must ask whether he seems logical, protective, or intelligent. If
so, she has a positive animus. If, on the other hand, he is threatening and
unattractive, her shadow self is coupled with the animus—and she's in
trouble with men! For example, there is the case of a vital, opinionated, and
decisive young lady who has her even-tempered and submissive husband
always wondering whether she will stay with him or return to the warm
nest of her parents. Before the dream her husband had clearly stated that he
hoped she'd never leave but that he would go along with her wishes. The
"projection" at work in this dream is evident:

> Bob and I were talking, no particular background, and I told him I had
> finally come to the decision that I definitely wanted a divorce; I felt it was
> the best thing to do. He said, "You've got to be kidding" and then he
> went on to say, "If you are going to go through with this I'm going to

make things so tough for you; you'll see, I'm going to fight you every step of the way."

Afterward she had "this warm fuzzy dream where this big kind older man was holding me. It was so sweet. . . . how could my child have awakened me when I was having such a lovely dream?" Daddy, in her unconscious, is all persona, so her husband has to bear the burden of her shadow.

An older man is generally a father image, as explained earlier. In a woman's dream he frequently appears in the role of doctor or employer. A son, or any young boy in a woman's dream, can symbolize her feeling about her real son, but very often he is a projection of her immature animus, perhaps memories of the "tomboy" stage of her own life or some other point in her ambitious youth.

In a man's dream a male figure of the same age as the dreamer usually embodies some aspect, positive or negative, of the dreamer's own nature. Unless some unusually strong emotion or conflict exists between the dreamer and his son, it is safe to assume that the appearance of a son in a man's dream represents his younger self. This would be particularly true if the dreamer believes that his son resembles him. Older males in a man's dream are figures of authority if not specifically father images.

The teenager, singly or in a group, in a man's or a woman's dream is usually irritating. His or her appearance may be an indication that an immature attitude, fixation, or urge is disturbing the dreamer's more mature self. A middle-aged professional woman with personality problems had the following recurring dream:

> I am just going about my business, trying to do my work, when a bunch of rowdy teenagers start aggravating me and make so much noise I can hardly think. I get mad and wish the police or somebody would get rid of them.

Sibling rivalry often appears in dreams because the instinctive resentment is taboo and not allowed to enter the level of conscious thought. Freud wrote that "many persons who now love their brothers and sisters, and who would feel bereaved by their death, harbour in their unconscious hostile wishes, survivals from an earlier period, wishes which are able to realize themselves in dreams. . . ." This was the dream of a loving and protective brother who to all appearances adored his little sister. His parents frequently mentioned with pride how tenderly he cared for her. The boy himself was charming and had before always been the center of his parents' attention:

> It was a real scary dream and I was sure glad when I woke up to find it wasn't true. I dreamed I was outside with my baby sister in her baby carriage. Our lawn is smooth but in the dream there was a drop-off, a high cliff in front of our house, and down below there was a river. The baby carriage started rolling toward the cliff and I tried as hard as I could to keep it from going over the cliff but I couldn't stop it. I woke up feeling terrible—and boy! was I glad to realize it was just a dream and my baby sister was all right!

He does try to stop her from going over the cliff. We try not to let our loved ones fall victim to our unconscious urges.

A baby is a very meaningful symbol in any dream and any dream containing one should be treated very carefully. A baby may represent something new, a new life or identity. No matter what the content of the dream, we can always start from the premise that the baby, like an egg, symbolizes the beginning of something.

A happy, healthy newborn in a dream is an indication that some "rebirth" is taking place within the dreamer, that out of the old self and old ideas a new sense of self is emerging. On a more prosaic level, a baby may symbolize a new field of study or the start of a new project that the dreamer has undertaken. A baby girl in a dream represents a renewal of the more emotional, feminine anima side of the dreamer's nature; the sturdier baby boy implies a renewal of the animus through, for instance, a new job or promotion. This is why a man can have a dream that he has given birth to a baby, which invariably puzzles and even shocks him. When reassured that it doesn't mean he's feminine but only that he is experiencing a kind of rebirth, he not only relaxes but is proud of himself!

Here is an example of a man who had undertaken, with the help of two other men, to build a forty-foot boat. After laboring for weeks at this Herculean task, he had this dream:

> I dreamed I had a baby to take care of. It was getting bigger and bigger, and was so heavy and unwieldy that I wondered how I would be able to handle it when it got still bigger.

Then there are dreams of pregnancy, in which the dreamer only feels the beginnings of a renewal. Here is an example. A seventeen-year-old girl, with almost no feminine identity because of rejection by both father and stepfather and a too-strong mother, began analysis. After several weeks she had this dream:

> I knew I was pregnant and I was very happy about it. Yet in the dream I said to myself, "How can I be? No man has ever made love to me, I am a virgin." Yet I was happy and excited over the baby on the way.

When asked how far along she was with her pregnancy she replied, "Five months," which was exactly the length of time she had spent in analysis; in other words, she had "conceived" her new self from the first session. Two weeks later she reported happily that in her last dream the baby had arrived, without pain, giving her much joy because it was such a lovely little girl. Finally, her attractive anima had emerged. From the "union" of the rational, masculine animus and the emotional anima, the true self is conceived.

If an unhappy, weak, malformed, or ill child appears in a dream, part of the dreamer's nature, because of trauma or neglect, has remained undeveloped. Here is an example. The dreamer was a lonely woman with a history of disappointing experiences with men who at the time of the dream was despairing of both marriage and motherhood. Although her parents had provided well for her materially they had been almost entirely unaware of her hunger for affection. Also, being the first-born, she had always borne a sense of guilt for not being the son her father had wanted. Her dream:

> There was a baby boy, uncoordinated and undeveloped. I didn't feel I could do anything for him. Then there was a lovely pool, and little babies were popping up out of it all over. They weren't mine but I was the guardian watching over them. Then a woman came up with a crying baby girl. When I took it, it was all right; when the mother held it, it cried all over again.

The baby boy was manifestly her undeveloped animus with which she could not come to terms. Despite the fact that she was naturally a gentle, almost timid girl, she had at her father's insistence taken up the study of business and law. After a period of time this brought on physical and emotional illness. She had this dream only after changing the direction of her life. The pool in her dream might be called her reservoir of feminine emotions out of which the babies (new ideas and creativity) were emerging. The baby girl (her early self) cries in the hands of its mother but the dreamer is able to make it happy.

A baby may embody the immaturity of someone else in the dreamer's life. For instance, here is the dream of a young woman engaged to a spoiled, self-indulgent young man:

> In my dream I was holding a baby boy on my lap. I guess it was mine; anyway, I felt I had to take care of it. It was almost as big as I was and was so heavy I hardly knew what to do with it.

Sometimes a starved love nature can appear in dreams as a starved and undeveloped baby. There is, for instance, the example of a young married woman who had been dreadfully inhibited by the combination of very strict parents and, later, a narrowly orthodox religion. As a result of this conditioning she had become sexually frigid. She eagerly sought help through counseling, responded well, and soon afterward experienced a revealing dream:

> It all took place in an old-fashioned, rather dark room. In the middle of the room there was a cradle and when I looked in the cradle what I saw was a baby—but it wasn't a whole baby. At first I thought it must be dead because its eyes were closed and it was very pale. But the worst part was that it didn't have any arms or legs. With an ache in my heart I started walking around and around the cradle praying and praying that the baby would live. When I looked again I saw a flush of color in its face. Then its eyelids fluttered! I kept on praying. Then I was overjoyed to see that tiny little arms and legs had started to grow, sort of sprouting out. . . . Before the dream was over it was a whole rosy baby and I woke up sobbing with joy.

Subsequently the dreamer's love nature continued to grow and she became an emotionally (and sexually) fulfilled woman.

Whoever or whatever enters the dreamer's room in a dream as an intruder represents something entering the realm of consciousness from the deeper levels of the self. This concept or problem is usually as unwelcome as any real intruder would be. But it demands attention; lock one door and it comes in another. If it doesn't come inside, it may be glimpsed peering through the window or lurking in the shadows. Shadow might be said to be its natural element because most intruding apparitions personify in some way the dreamer's shadow, or problem, self. Even if we have no desire to invite the unpleasant creature in, it behooves us nonetheless, once he is there, to bring him into the light, and, like nearly all other psychological and emotional problems, once faced he loses his power over us.

A simple example is the child who cannot go to sleep unless the closet door is closed or a light on; he fears something terrible will emerge while he sleeps and destroy him. Many children are afraid to hang an arm or leg over the side of the bed lest a creature lurking underneath do them harm. Of course one cannot simply tell a child he is afraid of his own shadow. This would probably add to the fear. Child psychologists have learned, however, that these children have deeply buried antagonisms toward a dominating parent or a sibling rival. If a child has an unconscious (or conscious) wish that his brother would drop dead so that he might have Mamma and Daddy all to himself again, he may fear that his destructive wish will emerge from an unlocked closet or from underneath his bed (his unconscious) in some frightening form and destroy him. And what is true of the child is also true of the adult.

A policeman in a dream represents the dreamer's conscience, his sense of what is right and wrong. Almost everyone has at some time dreamed of hearing the siren and seeing the flashing lights approach from behind, warning them of some transgression. This is as clear a sign as one could find that one side of the dreamer's nature, in this case the conscience, is "blowing the whistle" on some other aspect. Often, when an individual is undergoing analysis, he or she will project this role onto the counselor. In dreams the client may call for the police to come and arrest a "criminal," representing the problem with which he is wrestling. In this sort of dream, various facets of the dreamer's inner self can come into play. The "criminal" is the neurosis; the detective who tracks him down is the dreamer's own inner self, searching for what is wrong; the policeman is his conscience, which "arrests" or stops his wrongdoing. The "guilty party" is called into court where the opposing sides of the dreamer's nature come face to face: the defense lawyer represents the rational mind's attempt to establish alibis and excuses, and the judge is the dreamer's own inner judgment, his sense of honesty and integrity. Should he be found guilty, the jailor symbolizes the self-discipline by which he constrains his negative impulses to be sure that he doesn't repeat his "crime." Finally, after a period of atonement, the man who comes to release him is his welcome wiser self!

Soldiers in dreams symbolize warring instincts, conflicting emotions, a clash of personalities, perhaps two sides of the dreamer's nature fighting it out. Whatever the identity of the enemy in the dream, that enemy usually personifies negative characteristics within the dreamer's own unconscious self, some domineering or primitive instinct against which the dreamer struggles. Under certain circumstances the enemy may symbolize someone in the dreamer's life with whom he contends. And, of course, soldiers always appear in the nightmares of ex-soldiers reliving the trauma of war.

A clown in dream language means just about the same as in real life: comic relief, perhaps to compensate for depression.

A dwarf or other misshapen figure in a man's dream symbolizes stunted masculinity, undeveloped genitalia. In a woman's dream this would be a projection of her negative concept of the opposite sex. She might have such a dream when disturbed about the immature or underdeveloped sex organs of her husband. Or, if she feels abused or used by men, she can, to compensate, put her enemy in an extremely inferior role in dream. Carl Jung would say that such a woman dreamer was suffering from a sadly underdeveloped animus.

Foreigners, meaning any race or nationality other than that of the dreamer, may be significant in dreams. Free association is very important here. What characteristics does the dreamer associate with the foreigner and what does he dislike or distrust about such persons? Cultured or primitive, attractive or unattractive, through the process of projection the foreigner usually symbolizes some wish, impulse, or experience "foreign" to the dreamer's usual habits or attitudes. We might consider what various "foreign" personalities in a dream may represent. The American Indian appears in many dreams, and through free association is generally revealed to represent natural but primitive instincts, often (as a result of childhood ideas) in some way perceived to be pursuing or threatening the dreamer. The Nazi is a far more frightening figure, particularly if the dreamer is of an age or race with frightening memories. But we must remember that the dream is always trying to convey a message through the symbolic figure. The same is true of a Communist enemy figure. What is symbolized, not the symbol itself, must be faced and overcome. Often darker-skinned natives of warmer climes represent a simpler, more elemental side of the dreamer's nature to which he might like to yield.

The villain is usually clothed in a dark cape and hat, dramatizing a hidden, dark, but intriguing neurosis or attachment. This is illustrated in the following dream of a "Daddy's girl":

> I was parked in my little car in an alley behind our home. It was late in the day, sort of dark. A man in a dark cloak with his hat pulled down over his face approached me. At first I was afraid, but when the light caught his face I could see it was my father and I felt it was all right. So I opened the door for him to join me.

In other words, incest may be dark and clandestine, but with Daddy it is all right!

A married couple in dreams symbolizes the institution of marriage. How the dreamer feels about his own marriage is usually displaced onto the marriage of someone else and their conflict or harmony enacts the individual's feelings about his own marriage.

The teacher may be no more than a memory of a former teacher but usually symbolizes someone to whom the dreamer is turning for knowledge. The teacher may personify the dreamer's own inner and wiser self who could guide him if he would but listen.

The actor and actress represent role models, persons of importance in the dreamer's life. Free association is essential in deciphering such symbols; the dreamer must ask himself, "What characteristics of this person impress me; what roles do they usually take in a movie or play? What qualities do they project?"

The doctor appears in the dreams of many people undergoing analysis or therapy and represents the individual on whom they depend to diagnose their emotional problems and help them find a cure. The appearance of the doctor in the client's dream can reveal the dreamer's true feelings about the counselor and the counseling, and very frequently reflects the extent of progress toward a "cure." Here is an example:

> In the dream I was in a doctor's office. It seemed he had already operated on me, cut my abdomen wide open and left it wide open, bleeding. Never sewed me up. There I was, cut open and bleeding and then he said he'd see me next week, and walked out. I woke up shaking all over.

Fortunately this does not happen too often, but it seemed she had been through what is sometimes referred to as "psychic surgery." She reported the dream following a session with a psychiatrist who had really "cut into her." Fortunately a new counselor was able to "sew her up" emotionally and her psychic bleeding stopped.

Here is another dream in which the counselor appears as doctor. The dreamer was again a young woman who, after a period of emotional and physical depression, sought help. After some time she brought in this dream:

> It seemed I was in a hospital. I had gotten out of bed and felt I was fine. The doctor was coming down the hall and I went to him and reported to him that I was all well now and he could take a vacation. Then I added that he needn't worry about the other patients; I would take care of them in his absence.

The young woman interpreted her own dream. When asked what she thought the "other patients" represented, she replied, "Maybe any little aches and pains I have left, which I feel I can handle myself." After some thought she added, "Maybe it means I'm reaching the point where I can help others." In either event, her dream indicated no further therapy was needed from her "doctor."

Because any authoritative figure in a dream bears some paternal connotation, the "doctor" can also represent the dreamer's father.

The robber figure not only intrudes but threatens to or does rob the dreamer of something valuable. This could be peace of mind, self-respect, sexual fulfillment, or masculine or feminine identity. Many women have had a nightmare in which they fear a robber whom they may hear or see and who is always male. In this case one might suspect an overly dominant masculine aspect or animus or a negative concept of men. On the other hand, when a man dreams of a woman stealing his money, his sexuality is likely to be suffering because of an excessive passivity.

People with unseen faces represent an attachment or inner desire (such as incest or latent homosexuality) with which the dreamer has not or cannot come face to face.

Ancestors are personifications of inherited influences and sometimes superego figures.

Community in the dream represents social concepts, the dreamer's relation to exterior influences, the impingement on the dreamer's consciousness of his social environment.

When an insane person appears in a dream, in whatever guise, it should be given serious consideration. This would not of necessity imply encroaching insanity in the dreamer, but might instead symbolize an "insane" idea or impulse that alarms the logical mind. Or the dreamer may be so worried about something that he is "going crazy." If, however, the dream includes the walls of the home caving in, a ceiling crumbling, or electric wiring exposed and frayed, the psyche may be calling for help, perhaps psychiatric help.

The cripple usually embodies an emotional handicap. Because each part of the body has its own function and symbology, the dreamer must, through free association, discover what aspect of his life is limited or incapacitated. When a man has dreams of being crippled, the dream could indicate a castration anxiety.

A diseased person generally symbolizes the dreamer's fear that he will, upon psychological diagnosis, be found to be "infected" with a problem unacceptable to his conscious ego, perhaps latent homosexuality or incestuousness. (These neurotic fixations, common to some degree in all of us, seem to be the most taboo and therefore the most feared by nearly everyone.)

Black or white people often represent the dreamer's shadow self, which is projected onto a racial and "chromatic" other. If the persona is perceived to be "white," the shadow will be embodied by a black person, or, if the dreamer is black, vice-versa. Taboos such as incest and homosexuality are often symbolized by a racial otherness. A white man may express incestuous desire for his sister, mother, or daughter by dreaming of some emotional involvement with a black female. And since homosexuality has been, from biblical times on, a "dark problem" in the unconscious, the white man may express it by dreaming of a black man approaching him. We might consider as an example the following dream of a young black man, a college graduate apparently well adjusted in his relations with whites, both male and female:

> I have a recurring dream where a young white man about my age is getting very chummy with me, too chummy, and it makes me uncomfortable; it just doesn't seem right, and I try to get rid of him but he keeps hanging around.

He had, during early adolescence, experimented sexually with his male friends. He confessed that when he broke up with his girl friend he found his male friends a little too attractive. So in his dream the white man carried the burden of his shadow.

Religious figures usually personify the dreamer's early religious training and beliefs. Whether priest, minister, rabbi, Buddha, or other eastern mystic, the religious figure in the dream will conform to the faith that is familiar or acceptable to the dreamer. The dreamer's reaction is important: does the figure appear as an avenger or a healer? If the dreamer feels either guilt or fear, the religious figure may be an exaggerated superego image, reminding the dreamer of his faults or "sins"—a problem left over from an overly rigid religious indoctrination. More frequently, however, the religious figure is a symbol of hope and promise.

7

The Body in Dreams

Just as the different parts of the body each have their own identity and function, so do they have symbolic portent in dreams. The loss of or injury to some part of the body in dreams implies a loss of or injury to whatever that organ symbolizes.

Body Parts

The head emblemizes conscious thought, ego-identity, and sometimes, in the dream of a man, the tip of the sex organ. The face represents the image we present to the world, the persona. An "open face" is one without guile. To dream of a mask, therefore, implies secrecy. Blemishes such as pimples or warts on the face in a dream symbolize an eruption of guilt; the dreamer is "defacing" himself as a subtle form of atonement. An invisible or elusive face implies that there is attachment or emotion the dreamer is unwilling to recognize.

The first emotional stage of the infant is the oral or nursing period. This is the "I need and I want" period in which the individual depends on others to fulfill his needs. This is followed by the oral aggressive stage during which the child expresses frustration first by biting and later with words, by teasing, sarcasm, or quarreling. So the mouth in a dream can have widely varied meanings, all having to do with oral fixation. The context of the dream and free association are important. When eating and drinking, the key is that something is put into the mouth. Tooth brushing or cleansing of the mouth expresses a wish to "come clean" of guilt for what was said or done with the mouth. A sticky substance in the mouth connotes some guilt. If in his dream the dreamer has pins, broken glass, or other sharp objects in the mouth, these may represent sharp words withheld. To vomit in a dream is a cathartic attempt to expel rage or disgust over some person or situation, or sometimes it is guilt that the dreamer feels he "can't stomach anymore." To find the self in the dream unable to speak or "tongue-tied" enacts the unconscious wish to withhold some secret thoughts or feelings. The meaning of the tongue depends on the dream. But it is sometimes a phallic symbol, displaced upward.

Teeth, if bared or biting, signify aggression, but being bitten signifies masochism. Protruding front teeth can be phallic. Teeth falling out, usually into the hand, is a common dream image that connotes self-punishment for masturbation, a guilty feeling perhaps left over from adolescent years.

The nose is generally symbolic of the penis, displaced upward. The eye is related to the dreamer's ability to "see" the truth. Obstruction of sight (such as by fog, dirty windows, or broken glasses) indicates an unconscious problem preventing the individual from seeing or facing reality. Clarity of vision indicates an awakening of awareness. While such symbology is infrequent in a dream, the loss of an eye can have a sexual meaning, perhaps castration.

The significance of hair depends on free association. For instance, a woman's dream of having her hair cut very short might indicate a wish to be male. A man's dream of being shorn of his hair might mean a loss of virility. (Remember what happened to Samson when Delilah caused his hair to be cut.) Pubic hair in a dream has sexual significance.

Since all appendages may have phallic significance, the loss of an arm or leg in a man's dream may indicate castration anxiety. Occasionally, in either a man's or a woman's dream, loss or paralysis of a limb signifies an unconscious wish to be rendered helpless in order to be taken care of.

The hand is an important symbol, the interpretation of which depends on the context of the dream. Because our hands are our most important tool, their loss or injury implies that the dreamer is losing the ability to "handle" a situation, or that something has "gotten out of hand." Also, like the loss of an arm, to lose a hand or finger implies castration. Red or dirty hands signify guilt. A clenched fist means suppressed rage; palm upward, receptivity.

The feet in a dream tell how the dreamer "walks" through life. Bare feet imply a wish to return to an uninhibited infantile state, or get back to nature. The large toe in a man's dream is phallic. And there are occasions in which, through the process of transposition, the feet take on a sexual connotation, indicative of a foot fetish.

The heart, of course, is the center of the emotional nature. To be shot or stabbed in the heart implies an almost mortal injury to the dreamer's love nature. The stomach is another center of the emotional nature from the nursing period on.

The front of the body represents the outward self, the dreamer's persona. The back emblemizes less evident aspects of the self. Sometimes blemishes on the back imply hidden guilts that the dreamer has not faced. To dream of being stabbed in the back implies a sense of betrayal. A backache or injury to the back implies that the dreamer feels he is carrying too heavy a burden.

The anus usually has to do with psychical configurations associated with elimination carried over from childhood. In certain dreams the anus is symbolic of homosexuality.

The right side represents correctness, acceptability, morality, heterosexuality. The left side connotes negative impulses or desires, something "not right" (such as homosexuality or incest).

Blood is very meaningful in dreams, almost always as a sign of sadism or masochism, depending on whether the dreamer cuts someone else or himself. Internal bleeding signifies self-pity.

Physical States

Illness in a dream is a sign of emotional ill health. The locus of illness indicates the emotional center of the problem, and its seriousness symbolizes the intensity of the dreamer's maladjustment. On the other hand, to dream of being in a wheelchair or bedridden may express an unrecognized wish to return to infancy.

Infection, which causes the dreamer to feel unwell, unwholesome, even "unclean," can indicate a real or imagined guilt with which the dreamer fears he is "infected." There may be a fear of latent homosexuality or incest or the repressed memory of an unpleasant experience. Often the victim of some sexual aggressiveness carries a secret guilt for having enjoyed the stimulation.

A wound connotes emotional injury. In a man's dream it can mean castration anxiety; in a woman's, rape. The part of the body injured symbolizes the kind of psychological hurt.

Cleanliness implies guiltlessness, a sense of moral purity. Dirtiness means some type of guilt, real or imagined. Children are reproached not only for playing in the mud but particularly for "accidents" involving defecation. Discovery, exploration, or stimulation of the genitals brings the accusation of being a "dirty little boy" or "a bad girl" and the order to "go wash those dirty hands." Dirt can usually be expunged by confession, catharsis, or another cleansing experience, but a stain in a dream implies indelibility, something traumatic or a deep guilt that the dreamer has not been able to erase.

Whenever any force or energy, mechanical or mental, is immobilized, reason tells us that it could be stopped only by a force equal to itself. When in a dream the individual finds himself paralyzed, the crucial question is, what is the opposing force? Usually the dreamer is caught between a will to do and a will not to do. Usually, if carefully pursued, interpretation will disclose an unconscious desire, denied strenuously by the superego, the "Thou shalt not" part of the conscious mind.

Crippling, a handicap, connotes fixation or blockage that is keeping the dreamer from functioning at full potential. The part of the body afflicted symbolizes the emotional area in which the dreamer feels limited. As mentioned before, the incapacitation of an arm or leg in a man's dream indicates castration fear. Such a dream of either sex may express a wish to escape responsibility. The dream says, "I could not help myself." The following dream illustrates this point.

The dreamer was a handsome but somewhat passive young man. He was a part-time actor who, as is often the case, was always waiting for the big role. He felt that finding permanent work elsewhere would not suit him so he was getting by largely thanks to the largess of friends.

> It seems I was in a wheelchair; I don't know what was wrong with me but I was unable to walk. Some of my friends were approaching and suddenly I felt very embarrassed and tried to hide behind some bushes.

His free association:

> Q. Have you any idea why you had to be in a wheelchair? Have you ever been incapacitated?
>
> A. Never. And in the dream I really felt all right but I must have been crippled to be in the chair.
>
> Q. Then why were you embarrassed?
>
> A. I was ashamed to have my friends see the way I was. They were all so healthy and successful. [Pause] But if my legs were crippled, nobody could really blame me for not working, could they?

He saw that the dream was showing him his passivity and escapism. He learned, soon thereafter, to "pick up his chair and walk."

Because warmth is synonymous with security and love, the opposite in a dream may symbolize a lack of love, loneliness, and rejection. Occasionally, impotence or feminine frigidity also appears in dreams under the guise of ice. If the dreamer finds himself surrounded by snow and ice, these feelings are strongly implied. The following dream illustrates.

The dreamer was a young married woman with two small children. She had married impulsively after a broken romance and she and her husband were finding themselves constantly at odds, mentally and emotionally. Meanwhile she played the role of a cheerful wife and mother.

> It was the strangest dream. It seemed that our front yard was all green with grass, and bright flowers all around. But when I walked to the back of the house and looked out I saw that the whole backyard was covered with snow and ice. It was not only strange but depressing.

Her front yard represented her persona, the attractive and apparently happy role that she played for neighbors and friends, concealing all the frigidity of her personal life "behind the house."

We must not overlook the infrequent positive connotation of the frozen landscape. A devoted skier or skater will be delighted at all the snow, making the dream one of wish-fulfillment.

Drunkenness in a dream is symbolic of wanting to experience or having experienced some uninhibitedly lustful desire, usually an experience in which the dreamer feels he lost control and of which he is not proud.

Blindness symbolizes a psychological inability to see what is self-evident. Clarity of vision or the appearance of light indicates "awakening consciousness." Deafness represents an inability or unwillingness to hear the truth.

As the Bible puts it, "None is so blind as he who will not see or as deaf as he who will not hear." Often in the dream the person is trying to hear and cannot, the message never quite coming through. The dreamer may be unable to decipher an important phone call. The unconscious may be trying to convey an important message that the conscious mind is not ready to accept or is incapable of understanding. If the dreamer is open enough, there is a strong possibility that the message will come through again or in another way. This is like the dream experience of receiving a letter and not being able to read or remember it.

Being asleep in a dream indicates a lack of awareness. To awaken symbolizes that the dreamer is "waking up to the truth," becoming conscious of something not previously recognized.

Being lost indicates a lack of identity or sense of direction. "Who am I, what am I here for, where am I going?" Sometimes the dreamer can't find his way, fog or darkness obscuring the path. The goal that he hopes to reach is significant. Is he trying to get back home? Often the dreamer finds himself-explanatory. Home connotes love and acceptance, sometimes a regressive wish "to return"; school, of course, symbolizes learning and growing, skill at solving the problems of life.

Pregnancy represents incipient concepts, an inner awakening, embryonic potential, the germ of an idea not yet fully realized. This is a fairly common dream motif.

Nakedness is a common dream state. It can have two distinctly different meanings: real embarrassment at exposure, or a touch of narcissism. The first case, in which a man is "caught with his pants down" or a woman finds herself exposed in an awkward situation, often implies that the dreamer is feeling shame because some secret has been exposed or he or she feels naked to the criticism of others. The second interpretation of nudity is much pleasanter: an unconscious wish to give someone else a glimpse of the dreamer's body (usually an attractive one), while at the same time frantically trying to find some cover. Freud believed that the source of such dreams is the dreamer's memory of early childhood, when it was enjoyable to prance around naked, generally to the disapproval of parents and other adults. When it becomes conscious, this wish to bare the self is called exhibitionism.

Being late can be interpreted in one of three different ways, and only free association and the situation of the dream will make clear which is correct.

First, if the mood of the dream is one of depression or despair, lateness may reflect a sense that life has passed the dreamer by. Then there is the rather common dream in which the dreamer suddenly realizes that it is too late to keep an appointment with his counselor, or that he has overslept so that he'll be late getting to work or meeting some other unattractive deadline. Often he finds the clock in his dream is wrong, so, of course, it is not his fault. The escape mechanism is very apparent. The third dream of not being able to get there on time is frequently sexual. The woman who cannot reach an orgasm as quickly as her husband often dreams she is rushing somewhere to meet her husband, or to get the meal on the table in time for him, always with a great deal of frustration at her ineptitude. Since men generally are not as troubled with this problem as women, such scenarios occur less often in their dreams. If the dreamer is male, he might suffer from premature ejaculation and have dreams of getting somewhere too early. Or, being early for an appointment may simply reflect an over-anxiousness to "get ahead."

Feeling enclosed or trapped implies that the dreamer feels the burden of a responsibility or situation from which there seems to be no escape. Ordinarily such a dream really means the person is locked into *concepts* of entrapment and with help can usually find a key somewhere. When, as is often the case, in a later dream a door or gate swings open, the dreamer has been able to accept that his fear was more illusion than reality. But we cannot leave the subject of entrapment without recognizing that if the individual had suffered a severe birth trauma, perhaps a prolonged delivery, this claustrophobic memory can and frequently does repeat itself in dreams far into adult life.

Frequently a person will relate a frightening dream in which he cannot move, cannot, no matter how hard he tries, speak, cry out, or run. Sometimes he knows what he is trying to escape, sometimes not, and he awakens from his dream in a sweat. Hard as it may be for the ego to accept, such immobilization generally implies deadlock between some deeply buried desire repressed or paralyzed by the dreamer's superconscious. One way to reach the unconscious message is to ask, "From what was I escaping? What would have happened to me if it had caught and overcome me?" Rape, murder, or some unknown fate? A woman full of rage at an insolent daughter does not hit her ("Sometimes I'd like to choke her") because she wants to be a loving mother even if it kills her—and then has the nightmare that something is about to choke or kill her. She finds she cannot cry out for help in her dream because of her inner conflict. Many women have a paralyzing fear of rape in a dream. It would be too simple to interpret this as a result of reading too many lurid news reports. If such dreams are interpreted and understood, they usually do not recur. Often such a woman has an unconscious fear that her own masculinity, her aggressive animus, will overcome and "rape" her femininity, or gentler anima nature.

When a man, or for that matter a boy, has a nightmare in which he is frozen and being approached by a man with a gun or knife, we might assume that one of two problems is pursuing him: he may have a hidden wish to harm some enemy, from which his higher self holds him back and therefore turns it back on himself; or he may harbor an unrecognized wish to be approached sexually by another male. Always the gun and the knife are symbolic either of injury or the male sex organ.

Many people dream of the death of a parent, child, husband, or wife and even of their own death. The natural reaction is to wonder if it is a premonition. But virtually never does death in a dream imply the approaching demise of any person. Symbolically it represents the termination of a relationship, an experience, or a neurosis. Our grief in the dream is a reluctance to release whatever is coming to an end. Many people, when outgrowing their childhood attachment to a parent, will dream that that parent has "passed away." It would be impossible to visualize the death of one's own father or mother fixation, so the unconscious uses the image of the parent to enact the change. Here is a dream that frightened the dreamer until she got help interpreting it. The dreamer was an attractive young woman who had recently been widowed.

> In the dream I was alone in a room with a coffin in front of me. I looked inside and was shocked to see the corpse was a pretty young woman. The strange part of it was that she was all dressed in a white wedding gown, veil and all.

Her free association:

Q. Who did you think it was and how did you feel when you saw her?
A. I didn't know who she was but I felt terribly sorry that she had to die so young . . . Before we go further, I want to tell you I'm really scared. I told a friend of mine about the dream—he said he had read a

good bit about dream analysis—and he told me that was a warning dream, warning me that I might soon be going to join my husband. It got me so upset I can hardly sleep.

Q. If that were you in that coffin, do you think you'd be all dressed up in a wedding outfit?

A. Oh, no, that wouldn't be suitable.

Q. What does a wedding outfit stand for?

A. A marriage, of course.

Q. Then wouldn't it be logical to accept that the message of your dream was that your marriage is over, you must accept and "bury it"; you are no longer a bride. The bride is only an image, a memory you must lovingly release. After all, in the dream *you* are very much alive; she was only a symbol.

The emotional jolt she felt when her well-meaning but inexperienced friend attempted to interpret her dream is an illustration of how risky dream analysis can be, especially when dealing with such a serious subject.

There is another kind of death dream that can only be interpreted as a death wish directed against someone. In such dreams the dreamer has the satisfaction of observing the "comeuppance" of some enemy, imagined or otherwise. From such a dream the individual may awaken feeling that "they finally got what was coming to them." But of course the *dreamer* was not the wielder of justice; his ego makes sure somebody else carries that responsibility. And while we're on unconscious wishes, there is no question that a person who bears resentment toward a relative, whether a dependent parent or child, is perfectly capable of disposing of their responsibility in a dream by having the dependent "expunged." Strictly speaking, this is really a wish not for the death of the resented *person*—the dreamer must always be assured of this—but of the *problems* that person poses. Incidentally, the dreamer always awakens from these dreams with a sense of panic and grief, and is relieved to learn that the person is still breathing, which proves that they really didn't want them to die, after all!

Love, romance, or creative talent may in a dream be personified by a newborn babe or a lovely child. When it dies the dreamer grieves because "it died so early. It never had a chance to live, and it was so beautiful." Death in dreams, like birth, can wear many faces. Here is an example.

The dreamer was a young single woman, intelligent but much more concerned with her own happiness than the welfare of others.

> In the dream I knew I had died, and I was lying in my coffin. People
> were gathering around me and I was watching and listening to what they
> had to say. Some were grieving and some talked about how much they
> loved me. . . . The ones I was most interested in were those who were
> saying how sorry they were they hadn't treated me better!

No interpretation is necessary. The dreamer was simply telling everyone,
"You'll be sorry when I'm gone."

Actions

Through dreams we all act out that which we cannot or will not express
during our waking moments. Especially meaningful are those dreams whose
content is powerfully emotional or even physically violent. These dreams
are safety valves, outlets for suppressed emotions. They are sometimes
called catharsis dreams, and from such dreams we often awaken emotionally, even physically, exhausted, so great has been the effort to express—
or repress—our true emotions.

Laughter in a dream is generally not a sign of happiness but is an example
of subversion; that is, it expresses a reaction to shock, loss, or emotional
upset.

Flying is a delightful escape mechanism. Reality is terrestrial, so to leave
the earth and soar, by whatever means, is an expression of the wish to fly
away from the problems and responsibilities of everyday existence. The
dreamer is not only "free" but may look down on the earthbound creatures
below. The philosopher Manley Hall put it this way: "to fly in the dream
manifests an adolescent wish to escape the privileges of responsibility."

This dream makes meaningful use of the symbol of flying, and it revealed
to the dreamer truths about himself that he had not or could not previously
recognize. He—we'll call him David—is a pleasant, personable, middle-
aged man, intelligent and open to analysis. His infancy and childhood had
been troubled by illness and a lack of communication with his parents. For
whatever reason, he had been afflicted with the problem of stammering all
his life, and despite having undergone treatment for it, when under stress
he still had to struggle to get his words out.

At the time he came for counseling David was, one might say, "float-
ing" along through life. He was unemployed but emphasizing—over-

emphasizing—that he really didn't want to work, couldn't stand taking orders from men whose intelligence he didn't respect. He was living with a woman whom he didn't really love and was considering leaving because she wanted a commitment. He spent his days at the beach, observing "people and life" and enjoying various recreations, living what he maintained was the good life, without work, responsibility, or self-discipline of any kind. When told that work can be a fulfillment, that circumstantial necessity requires that we earn both our keep and what love we want to receive, he replied that he was convinced his life-style was the right one, and nobody could convince him otherwise.

His psyche, however, must have found a chink in his armor, a way around the censor that had been protecting his ego. He had this dream:

> I was in Las Vegas, going to dinner, but it turned out to be a testing laboratory. [His "fun and games" kind of life ended up in the analyst's office, also a kind of "test."] They tested people's intelligence and abilities.
>
> In the next scene I am in a borrowed airplane, a two-seater. I'm going to fly the plane to get advertising time for this good cause. At first I am at the park in Long Beach [pleasure again] but it turns into an airport and I am trying to take off and I'm trying to find the radio to talk to the tower for takeoff instructions. Unfortunately I don't know how to operate the radio and I am real afraid to use it because of my stammering problem. I sit there for some time and someone is urging me to take off, with the radio or not, saying, "Look out! A black dirigible is coming over the horizon." It is obviously out of control and crashes close to where my plane is and blows up with a loud explosion. I am sitting there; I am not sure whether I am going to die or be injured in the explosion. The thing that really happens is that the explosion merely causes some oil drops to hit my airplane. That's all.
>
> The next scene the plane is parked in the back of a lunch room and my new girl friend I've been seeing on the side and I are sitting in the front of the lunch room eating and drinking. After we are through I go back to check on the plane and I find it has been stripped by thieves, leaving only what looks like a bicycle frame with a few nuts and bolts and that sort of thing.
>
> My girl friend says to me, "Don't be silly, it can't be; it's only your imagination." At this point I am examining some keys to prove the reality of the situation. I am looking at some straight keys and they all have one notch on them, and somehow that notch proves to me that I am not

dreaming, that the situation is real and I am responsible for that plane. How can I pay for it? What can I do about it? How can I make amends?

Meanwhile, I am really hoping it is just a dream, so I can get out of this problem—but I am really convinced that it is not a dream, and it is really happening.

He saw that his "flying" was symbolic of fantasy and escape from "down-to-earth" reality, and then added: "This is how I understand this dream: Here I am looking for the radio to call—I need to do something in my life. I have been trying to push myself into being a salesman and can't do it because it is uncomfortable for me with my stammering. I am a man fifty years old with nothing meaningful in my life; I know I have to do something. What kind of a price can I pay for it? I know that is the biggest thing in my life; I don't know how to proceed. When I start actively looking for a job and responsibility, because of my problem, I get such a feeling of anxiety you can't believe. My experience has been in the electronics field, but that was years ago and the technology has passed me by." The "big black dirigible" was the anxiety (mostly "hot air") that had floated over his head and finally come to earth with a bang, but with the fortunate and hopeful result that he was unhurt. We came to the simple dream statement that, from the wreckage of the plane, which he couldn't have flown in the first place, he was left with "the frame of a bicycle," its nuts and bolts. While this wasn't what he wanted, his dream told him that he had something practical with which he could proceed through life if he would go to the trouble of putting it together. The value of this dream was the emotional release it afforded, starting a decent individual on his way to a constructive life.

Many and varied are the methods by which the psyche takes flight in a dream, and they are all significant. To float lazily on the back expresses passivity and a wish to enjoy life without effort. The person who zooms vertically in his dream at great speed is expressing a wish for control, power, and to get where he wants in a hurry. Flapping the arms like a bird and soaring gracefully, seagull fashion, would express a yearning for harmony and natural beauty instead of the discord of everyday existence. Also common is the dream of a swimming motion with the arms, a breast stroke, as though the air were water. People who fly in this fashion seem to have a greater than usual wish to "return to the womb," often from having experienced traumas at birth or in early infancy. Freud saw flight as expressing a sexual impulse. Experience in interpreting dreams rarely conforms with this view, however.

Running from something indicates the wish to escape some threatening problem (usually within the dreamer) that appears embodied as man, beast, or monster. Running a race in a dream connotes what it seems to: ambition and competitiveness. The following dream is an example.

The dreamer was a seventeen-year-old boy. His life had been sandwiched in between a clever and successful older brother and a younger sister who had always been his parents' favorite.

> I was running a race and felt good when I had outstripped my younger sister. My brother was a little bit ahead of me but I knew in the dream I was about to catch up with him.

His brother had always excelled in athletics but now this young man was making such good grades in school he was receiving as much or more attention and praise as his brother. This was a race in which he could set his own pace.

Dreams of unique physical performance include taking magically long steps or any unusual physical act. The dreamer is often impressed with his unique ability. One woman dreamed that by turning her feet at a certain angle she could slide over the edges of a stairway from top to bottom, landing on the ground floor with a great sense of accomplishment. A man was equally surprised and pleased that he could perform a dance all by himself. Such dream experiences relive the adolescent discovery of masturbation.

Climbing always symbolizes the dreamer's effort to accomplish something. What the goal might be can be revealed by free association or be deduced from the waking content of the dreamer's life. If the goal is a mountain top, it could represent career ambition, but more frequently it means a spiritual yearning for growth and awareness. Climbing in a dream often symbolizes a much more earthy, physical drive, particularly if the dreamer is climbing stairs indoors. The effort in this case is toward sexual fulfillment, the summit symbolizing orgasm. The following dream contains just such a struggle.

The dreamer was a middle-aged married woman. While intelligent and attractive, this dreamer was unhappy and dissatisfied with her marriage. She was both irritable and critical with her husband. While he had been successful and provided her security and a beautiful home, he still had a self-effacing, almost apologetic manner.

> This is a dream I have had many times. In it I am always trying to climb some stairs. I climb and I climb and I never seem to reach the top. I stop at the landing and rest awhile and then I start climbing again. The last time, I looked up and saw that I was still a long way from the top, so I just said to myself, "I am too tired to go on" and sat down and started crying.

The same day her husband had occasion to relate a dream of his own, and it turned out to be related to hers.

> In the dream I was out in the front yard and decided I should water my wife's flowers. So I got the hose and turned on the faucet. But not a drop of water came out.

These dreams scarcely need interpretation, only understanding and sympathy.

Falling is always indicative of insecurity, a sense that there is nothing to hold onto. It may result from loss of work, the break-up of a marriage, or the departure from the dreamer's life of someone who represented security and protection. When a child hears the parents quarrel and one threatens to leave, the child may dream of falling into a deep hole. If a woman's husband tells her he has fallen in love with another woman, she may dream of falling from a cliff into the ocean. The dreamer almost invariably wakes up before hitting bottom, although there were two instances in which the dreamer hit the ground, hard; one bounced, and the other said the breath was knocked out of him!

If in dream a person is sliding downhill, with nothing to hang onto, he is in some way "losing ground," experiencing a sense of failure because his life is "going downhill." There is also the fear of "falling from grace" experienced by individuals from a strict religious background, particularly after a wish or act that they feel is immoral.

There is another, entirely different, dream of falling—different at least in its cause. Since a man's ego-identity and sense of manhood is naturally quite dependent on his sexual virility, one of the greatest dreads he has is the inability to achieve an erection. When this happens, it may be followed by a nightmare of falling.

Inasmuch as water almost always symbolizes the unconscious, diving in a dream implies a desire to discover or experience some repressed impulse. The questions to ask are how deep is the water, is it clear or murky, and how does the dreamer feel about the experience? The following dream is simple—but the solution to it wasn't.

The dreamer was a very disturbed young man starting analysis. He had a strong mother, head of her own business, and his father, a very weak man, had recently committed suicide. Although he was a strong, athletic, strikingly handsome young man, he was confused and had a poor sense of identity.

> I keep dreaming over and over that I'm diving into a deep pool. I feel there is something at the bottom that I must find; I don't know what it is but I feel it is important that I reach it. The water is so cloudy I can't see the bottom and I never reach what I'm trying to find.

It was quite awhile before he was able to bring "it" to the surface. When he did, it was comprised of several things, one of them being his confusion about the male and female poles in himself: he didn't want to be like his father, and his concept of womanhood was awry.

Freud believed that diving was symbolic of the birth sequence in reverse, so that instead of emerging the dreamer is entering, though it seems a bit more like the wish to return to the womb.

Unless the dreamer is re-experiencing the trauma of an actual near-drowning, a dream of drowning (and it is a fairly serious one) implies that the dreamer feels overwhelmed by an ocean of problems, that he can't "get his head above water." To carry the analogy a little further, one might say the dreamer's psyche is calling for a "lifeguard" in the form of some sort of counselor.

Fighting is always an expression of aggression withheld during waking moments. The appropriate question is, whom is the dreamer fighting, and why? It may be some real opponent in his life. Generally, however, the opponent is the personification of some negative aspect of his own nature, some aspect of his alter ego he does not want to submit to. In such dreams there are always the "good guy" and the "bad guy." Fortunately the better nature almost always wins.

Quarreling is a milder expression of conflict. In such dreams men usually express their frustration and aggression physically, while women generally "tell somebody off."

Cutting the self, hitting one's head, or other forms of self-injury are forms of sadomasochism. The purpose may be self-punishment as atonement for some real or fancied guilt. This sort of dream can express a sense of unworthiness resulting from the failure to live up to an impossible religious ideal. Fortunately such destructive impulses usually go no farther than a dream. However, if a man consciously or unconsciously fears that he has incestuous desires or homosexual inclinations, he may consequently think he has no right to a good sex life. In his dream he will symbolically castrate himself by cutting off a finger or a foot or injuring his leg. If his problem is deep enough, he may dream of cutting off his penis in expiation of his guilt.

Killing expresses a suppressed wish to destroy a real person or a problem. Whom and what is being killed is the key to the dream. If it is a person who is truly despised by the dreamer, then the dreamer is in a serious neurotic state and needs help to dissipate his rage. In most dreams, however, whatever is being destroyed symbolizes something perceived as negative within the dreamer. If an animal, it may be some aspect of his instinctual nature that he feels is "untamed"; if a snake, a sexual habit or problem he wishes desperately to "stamp out." Perhaps it should be eliminated, but the dreamer should realize he doesn't have to resort to violence. Understanding may be quite enough to eliminate the problem.

Beheading means, quite simply and obviously, castration, physical or intellectual.

Hiding indicates that the dreamer has a problem that he wants to conceal. It may happen in analysis that, as the counselor approaches some hitherto undisclosed aspect of the dreamer's life, he may have a dream of hiding. If the dreamer is hiding from a detective or policeman, these may well represent the dreamer's own superego.

The significance of playing games depends on the kind of game and who the players are. Bats, clubs, rackets, and balls are phallic symbols. Since the games involved are predominantly "masculine" sports, in dreams they are nearly always sexually charged. Sometimes these games are an unconscious reference to early adolescent homosexual play with male friends. The following dream shows a man attempting to work through such an early experience.

The dreamer was a young businessman, successful in everything but his sex life. He and his wife genuinely loved each other and he was deeply disturbed by his sexual inadequacy, which had not been helped by the various medical treatments he had tried. He had never thought of it as a psychological problem.

> Somehow I feel this is an important dream, but I don't know why. In the dream I was driving home from work. Halfway home my way was blocked by a bunch of teenage boys playing baseball. I tried to get them to get out of my way but I couldn't get through them. I knew I had to clear them out of my way or I would never get through to my wife. I awoke feeling very frustrated.

After the symbology of the boys playing baseball was discussed, he recalled and willingly related his rather extensive sexual experimentation as an adolescent with other young boys. Since this had gone on for a period of time, it had left quite an impression on him. He had in fact found it very stimulating and, as is often the case, wondered many times since if his homosexual interest was more than latent. The more he thought about it the more clearly he understood that this problem—like the boys' game in the dream—was something he had to clear out of the way before he could "get through" to his wife. Because the dream was entirely his own he could accept the message more easily than if it had been told him by someone else. His recognition of the problem was, of course, of great help in his therapy.

Card games in a dream, as games of the mind requiring cunning and a good memory, may symbolize the game of life itself. However, the name "poker" lends itself easily to sexual interpretation.

Partying, because it involves alcohol, perhaps dancing with a partner and release from inhibitions, usually indicates that the dreamer is wishing for or remembering a happy sexual relationship.

Eating and Drinking

The first thing we do at birth is take a breath and cry for food. We can breathe on our own, but we depend on others for food. A baby is at that moment entering what is called the oral stage of receptivity and dependence. If well nourished, he feels secure and content; if hungry, he feels neglected and unloved. From that time on in the unconscious of the individual the connection between nourishment and love is indelibly intertwined. Later, a person will say, "I am hungry for affection" or "I am starved for love." Dr. David Seabury, well-known author and psychologist, has said that "we must remember, the baby was a stomach before it was a brain." This introduces the importance of eating and drinking in dreams.

A banquet in a dream indicates that the dreamer has had some rich emotional experience—he feels his life is laden with good things. A bare table signifies a barren emotional life, emotional emptiness. No place at the table for him means self-pity, rejection, a feeling that life is good to others but not to the dreamer.

The kind of food, whether infantile or adult, a "square meal" or a sweet dessert, is important. The sort of food can reveal the age level at which the dreamer yearns to fulfill his hunger. Milk (and cheese, which is a milk product) connotes the nursing period. Sharing a complete meal with a member of the opposite sex would indicate that the dreamer has experienced a fulfilling emotional and probably sexual satisfaction. When two members of the same sex share something cloyingly or sickeningly sweet it might be wise to look for covert (or overt) sexual sharing.

As discussed earlier, any act of expulsion such as vomiting on the part of the dreamer has energy behind it: either a cathartic wish to expunge some inner guilt, or an expression of suppressed rage at a person or situation that makes the dreamer "sick." Spitting is an expression of contempt or even, if directed at someone, defilement. In a man's dream there is the occasional displacement upward of ejaculation into such a symbol.

Being eaten occurs most frequently in a child's dream. Some huge creature poses the threat. This indicates that the dreamer feels he is about to be "consumed" by some overwhelming emotion against which he feels small and inadequate. The dreamer's free associations with the animal and its characteristics will help uncover what fear or other hidden emotion might be threatening the dreamer. In a child this could be jealousy or sibling rivalry.

Drinking lends itself to many interpretations. It is important to note what is being drunk: water, milk, coffee, alcohol? Each of these carries its own symbolic charge. Milk connotes infancy and mother; coffee, social situations; bottled sweet drinks, the infant's identification of sweet liquid with the bottle. Alcohol usually relates to sexual excitement. Thirst in the dream that is quenched by a drink of cool, refreshing water would imply that the dreamer has "drunk at the fountain" of some source of "truth." To be offered a drink or have one forced on oneself (depending on the container) may refer to an oral sexual experience. Mucus and saliva often symbolize semen.

Urination and Defecation

After the nursing period, the second most important stage in the development of the baby is called the anal stage or the period of toilet training. The child's focus of attention is transferred from what is put in his mouth to what goes out of his body. This is his first attempt to gain control over his bodily functions. And because great emphasis is often put on his success or failure to perform according to mother's training, a feeling grows in him that his feces are a present to mother. The consequence is that when she's good to him, he goes to the bathroom on schedule; when she's cross, he withholds. The result is constipation. When angry enough, the child may express that rage by bowel accidents that mother has to clean up. This can never be attributed to a conscious expression of rage; it, like other bodily functions, is stimulated by subconscious emotion.

Dreams of the process of elimination are common. Sometimes the dreamer can't find a toilet, or is embarrassed because there is no privacy and he is being observed. While such dreams may replay a childhood experience, in general the discharge of waste matter from the body, especially when the feces or urine is in great quantity, represents catharsis, eliminating some guilt and/or rage. Because bowel movement is both consciously and unconsciously unattractive the dreamer may have been told as a child that he was "dirty"; certainly feces in a dream always connote something the dreamer feels guilty or ashamed of.

Urination means more or less the same thing as defecation but with a stronger sexual charge because the urinary tract is more closely associated with the genitals. In an adult male, a dream of wetting the bed may be related to a problem of premature ejaculation. Also, the act of urination in a dream may express aggression. The instinctual use of urination as a weapon of contempt or revenge is typical of animals—the dog that "kicks up" on the wheel of the car that took him to the vet, or the cat that leaves a little puddle on the bed of the mistress who punished him. This rather primitive instinct is evident in the following dream, though it was completely unrecognized by the conscious mind of the dreamer. In his waking moments he would of course never do such a thing. The dreamer was a genteel and devoted husband with a frigid wife who barely tolerated his sexual advances. Despite his protestations that he dearly loved his wife and did not worry about her rejection, he had this dream:

> This was the strangest dream. In it I was standing, hugging my wife. We were hugging each other face-to-face when suddenly I felt the flow of warm moisture between us below the waist. When I backed off and looked I was shocked to see a wet yellow stain running down the front of her white skirt.

The little boy inside of him was saying, "So there."

Other Actions

It sounds like an over-simplification, but *motion* in a dream symbolizes some kind of *emotion* in the dreamer. Since one cannot dream of abstractions, they appear in dreams as actions or as people, animals, or places.

Dancing, because of the rhythm involved, usually relates to love-making; if with a partner, it means harmony with the opposite sex. To dance alone has two implications depending upon the connotation of the dream. If spontaneously and exuberantly, it symbolizes freedom and self-expression. Otherwise it can express the pleasure of sexual self-gratification. The following dream of a virile young man, recently divorced and living alone, is revealing:

> I was dancing alone, in fact doing a ballet all by myself and enjoying it very much. I must say I was surprised at how well I could perform alone.

If the dreamer is a ski buff, then a dream of skiing may be a wish fulfillment or it may recall an actual experience. Otherwise, to ski alone is somewhat like dancing alone, but with no music, surrounded by snow and ice. There is an implication of loneliness.

Despite the possibility that the dreamer is musically inclined, a dream of playing a musical instrument is nearly always sexual. One man dreamed he was trying to play a ukulele, which he had played well in his youth, but in his dream he could not get a sound out of it. In free association he said he was afraid "a string was broken." Another young man, sexually inexperienced, had the recurring dream that he was playing a great pipe organ, from which he elicited fine music.

Riding, if on a roller coaster, may simply symbolize the ups and downs of life, or can be related to sexual movement. A horse can symbolize masculine strength and energy, implying that its dream-rider is carried through life by such virility. Again there may be sexual content. To fall off a horse can mean impotence.

Another dream involves finding that it is time to take part in a play but in a panic the dreamer discovers that he doesn't know his lines and is unprepared for his role. Freud related such anxiety to the child's reaction to the "primal scene," the act of lovemaking by the parents, a "play" for which he instinctively feels totally inadequate. The infant in his bed, like the actor in the wings, sees the play, identifies with the players and the excitement of the action, yet feels helpless and inadequate in the presence of such excitement.

Watching a play or film generally symbolizes the "replay" through projection of some emotional experience. There are also wish dreams, in which the dreamer, from his seat in the theater, watches himself perform, center stage, and always brilliantly! Frequently during analysis, when the dreamer is more conscious of all his feelings, his conscious mind stands aside in sleep and watches the performance of his inner self, projected clearly before his eyes. And even in the dream he may say to himself, "This is fascinating. I must remember and tell my counselor about this."

Many theories have been advanced about talking and walking while sleeping but, simply stated, they seem to be manifestations of "dream overflow." People who talk in their sleep do not usually, on awakening, remember dreaming, despite the fact that the tone and the words of their sleep talk may have indicated intense emotion. Rarely does the sleepwalker have any recollection of the dreams or impulses that stirred him into motion. However, it is often possible to recognize a wish fulfillment pattern in the direction or object of the nightly perambulations. Is the dreamer going toward something or someone, in desire or resentment, or away from someone or some place?

Position of the Body

Anything to the right of the dreamer represents morality or heterosexuality; anything to the left represents homosexuality or perversion or some wrong choice. Anything in front of the dreamer is something to be confronted, some experience or problem with which the dreamer is soon to be faced. Whoever or whatever is behind the dreamer personifies a memory, fear, or guilt that the dreamer has tried to put behind him, to ignore or forget. If what is behind poses a threat, is an enemy or attacking animal from which the dreamer tries to flee, it can usually be interpreted as a repressed desire that the dreamer fears might overtake and overwhelm the higher self. Once understood, the dreamer no longer runs in panic from such "pursuers."

In relating a dream a person will often say, "There was someone with me, walking along with me, I don't know who." This figure usually embodies the dreamer's alter ego or unconscious self, particularly if of the same sex as the dreamer. If of the opposite sex, such a figure may symbolize the animus or anima. Often this figure criticizes the dreamer, or gives advice. Free association helps to identify which facet of the dreamer's nature is making itself known in this way.

Anything above the dreamer is someone or something respected or emulated, real or imaginary, while anything below is inferior, perhaps a "lower" part of the body. Nearness of people or objects means they are close in time or affection; distance therefore implies remoteness.

8

Sexual Symbols, Male and Female

Sigmund Freud once said that he had found our dreams are involved primarily with five basic instincts or emotions: birth, death, relation to the parents, rage, and love (which includes sex). Of them all, the concern with love and its fulfillment through sex seem to occur most frequently in dreams, whether in the form of a problem or a wish. No other natural instinct seems to wear so many faces or masks as the mating urge. The mechanism of displacement is used to bypass our censor, or conscience, or whatever label we wish to give the screening mechanism that the unconscious uses to protect our social and religious concepts. From early childhood the natural curiosity and instincts regarding the nude body and the mating process have been considered taboo; therefore, they become inhibited and are driven "underground." That which is not of the conscious mind or acceptable to the ego can emerge from the unconscious mind only in a dream state through the form of symbology.

Most dreams with sexual meaning are in some way related to a problem of some kind because if one is emotionally fulfilled there is no need to dream about sex. If one has dined well, one does not dream of food! So sexual problem dreams can be the expression of a yearning or wish, unhappy memories, frustration, castration, frigidity, incest, masturbation, and homosexuality, with all of their attendant guilts and anxieties. It is as though the inner self is saying, "There is a problem down here; do something about it."

And no one should be embarrassed to reveal or confront sexual symbology, because the will to love is almost as strong as the will to live, and had we all grown up in a more natural culture we would have developed fewer inhibitions and frustrations and therefore have less need for release of anxiety through dreams.

In the interpretation of such dreams it is first necessary to recognize the basic symbolic forms. While these have been pointed out by Freud and those who have followed him, they were in truth first established by nature itself: that which protrudes and conquers is male; that which receives and surrenders is female. Physically the form that is erect, straight, and firm is masculine; whereas the forms that are soft, round, and yielding are feminine. In addition to the form we have energy and movement: things that project, propel, have force, drive, and initiative fall under the masculine principle. At the other end of the polarity we find receptivity, conception, tenderness, and nurturing under the female symbology.

Here are some examples of female sex symbols: anything that receives or contains, such as a purse, a bowl, a basket, a vase, a flower; something that opens or closes, such as a shellfish, a gate, a front door, a broken window (deflowering), a refrigerator (frigidity); parts of the body (vagina displaced upward), such as the mouth, the ear, and sometimes the eye; any opening like a cave or a fireplace; something that nurtures, such as a kitchen, milk or a milk bottle, or ice cream. Idealized feminine symbols include a rose, a pearl, or a lily, and breast symbols include cushions, smooth rounded hills in a landscape, apples, peaches, and cupcakes, especially with cream inside.

Male sex symbols include anything that is straight and erect, such as a telephone pole, a pine tree, flowers on straight stems, or the limbs of trees. Male symbols can also include anything that moves forward, such as a plow, an engine, a pen, or a pencil, as well as anything that protrudes or ejects, such as a gun, a garden hose, an unfolding camera, a faucet, a slot machine, the nose, or the tongue. Anything that is long and round can also be a phallic symbol, such as a snake, a hot dog, a banana, a mouse or a rat, a bottle, a cigar or cigarette, baseball bats and golf clubs, a fish, a whale, a bird, or a lizard. A key, because it enters and unlocks, is also a male symbol. Testicle symbols include grape clusters, potatoes, figs, avocados, soft bags, or balls used in games.

Here is the dream of a young single woman, lonely and anxious to get married:

> I was with somebody, a young man I liked. He took me into a gift shop where he gave me some diamond stud earrings. Then he sort of turned into my insurance man and he asked me to stay and eat. He had prepared a snake for dinner, had broiled it. I didn't want to offend him and although I didn't really want to, I started eating the snake. As I was cutting it, he remarked to me that it was really like steak, sirloin steak. The thing that bothered me about eating it was that I could see the tail of the snake and it was over-cooked, too brown.

The phallic implication of this dream is obvious. The dreamer's free association was that she would have preferred an engagement ring instead of something to go in her ears (promises, perhaps?). Also, that he took on the identity of her "insurance man" might be interpreted to mean that she wanted the insurance of a marriage—the reason, doubtless, why she was willing to eat such an unpleasant meal!

The phallus appears as a bird in the following dream of a married woman. Her sympathy for her husband is also apparent:

> It was a parrot or large bird. It was just gorgeous. I was holding it and looking at it. The next thing I knew, the feathers and all of the skin seemed to come off and it was just like a little broken chicken. I felt so sorry for it; it was such a skinny little thing when it had been such a beautiful bird.

A classic symbol of sex occurring in dreams of both males and females is that of money and objects used to contain it—purses for women, billfolds for men. These express sexual poverty or plenty depending on whether they are empty or full. This was a man's dream:

> It seemed I was starting out on a very important journey and when I opened my wallet I found I didn't have enough money to buy my ticket and I became extremely depressed and frustrated.

Many, many women, no matter how affluent, have had the experience of dreaming that they discovered, much to their dismay, that they had only a few pennies in their purse. When the dreamer is in reality financially secure, the dream can be interpreted only as an indication of her lack of sexual desire or ability. How fortunate when, after working through the cause of her frigidity, a dream emerges in which the dreamer opens her purse and is delighted to find more money than she ever had before!

The next dream uses the symbology of the purse. A father attachment appears to be depriving the dreamer of love and sexual expression.

> At the beginning I was in my father's car. When he stopped the car I got out and as I walked away I suddenly realized I had left my purse and all my money in his car and he had driven away with it.

Then there are the movements relating to the act of lovemaking: dancing, swimming, making music. Generally where pleasurable rhythm occurs in a dream there is some sexual connotation. Other symbols of intercourse include riding a horse, using a sewing machine, enjoying a full meal with a partner of the opposite sex, having a party, playing games, or performing gymnastics.

The above symbols are relative to the dreamer's own personal experience or concept. But what about the person who dreams of having witnessed the act of intercourse? The childhood memory, conscious or unconscious, of watching the act of lovemaking by the parents can, because of the excitement of the experience, emerge symbolically in dreams much later in life. Sometimes it occurs as an athletic event, other times (depending on the intensity of the movement) as some kind of animal performance. The following is the dream of a young woman who had slept in the same room with her parents until she was two or three years of age. For interpretation, it helps to understand that her father was much older than her mother.

> In my dream I was watching an oldish kind of horse pulling a buggy along a very bumpy road. As I watched him go up and down over all the big bumps he seemed so tired and I was sorry for him and wished he'd just stop.

Even at that age she was feeling her childlike concern for "poor Daddy."

Impotency and Castration Fears

If impotency is symbolized by something that won't start, premature ejaculation is represented by something that should go further or last longer, as the golf ball that goes only a short distance, the bullet that falls from the gun barrel, or the garden hose from which only a little water trickles.

Sexual anxiety appears more frequently in men's dreams than in women's.

The male by nature bears a greater responsibility for the sexual satisfaction of himself and his partner. The ego and the identity of the male are deeply involved with his sense of sexual potency; there is rarely a more profound hopelessness than that of a man who has become impotent.

Here are some of the various symbols of sexual anxiety that appear in the dreams of boys and men: a car that won't start, a gun that won't shoot, a bullet that barely falls out of the barrel, or a barrel that is limp, a plow that is broken, a musical instrument that won't play, a tool that won't work, a broken key, a pen that is dry, a golf club that goes limp, a flat tire, no money in a billfold, or a man who cannot stand erect.

When a man is troubled with a sense of sexual inadequacy, his unconscious will express the problem, using the mechanism of displacement, through the tool or instrument with which he is most familiar. Therefore, the farmer will dream his plow is broken; the musician finds his violin unstrung; the writer, no matter how hard he tries, can get no flow from his pen; and another man will find the starter in his car has gone dead. If his car is out of gas, the message is quite different: he is being told he has lost physical energy and drive. In that case a visit to an analyst or counselor will appear in a dream as a trip to the filling station.

Whenever a man has a sexual blockage it is important to watch for its symbolic representation in his dreams. The following dream is an example of such emotional interference. The dreamer was a married man incapable of starting intercourse. Before reading the dream, it is helpful to know that in reality his mother lived in a distant town.

> I have had this dream a number of times. Each time in the dream I am starting to make love to my wife and just as I am getting ready to start, the bedroom door opens and my mother enters the room. Naturally I withdraw sexually. I can't possibly make love with my mother puttering around in the room.

All one needs to do is change "mother" to "mother attachment" to understand why he cannot give his love and sex to his wife.

Another man's dream of frustration ended in a sense of hopelessness:

> Although I used to play golf, I haven't for years. But in the dream I was out on the golf course. I used to have some fairly old golf clubs, but in the dream they seemed to be more rusty and decrepit than before. I was deciding how many golf balls to take with me; decided to take two in case

I lost one. I teed off and went into the rough. Then teed off with the other. Lost that one, too. By then I was out there without anything to play with, so I just quit and went to the golf club.

Given that all males have a strong ego identification with their ability to procreate and to conquer any competitor for the favors of a mate, as well as the natural vulnerability of the male genitalia to injury or attack, it is easy to understand their instinctive fear of castration. Through displacement this fear may appear in a dream as loss of some part of the body—any part essential to his functioning as a complete man. This fear is instinctive and may not be conscious, but can be activated by an accident or injury in early childhood. (One man's anxiety was traced back to a circumcision problem: the development of too much scar tissue had necessitated a second circumcision with much pain and anxiety, of which he had no conscious memory. It was only after his fear emerged in a dream that his mother told him what he had undergone before he was a year old.) Also, as is illustrated in some of the following dreams, a man may feel buried guilt for some real or imagined sexual "sin" that has produced a fear of sterility or other loss of masculinity as punishment or atonement.

Without some awareness of symbology, it might be difficult to understand the meaning of the dream given below, that of a healthy young man:

> I was riding in a car with my brother. Suddenly his head rolled off, screaming, into a ditch. It was all bloody and it just kept screaming. I woke up shaking all over.

When asked, on a hunch, if he had recently undergone a circumcision, he replied that he had, at the urging of his doctor. "But," he added, "everything went all right and while it was very painful, I wasn't too worried about it." Consciously, that is, but his unconscious self, his alter ego that appeared in the dream, was screaming over the shock.

The next man was troubled not only with sexual inadequacy in his marriage but a lurking sense of guilt (which may have been the cause of his inadequacy) for many early homosexual encounters.

> I was playing baseball. Somebody hit me in the groin. They weren't playing according to the rules or were too close. I woke up worried about my genitals.

His next dream:

> Someone was showing me a book, a brand-new book. In it was a picture of a man having his head chopped off, like a tribe of headhunters would do. Then his testicles were ground up and given to animals to eat.

These are rather primitive symbols of sadomasochism as atonement for his sense of guilt and also some indication of oral sex.

Here is another young man's dream that can be interpreted to imply impotence and/or castration:

> I was sitting on top of a palm tree and it fell down with me. Then I was mad at somebody for pushing down another tree, an avocado tree. Right after that I was looking at a chimney that fell down.

Male Castration versus Female Rape

Why, in the interpretation of dreams, is much more mention made of male dreams of castration than of female dreams of rape? The answer seems to lie in several directions.

If one approaches the subject from a conscious and *physical* standpoint, far more women are raped than men are castrated. But dream content is not always coincident with conscious physical experience. Many men carry unconscious castration fears implanted by childhood injuries or threats: scar tissue from circumcision, bruises from injury in a game, anxiety about the result of having mumps (an overheard remark by the examining doctor or one of his parents), or—and this is of extreme importance—concern over whether the penis is of normal size. ("Organ inferiority" produces an anxiety in the male that amounts to a castration fear.)

A man, if sexually injured or impaired, is robbed in two ways: first, he feels he has "lost his manhood," his sense of identity and worth; second, he has lost his ability to satisfy his partner and give her children. The depression that results from such injury is often very deep, and has been known to result in suicide. (Rarely if ever has a woman ended her life because of frigidity.)

Many young boys have been warned by well-meaning parents or religious figures of punishment that may descend upon them later in life for natural curiosity about sex and masturbation. Many are the youths who approach sexual maturity with a deep guilt, sometimes involving castration anxiety, which results in the belief that they have no right to a good healthy sexual fulfillment.

While women often suffer serious injury as a result of rape, the most lasting result of the experience is emotional and psychological. Her enjoyment of sex as well as her trust of males may be shattered for a long time. However, she is still capable of loving her husband, giving him sexual satisfaction, of conceiving, and having the fulfillment of motherhood. In this way she is more fortunate than the impotent or "castrated" male.

When women relive the trauma of rape in dreams it rarely takes the form of the physical act itself but appears through displacement as a stain or tear in a garment, usually the skirt, or sometimes as a shattered window of the dreamer's bedroom. "But what about," one might ask, "all of the dreams women have of being pursued by a threatening male figure whom they fear is going to rape them?" Here we encounter an entirely different kind of threat. Almost never has this dreamer been actually threatened by rape. Instead she finds herself attempting to flee in dream from her own aggressively threatening animus, projected in the dream upon the pursuing male figure. Then again, on a still subtler level, a dreamer might have a deeply buried unconscious wish to be captured—against her conscious will, of course! If caught, which fortunately she never is, she could declare on awakening, "God knows I did my very best to get away from him."

Female Sexual Inadequacy

Symbols of female sexual inadequacy or frigidity can include an empty refrigerator, blocks of ice, an empty purse, a cold kitchen stove, a boarded-up fireplace, an inability to prepare food on time or an inability to meet the husband on time, or a locked front door. Here is the dream of a young woman, recently married:

> I was in my present new home and I was looking at an old-fashioned ice-box or freezer and thinking it was just like the one my mother had when she was a little girl. In reality we have a new modern refrigerator, but in the dream I said to myself that if the ice-box was like my mother's, it would be all right.

Another young woman's dream:

> I was looking at a lovely young lady doll. I love dolls. She was very pretty and beautifully dressed. But when I lifted her skirt I found she was all hollow below the waist, with dangly legs. It was very depressing.

This young lady needed help in realizing that despite a recent partial hysterectomy, she had not lost her femininity.

One can hardly read the next dream, that of a pretty wife, without feeling some sympathy for her husband:

> It all took place on a big ship, a battleship. There was a big block of ice on the deck and locked in it was a beautiful young woman, nude. The captain of the ship, an older man with a mustache, came over, placed his hand on the ice, and then it began to thaw.

It is scarcely necessary to report that "Daddy" had a mustache!

Many women have the frustrating dream, already mentioned, of being late to meet their husbands or being unable to get meals ready. Such dreams express her concern over her sexual slowness, or not being as "quick" as her partner.

Here is a pair of dreams in which the purse appears as a sexual symbol. A young woman who in her eagerness for love and attention had given of herself, emotionally and physically, much too freely, was plainly informed by her unconscious how she was wasting herself:

> I was just leaving a cocktail bar when I discovered I did not have my purse with me. I went back to the bar to see if I could find it. Sure enough, it was there. But it was lying wide open on top of the bar and I realized somebody had robbed me; I had nothing left.

The dream that followed not only re-emphasized the problem, but sadly illustrated her poor sense of worth:

> I was riding on a bus and discovered my purse was lying in the aisle. Everybody was stepping on it.

Frustration dreams can be due to a sexually inadequate husband or lover. Here is one example:

> I was at a banquet and a lot of people were dancing around with ballet-like motions, happy. They were preparing this food and were going to serve it to me. One young man brought this bowl to me. Inside of it was a yellow bird, like a canary. The poor thing was lying on its side. They

were drowning this bird in wine and were acting like I was supposed to eat it.

Before we consider the next dream, it is well to remember that a cap or hat signifies identity, and that lifting something up and looking under it (a rock, for instance) means discovering something previously hidden that the dreamer has not wanted to face. The dreamer was a married woman, and it is not difficult to deduce from her dream how she felt about the entire business of sex!

> There was a Navy cap lying there, a cap like my husband used to wear. I lifted it up. Underneath it was a worm and it was all slimey. It was rather small. I thought, "What is that?" It was repulsive to me.

Another example:

> Bill was uprooting our avocado tree, which was apparently dead. When he got it up I noticed it had only two branches growing and they fell off. I said, "It was dead, anyway." Then I noticed one branch that had fallen off had some very small avocados on it, and I was sad—now they would never be able to grow. I picked one up and it was soft.

The next dream, of an unhappy wife, contains not only frustration but suppressed rage:

> I looked out the back window of an old house, not our present one, but one like we had ten or fifteen years ago. The grass was dry, high and neglected-looking. I went to turn the sprinklers on to water it and saw a lion hiding in the grass. I became terrified and ran into the house, but felt somehow it had gotten into the house, too, and was hiding someplace.

The old house represented the past; the backyard, that which is private, not known to others; the neglected grass symbolized pubic hair. The sprinkler was a phallic symbol, and the lurking lion was her own rage, which followed her into her home.

"Penis Envy" Symbols

Sigmund Freud held that all females at some time envy the male role, a phenomenon that he succinctly called "penis envy." And since little girls—and for that matter big girls—for generations have been impressed with the idea that boys were not only more desirable to the parents but more fortunate in life's opportunities and experiences, it is easy to understand why many girls and women have not only envied the male sex organ and tended to imitate the masculine role, but have attempted in their dreams in compensation to produce a penis symbolically. Here is an example. The dreamer was a middle-aged woman who dominated her passive husband and her teen-aged children:

> I was driving along in my Cadillac with my daughter beside me when I became aware of a long hard lump on the underside of my hip. Disturbed, but not wanting my daughter to know about it, I pulled into a filling station and went to the restroom to investigate. What I discovered was a hard object, like a bone seven or eight inches long, right under the surface like it was trying to work its way out. I knew I had to get rid of it and was calling a doctor to have it removed when I woke up.

The "doctor" in this dream symbolizes (as frequently happens with people under analysis) the counselor to whom the dreamer was turning for help. What more graphic symbol could there be for her strong animus than the "long hard lump," which she knew she "had to get rid of."

Here are two more equally clear examples:

> I looked in the mirror and saw an ugly-looking growth coming out on the side of my neck, sticking straight out. Somehow I knew it was full of pus and unhealthy and that I must get rid of it as soon as possible.

The next dreamer was a woman in her early thirties, never married, and almost strident in her need to prove her mental and physical strength. Her earliest memories were of the disappointment her parents had expressed that she, the first-born, had not been a boy. Naturally, after her little brother did arrive, she did everything she could to outstrip him.

> I dreamed I went to the bathroom and discovered beneath my underpants a large penis. I wasn't particularly worried, but wondered what I should do about it.

When asked what her first reaction was, she replied that "I thought the growth had come back," and then related that a few years before she had found a slender fleshy growth protruding from her own sex organ that had to be surgically removed. In this rather sad case the female was trying physically as well as subconsciously to compensate for having disappointed her parents!

The Castrating Woman

Many women, whether from fear or dislike of men, have a conscious or unconscious urge to emasculate them. They attempt to do this by getting the better of them intellectually or emotionally. In other words, they attempt to achieve supremacy over their imagined enemy by mental or sexual castration. Frequently this urge is more manifest in their dreams than in their waking moments. It came through clearly, represented by displacement, in the following dream. The dreamer was a young woman:

> I was with my best girl friend [her alter ego or unconscious self] whom I really don't like at times. In the dream it seemed that her boyfriend had rejected her somehow. Before that, two or three other men had hurt her in some way. She was with her last boyfriend in the dream, and as I watched she took a nail and pounded it straight down in his head. After that I was afraid of her, afraid she might turn and hurt me.

Of course, the dream was about her own antagonism toward men, which she instinctively feared could in some way be turned against herself.

The young woman who had the next dream had been enduring a frustrating relationship with a sadistic husband and was at the point of withdrawing from his sexual advances:

> In the dream my husband was kissing me, and I knew he was trying to work up to sex. While he was doing this, I became aware that our dog (a female) was creeping up on him and getting ready to bite his genitals. My husband didn't see the dog and I was secretly enjoying what was about to happen.

Another castrating symbol appears in the next dream. The dreamer was a frustrated young woman who felt that despite doing and saying all of the right things to hold a man, the attractive ones lost interest and soon drifted away. With the help of dream interpretation she got a glimpse of the source of her problem. Her dream:

> I was going to a party or dance, accompanied by a very attractive man. I was well groomed and had on a lovely dress. And I was carrying a soft black velvet purse. As we walked along, I decided to put some lipstick on, but when I opened my purse to get my lipstick I saw a sharp knife shining in the bottom of my purse. I snapped it shut as fast as I could for fear he would see it.

No matter how she attempted to hide the sharpness inside her outwardly soft "velvet purse," apparently her male friends saw it and went on their way.

This final example might be called the castration dream to end all castration dreams! The dreamer was a middle-aged widow.

> I was sitting between two buckets or pails. I had a knife in my hand. In the bucket at the left were penises. I would pick them up one at a time, slice them with my knife, then drop them in the bucket on my right.

The reason for her husband's demise was not discussed but one can be sure it wasn't from sexual over-indulgence.

Bisexual Symbols

Dreams that contain symbols of bisexuality must not always be interpreted as indicating homosexual tendencies. Many women have dreamed that they discovered a male sex organ underneath their skirts. Generally this implies what Freud called "penis envy" and maybe developing masculine characteristics. The boy who dreams his mother has a male organ is getting the message that his mother has "worn the pants" and robbed him of some of his own male identity. The man who dreams he has female breasts may have over-identified with his mother, or he may have been made to feel that he disappointed his parents by not being a girl.

This dream is that of a woman who by inclination and experience was bisexual. She had been an only child and almost from birth had heard that her parents had wanted a boy instead of a girl. And she had done her best to fulfill their wish.

> I was in this house with a boy nine years old. It seems his parents were waiting in the driveway for him to come out. He was sort of fooling around and I decided to go out as a delaying tactic—I thought that per-

haps when they first saw me they would think I was their son. When he finally came out and I was about to say good-bye, I noticed that he had fluffed his hair up in the back with a kind of lacy ribbon in it. I wondered where he was getting these odd transsexual ideas, a nine-year-old child. His parents seemed to think this was the last straw, and just drove away and left him.

So, he and I were standing there in the yard watching them depart. All of a sudden he kissed me and put his tongue in my mouth, a "French kiss." This was quite startling to me, but I made up my mind instantly to keep my calm. I was thinking this child is really mixed up and maybe I can talk with him and sort of set him straight on a few things. When I asked, "Why did you do that?" he said, "Well, I have always gotten away with it before." I decided I must tell him about sexual things you just don't do "to get away with" and to make him realize what unwholesome ideas were forming in his mind. I thought, "We will go in the house and have a little talk." We went inside and were lying across the bed, kid fashion, and I was going to tell him these things that were wrong when the phone rang and woke me up.

This is an expression of confused identity. The young boy is her immature and undeveloped animus, which, despite a ribbon in his hair, attempts to function sexually. The rejection and neglect of her parents is apparent in their disgust at her masculine side and abandonment of both her feminine and masculine sides. Her inner common sense and wish to be both mature and moral comes through clearly in her desire to teach the young self things "you don't do." In contradiction of her previous conscious avowal that she was entirely satisfied with her bisexuality, her inner self was deeply troubled by the wish, expressed in the dream, to clear up "unwholesome ideas."

Objects that symbolize bisexuality are usually objects that can be changed from an enclosure (female) to a projection (male), such as a convertible car or a turtle.

Homosexual Symbols

Since everyone in the process of growing up goes through the latent or homosexual period (roughly from seven to fourteen years of age), at the time when all little boys prefer their buddies and think girls are a waste of time, and all girls of the same age have crushes on their girl friends and consider boys a pain in the neck, it is natural sometime later in life to have dreams that derive from that period of development. If there has been overt sexual contact with a member of their own sex during that period there would naturally be fear or guilt later. The important point to remember is that dreams containing homosexual symbols do not always indicate a serious problem; they often bring to the surface some emotional experience during the latent period. Where the dreamer is an active homosexual the symbology of his dreams will be more vivid and usually more frightening (despite the usual avowal that he consciously feels no problem about the direction of his love life).

The snake is the symbol most frequently used by the subconscious to convey a sexual problem, and of course the larger and the more poisonous the snake, the greater the threat to the dreamer. A great fear of many otherwise well adjusted men is that they will be found to have a taint of homosexuality, particularly if they indulged in some experimentation with it in their youth. Here is a case in point: a religious, faithful husband, thrashing around in the bed, awakened night after night with the following nightmare:

> There is always a rattlesnake wrapped around my leg in the bed. And I am scared to death. I try and try to kick it off and keep thrashing around in the bed yelling to my wife to help me get rid of it.

He "confessed" a youthful sexual contact with male friends and was assured that, inasmuch as he was now successfully heterosexual, he had nothing to worry about. This, with the comforting thought that God had probably forgiven him for his youthful transgressions, allowed him to go home and sleep peacefully through the night. It is significant that in his nightmare struggle with his tormentor he was calling for his wife's help, indicating that he had believed lovemaking with his wife would rid him of his fear and guilt.

The young man who had the next dream, totally unaware of dream symbology, had interpreted previous nightmares as simply dramatizing his strong conscious fear of snakes. When he had this dream, in which the snake appeared in a more attractive form, he reasoned, "It must mean I'm getting better because in the dream I'm overcoming my fear of snakes." It should be mentioned that this healthy young man had found himself incapable of performing sexually with girls.

> There was a huge warm soft snake coiled around me. In the dream I said to myself I should be afraid of it, but I was not; even if it might be poisonous, it was so warm and soft and comfortable. Its coils somehow reminded me of buttocks.

When we remember that in almost all cases the snake is a phallus, it follows that a poisonous snake symbolizes a sexual problem; in this case, borderline homosexuality. This dreamer had at the time not only accepted this "snake," but found it comforting and attractive, though he still viewed it as poisonous.

Here is another dream example of a man's attempt to overcome a latent homosexual problem through the experience of marriage. This man (who did in fact raise flowers in his backyard), quite disturbed about sexual inadequacy with his wife, had this dream:

> I went out to my backyard and saw a very beautiful but strange-looking flower. It was lavender colored, rather exotic looking, and was blooming at the top of a tall straight stalk. Somehow I felt it was a poisonous flower and I picked up a stick and tried to beat it down to the ground. But no matter how I tried, I couldn't seem to kill it.

There are two phallic symbols here: the stalk on which the unwholesome flower was growing (homosexuality), and the stick with which he attempts to fight it (heterosexual relations with his wife).

Other homosexual symbols include dancing or making music with a member of the same sex, playing games with bats and balls with male friends, playing poker with males, exchanging cigarettes or bottled drinks with other males, eating a hot dog, or taking drugs (illicit stimulation). This is the dream of a very emotionally confused man whose problem is apparent:

> I was going on a picnic with a football team. Then I was playing cards with some of the guys. The cards kept changing on me and I thought I was going crazy. I asked one guy if he had given me a drug and he said yes. I felt like I was hallucinating. I asked him how he had given it to me because I didn't realize how it had come about, and he said he slipped it into my mouth. I felt I was under the influence of LSD, which I have

never taken, and when I walked away I thought everybody was looking at me and could see that I was under the influence of a drug.

Lesbian Symbols

As with males, female dreams that contain lesbian images and experiences do not always imply overt lesbianism. However, when such dreams do occur it is best not to brush them aside too quickly. In addition to dreams in which actual sexual contact between females occurs, a number of displacement symbols have lesbian connotations. These include sharing sweet food or drinks with another female, dancing or making music with a female friend, or even the symbol of the snake.

A beautiful young woman who had been troubled by intense anxiety of unknown origin had this dream:

> I went to the dresser in my bedroom, opened the drawer, and reached inside to get my silk hose. I felt something soft and as I pulled it out, instead of my hose I was horrified to see it was a rattlesnake. I woke up in a cold sweat.

When we remember that the drawer could symbolize only a very private compartment of her unconscious, the meaning of the snake, a phallic symbol, and in this case a poisonous or dangerous one, becomes clear. After discussing the dream she brought up the memory of sexual experimentation with another girl in her youth, in which she said she always pretended to be the man, and then added that for some time she had been afraid that she would find out she was too attracted to women.

The meaning of this next dream is much more subtle, but nevertheless brought to the consciousness of the dreamer something she had suspected but never faced. The dream is that of a young woman in the employ of an older woman. While there had never been any overt act, the younger woman was occasionally embarrassed by the attentiveness and very personal solicitation of her employer.

> I was talking with my boss and suddenly, despite my protest, she—of all things—reached over and put an egg in my pocket! I was annoyed and a little disgusted. Besides, I didn't want it.

The rhythm of music takes on a sexual connotation in the next dream. The dreamer was a young woman living in close contact with another young woman:

> This was a frustrating dream. In it, my roommate and I were trying to play a duet. We each had separate pianos. I could get the rhythm but my roommate just didn't seem to be able to catch on, and I got very irritated with her.

Nothing could state more clearly the conflict between the outer life and the inner yearning than this next dream, that of a young woman who sought counseling but stated at the outset, almost defiantly, that she was lesbian and had been living with another young woman for several years. She was happy with the arrangement, she said, and had no desire to change it. Assured that no one wished to change her life, she went on to other matters, starting with her childhood. After some time in counseling, she had this dream:

> I was in a very small car driving up a narrow street. As I progressed the street became narrower and narrower. Suddenly I realized that the street was closing in on me and there was barely room for my car to squeeze through. A feeling of anxiety came over me and I had a strong urge to turn back—but now it was impossible to turn my car around. I could not back up or turn around, so all I could do was go forward. Then I looked up and saw a big sign up ahead of me, DEAD END. A panic swept over me and I cried out for help, "Why didn't somebody tell me? Why didn't somebody tell me?"

She was the first child of European parents who let her know very early that her birth was a disappointment; they would have preferred a son. After two brothers were born she had tried every way she could to compensate for the handicap of being born female. One memory stood out painfully: one of her brothers had done something that the father had thought was cute. With the hope that she, too, might amuse her father, she repeated exactly what her brother had done. Her father slapped her and told her to stop being silly.

When asked what, at the age of eighteen, she had wanted more than anything in life, she said her greatest wish had been to be married to a good man and have children and a home. But her father's rejection had scarred her femininity too deeply. In compensation, she became "butch" herself and found companionship with a girl. Yet how clearly and painfully her dream revealed her true nature and the panic she felt when she thought it was too late to "turn around." Though she cleared up other problems, in spite of her dream she made no real effort to "back up" or "turn around" in her sexual life.

Masturbation

Dreams about masturbation usually relate to some adolescent memory or guilt. Here are some common symbols of masturbation in dreams: playing a slot machine (pulling the handle and catching the coins), writing checks (especially for five dollars), imitation money, finding coins or jewels, riding a bicycle, dirty hands, teeth falling out, doing any kind of dance alone, or taking extremely long steps or otherwise performing in some magical way, where the dreamer is amazed at his ability to perform something very unusual.

The dream of riding a bicycle occurs fairly frequently, and while it can relate to the actual experience, if the dreamer remarks, "I don't know why I'd dream of riding a bicycle; I haven't been on one in years," it might be wise to explore the possibility that he or she is expressing an urge to masturbate.

Sexual anxiety, apparently as a result of an attempt at masturbation, appears in the next dream, that of a young man:

> I was at some kind of slot machine that had wheels turning but not the usual bells and cherries when you hit the jackpot. Wheels were turning and lights flashing but no bells and cherries. I seemed to be egged on by some female voice behind me. Then it seemed I had won—but there was no money! I said to somebody, I don't know whom, "Where's my money? Where's the jackpot?" They said, "The girl has it; she took it."
>
> I seemed to go looking for this girl; she was no one I knew or could recognize; it was just myself looking, trying to find who had taken what belonged to me. I found a girl, she was having her car pulled out of the water [the unconscious] where it had fallen. An old car, about 1955. I say to her, "Where's my money?" She throws it down on the ground and I have to stoop to pick it up. It's all in coins, small coins.

The girl behind him in the dream could be considered the personification of his feminine side, which he had never faced and which had been robbing him of his masculine potency. The 1955 car being pulled up from his unconscious would indicate the approximate date in his life when his problem became submerged in the unconscious. The small coins often symbolize semen. He had to "stoop to pick them up," a gesture that often appears in dreams about masturbation.

The discovery of masturbation during puberty is now recognized as a natural development and harmless unless excessive (which may indicate a psychological problem). Until fairly recently, however, this practice had been considered a "mortal sin" by some parents and religious figures, threatening not only the physical health but the very soul of the transgressor. Young people were warned that God was watching them, that they would go insane, or that they would become blind. One young man, before receiving help, was seriously contemplating cutting off his right hand to atone for his "mortal sin"; better, he thought, to go through life with only one hand than to eventually "burn in hell." And one young married woman was ready to take her own life to be rid of her burden of guilt: she had previously given birth to an undeveloped fetus and was immediately stricken with the belief that God was punishing her for having "played with herself" in adolescence.

In 1898, Mrs. Mary Wood Allen, M.D., published a book entitled *What a Young Woman Ought to Know*. Here is a short excerpt that may show where such attitudes originated:

> A certain wise physician has said about this habit . . . He is convinced that it causes a great many headaches and backaches and other aches, tenderness of the spine, nervousness, indolence, pale cheeks, hollow eyes and languid manner. He says he can always tell when a girl begins this habit of solitary vice, or self-abuse as it is sometimes called, for she will suddenly decline in health and change in disposition. Instead of being happy, obliging, gentle and kind, she will very soon become peevish, irritable, morose and disobedient. She will lose her memory and love of study. . . . She will manifest an unnatural appetite, sometimes craving mustard, pepper, vinegar, and spices, cloves, clay, salt, chalk, charcoal, etc., which appetites certainly are not natural for little girls.
>
> Sometimes there is an eruption found around the roots of the nails,

and the eyes will look blank. This is a very serious penalty to pay for any pleasure that one may derive from this habit.

In 1945, Dr. Otto Fenichel, in his book *The Psychoanalytic Theory of Neurosis*, wrote:

> This is perhaps the moment to insert a few general remarks about masturbation. Masturbation, that is the stimulation of one's own genitals for the sake of sexual pleasure, is normal in childhood, and under present cultural conditions, is also normal in adulthood as a substitute when no sexual object is available. If a person whose sexual activities are blocked by external circumstances absolutely refuses to make use of this way out, analysis always reveals some unconscious fear or guilt feeling as the source of the inhibition. Patients who did not masturbate during adolescence likewise reveal that their sexual urges were overcome by fear and guilt feelings . . . this is usually due to an especially deep repression of infantile masturbation.

Pubic Hair

Pubic hair can take many forms in dreams. Here are some examples: hairy animals, a fur coat, feathers, tassels, brushes, moss, grass, or ferns. A mature woman, weary of the sexual demands of her husband, dreamed that she had an old fur coat that was worn out in patches and she wanted to get rid of it—a clear instance of pubic hair, as a figure of sexuality, represented in symbols.

The next example is not pleasant. It is the dream of a very proper married man. Both he and his wife are very concerned and puzzled over its meaning:

> Several times I have dreamed that my wife is trying to get me to eat a mouse. I want to please her, but the idea is disgusting to me, particularly because of the mouse's hair. Now why in the world would I dream that?

The next dreamer was a young woman, an only daughter with a doting father. She had this recurring dream:

> In the dream I keep feeling something disturbing is behind me. I am afraid and at the same time not afraid, sort of fascinated. Then in my

dream I glance behind me and there is a big old brown bear, very hairy. I want to run but can't.

Through the process of free association she recalled that as a small child her father often put her in the bathtub with him, placing her in front of him between his legs. She said he was a large man with thick dark hair. She could remember occasionally turning around and glimpsing the dark hair in the water behind her. This made it easy to understand why in the dream she "was afraid and yet not afraid, sort of fascinated."

Madonna/Prostitute and Saint/Satyr Complexes

Occasionally a man or woman will grow up with what might be termed a "split image" of the other sex. The opposite sex may appear to them as undesirable, even evil, and therefore not to be trusted, or, on the other hand, as idealized, so pure as to be unattainable. When a man sees women this way it is called the madonna/prostitute complex, while the female version is termed the saint/satyr complex. This is a neurosis that is believed to start in early childhood. A child forms its first image of the opposite sex according to the kind of parents he or she has: the little boy yearns for a loving mother whom he can look up to and give his devotion—the madonna image. Should his mother fall short of this by being coarse, cruel, or even sexually promiscuous, she not only topples from his heart's throne but implants in him a distrust of females in general. Later in life he is suspicious, critical, and frequently disappointed in his involvement with women, meanwhile yearning to find the lovely virginal creature who would measure up to his very high and rigid standards. He often lives a disappointed and lonely life, with one love object undesirable and the other unattainable. The same pattern of emotional disappointment and yearning frequently develops in the young girl. She may be afraid of closeness with a man lest she be shocked or hurt, or she may go through life longing for an "ideal" man, the Sir Galahad who never seems to appear. It is as though the child, after seeing the parental image shattered, in compensation creates an ideal, a fantasy figure, which he or she then seeks and too frequently never finds.

There is a tendency on the part of such people to classify everything (themselves included) as either good or bad with no gray area in between.

This rigidity can be strong indeed if the individual also embraces a strict religion, resulting occasionally not only in emotional inhibitions but frigidity or impotence as well.

Below is the dream of a young lady whose history followed the outline above: her father was a dominating man with coarse manners, very "macho," who boasted of his exploits with women. What embarrassed his daughter the most was that he asked probing questions and made crude remarks about her nonexistent sex life. In contrast, her mother was a genteel and reserved lady who not only attended church regularly but sang in the choir. Her parents eventually divorced. Meanwhile the dreamer clung to her college friends and chose new friends only from the young men and women she met at her church. They were all people, she reported, of "clean" habits and high standards with whom she felt morally and physically safe. The young lady was intelligent, attractive, vivacious, and had a sincere desire for love and marriage. No matter how many parties she attended or dates she had (not many) she always felt like "the bridesmaid and never the bride." Her male friends all treated her like a friend or sister, parking her on her doorstep after each outing. Frustrated that at the age of twenty-three she had never had a real romance of any kind, she sought counseling. Soon afterward she brought in this dream, in which her saint/satyr problem was easy to recognize.

> It seemed that one of my girl friends [her alter ego] told me that this man wanted my phone number and she gave it to him. This person called and we made a date to go out. When he came to the door he was a fifty-five-year-old man, partially bald, big beer belly, looking awful, and dressed like he had been at work all day. I said to myself, "This is awful," but we left. As we were driving down the road, I saw a station wagon on the side of the road with a flat tire. We stopped to see if we could help them change the tire. They were all friends of mine, and we all stood around chatting about what they were doing and where they were going. It seems to me they were going on a water skiing trip. They were all friends of mine from the Bible study class. The next thing I remember I was talking on the phone with my good friend Lucille, an attractive married woman, and she asked, "Who have you been dating lately?" I said, "Funny you should ask," and then I remembered when we finished talking on the phone that my date, the older man, had disappeared, as though it had been a dream. I didn't remember his bringing me home

because we never continued the date. The others were back at the station wagon and I realized I was all alone again.

It is easy to see her negative father (satyr) image in the slovenly older man who wants to date her. The nice guys, on the other hand, have a flat tire and are going nowhere. Their supposed destination involved water skiing. Symbolically, this would connote skimming over the surface of the water (the unconscious), each on his own. As the dream progresses she puts in a call to her friend, the married woman, who embodies what the dreamer yearns to be, and is confronted with the question, "Who are you dating?" She then realizes that the unpleasant father relationship has faded out of the picture, her group of religious friends are still back with their flat tire, and she is alone. This dreamer added the healthy confession that she had always been secretly intrigued by more devilish males. She really would, she said, like to meet "a red-blooded young man who raises a little hell now and then" and would be masculine enough to try to seduce her.

Here is another example of the saint/satyr complex. The dreamer started life as a strict Catholic, and, being sensitive and idealistic, tended to idealize her father. Too much criticism from her parents robbed her of a sense of worth, and because her femininity was poorly developed she had experienced a series of disappointing relationships with men. At the time of the dream she was living with a married man who, although separated from his wife, said he would never divorce her. The young woman confessed that she knew it was a "dead end street" but she was grateful to have a man care for her and dreaded being alone. Her dream:

> My mother and I went to church, and there was an overweight priest. During the ceremony he took off his robes and stuck his head out of the curtains behind the pulpit. When he came out he had on a white T-shirt and underpants. I left my purse in the church and went out. Then it seemed I had parked my car illegally; it was in the church grounds but somehow I knew it was against the rule.
>
> I called a girl friend and we went to an AA club, and I told a man friend there about my car—but then I couldn't describe it because I couldn't remember what it looked like. I knew I had parked it in the church parking lot but I just knew there was something wrong.
>
> After I told him about my car, this girl friend and I went to the back of the club and an overweight couple was talking to my friend. The woman was curled up like a child in a chair. She was coming off a drunk, trying to

sober up. He was fat, with a full face and black-rimmed glasses. He said he remembered my girl friend as a child; he used to drink in front of her, and then he repeated himself.

All through the dream I had feelings of anxiety, very intense anxiety.

Here is her free association: "The man I have been living with is big with a tendency to be overweight. He is an alcoholic and I had a drinking problem, too; we met at an AA meeting, but neither of us drinks now. As for the priest in the dream: I was very religious when I was young and hoped to find a good man, but they always turned out to be interested only in sex and ended up taking advantage of me. I can see where my girl friend in the dream can be the better part of me; we have always gotten along well, and she's warm and sincere, an understanding and loving person. Also, she has been involved with a married man for several years. And as for the priest in the dream defrocking himself, I know he symbolizes the man I've been living with. I thought he was so fine when I first met him, but now I don't trust him or really respect him; I'm constantly afraid he'll go back to his wife—or find another woman. Now I believe that was the reason for my anxiety all through the dream."

It is easy to recognize the sexual implication of the man's head emerging from between the curtains. From there, everything seems to go wrong. She left her purse (her own feminine sexuality) in the church; although her car was in the correct parking lot, she knew she had done something wrong; she could not even identify her car (her way of life); and she ended up with a pair of alcoholics. She herself added, "And the woman coming off a drunk, curled up in a chair like a child, is the childish side of me." The dreamer, despite her problems, is a gentle and intelligent woman and became aware of her worth. She broke off the relationship with the married man and moved into her own apartment after finding a good job. Her "satyr" took a good look at himself and decided to put his life in order. She is waiting to see if he can become, if not a "saint," at least the decent man she needed in the first place.

Here is a dream that illustrates a man's madonna/prostitute complex. The dreamer was a young man, married to a faithful, slightly older wife. At the time he was carrying on a secret affair with an attractive younger woman. This woman had accepted his story of unhappiness with a cold dull wife, and believed that he planned to get a divorce and marry her. But how different were their images in his dream:

> I was in a living room talking with some woman. I can't remember what we were talking about or exactly who she was, but I knew somehow she was a very fine person and I respected her. While we were talking I became aware that there was another woman, younger, in the next room and I knew she was waiting for me. I hoped the nice woman I was talking to wouldn't see her because I knew the other woman was a prostitute. I was kind of pleased that she was waiting for me, but I was ashamed at the same time.

He understood the meaning of his dream. Bored as he was with his wife, "the madonna," he respected her after all. When asked about the "prostitute," with no compunction whatsoever he stated, "While my girl friend is attractive and all that, after all I have to be honest, she is a single woman having an affair with a man she knows is married!"

Incest

Incest is another common sexual motif of dreams. The young woman who had the next dream refused to accept it and closed the door on any solution. An attractive married woman, she was not only frigid in the bedroom, but was constantly bored with her hard-working husband, frequently comparing him unfavorably with her more than perfect, loving daddy. Two weeks into her analysis, she had this dream:

> I dreamed I was in bed with this man, having intercourse, and it was very exciting. And I had an orgasm—the first one in my life.

On being congratulated that she had discovered the joy of lovemaking and was not frigid after all, she added irritably, "But that wasn't all there was to it. After it was over, I saw his face, and it was my father! I woke up sick to my stomach and with an awful headache." Then after a pause she added with disgust, "I never had such awful dreams until I came here for counseling."

Assurances that she need feel no guilt, that the dream only expressed a little girl's father fixation, had no effect whatever. Believing that the dirty-minded analyst had caused it all, she brought an end to her counseling, and also no doubt to any possibility of sexual adjustment and fulfillment.

Here is another, similar dream, again that of a young woman who was cool to her husband both in and out of bed:

> It seemed that my husband had gone out of town on business for several days. In the dream I had gone to bed, and felt secure that the front door was safely locked. Then I decided I'd better get up and unlock the back door, just in case Daddy wanted to come in during the night.

The next dream is an extremely graphic, even shocking example:

> It seemed like I was trying to wake up. My husband was sleeping in the bed next to me. Then it seemed I was holding his sex organ. I just touched it and it started to get large. He ejaculated and it startled me.
>
> Then I looked and it wasn't my husband at all, it was my father, lying on his side. He looked very gray.
>
> Then I had a finger in my mouth; I don't know whether it was his finger or not. I thought, "I know it's a dream; I must wake up." As I was pushing him away and as I looked down, they weren't my hands, they were a little kid's hands pushing him away. I was struggling to get away.

Incest dreams seem to occur more frequently to males than females, perhaps because of the close physical and emotional ties between many mothers and sons. Sometimes latent incestuous desire appears in a dream in very mild form, as in the case of this thirteen-year-old who dreamed, after his father had left the home prior to a divorce, that he was now driving his father's large car at high speed and that he was "taking care of Mother now that Dad is gone." Quite frequently, however, young men, and sometimes those not so young, are shocked to find themselves sexually involved with their mother in a dream, something altogether unacceptable to their conscious mind.

Sexual symbols are often intertwined with those of birth and death, and it is to these that we turn in the next chapter.

9

Birth and Death Symbols

There are several kinds of dreams relating to birth. In the first, the dreamer re-experiences his own birth. The emotional memory of our entrance into the world is recorded in the subconscious mind and has been recalled by persons under hypnosis. So it is possible, particularly if the birth was difficult, for the trauma of birth to be expressed in dream.

The first example is the dream of a young man who knew almost nothing about the beginning of his life, but assumed his birth was normal. He also did not know whether he was breast fed or not.

> It seemed I was in a cave, a dark hot cave. Ahead of me I could see a tiny glimmer of light. I wanted to get out of there and I was trying to crawl toward the light. It was very difficult. Then I heard a rush of water coming from behind me and I was afraid I would drown. With great effort I managed to push my head through the tight opening of the cave. I woke up wringing wet with perspiration.

A week later he came up with a further chapter to his subconscious serial:

> In this dream I had just crawled out of the cave that I was in before. There was a man standing there in a white coat. I asked for two bottles of milk and he told me there wasn't a drop to be had!

Shortly thereafter, his mother came from the East to visit and supplied the details of his birth. He was a very large baby and had a difficult birth. And his mother had absolutely no milk for him.

Here is the dream of another young man:

I was inside something like a plastic sack; it was sort of smothering me. I kept trying to free myself, struggling to break out. It was so vivid that when I woke up I was turning and twisting in the bed.

And still another man's dream:

It seemed like I was in the hold of a very small ship or more like a boat. The space I was in was dark and snug. There was a hole—I guess you'd call it an escape hatch. While I felt all right where I was, somehow I knew I must climb out through that hole.

All of these dreams deal with memories of actual birth. But perhaps more prevalent are dreams of psychological or metaphysical rebirth. In such dreams the dreamer may often feel he is moving from the dark to the light, perhaps the light at the end of a tunnel. When a dreamer is moving into light or freedom, his psyche is emerging from the chrysalis of old and outgrown beliefs.

More frequent than any of the above-mentioned dreams of birth are those in which the dreamer is producing a child. He or she may be pregnant, giving birth, or simply realize in the dream that the baby is already there. Generally these dreams are puzzling to men and to the female dreamer who have never been pregnant or thought of having a child. There are wish fulfillment dreams of the sterile woman who yearns for motherhood, but these are exceptions.

To give birth to a new life in a dream can be one of the most hopeful messages from the subconscious to the conscious mind. But, just as in real life, when a baby is born, the first questions are: "Boy or girl? Is it healthy? Is it attractive?" We must, in interpreting a birth dream, determine what the new baby signifies.

To understand the meaning of gender we need to recall the Jungian concepts of animus and anima, the male and female polarities in each of us. The animus represents the mental, physical, and productive aspect of the personality, while the anima represents the spiritual, gentle, more yielding tendencies. With this in mind it is easy to understand that if someone has started a new project, a new class or study, the baby in the dream is more likely to be male than female. But if the baby is a little girl, analysis will generally discover that the dreamer (usually in this case female) has been discovering her femininity, feeling more receptive and nurturing.

If, however, the newborn baby in the dream is not healthy, or is crippled or deformed in any way, the dreamer is being informed that some latent aspect of himself, some creativity, has been stunted or injured or has remained undeveloped due to early trauma or privation. But on recognition and catharsis of the traumatic conditioning, the dreamer may find later that that which was crippled has become whole.

Womb Symbols

Otto Rank believed that everyone at some time has a wish to return to the womb. This is often interpreted as a death wish. But Dr. David Seabury has said that "nobody really wants to die, ever; instead they would like to escape life's problems by returning to their source and starting all over again."

One might say that the security of the infant is dependent on two kinds of wombs: the warm, physical enclosure of the mother's body and the later emotional enclosure of the mother's protection and nurturing. When this urge occurs in a dream one must be careful to ascertain which sort of "womb" is symbolized. Here are some womb symbols.

While a cave in a dream usually represents the womb, it can also represent the dark, unexplored area of the dreamer's unconscious. If the dreamer feels a desire to curl up and go to sleep there, a wish to regress is apparent. But if the cave in the dream represents an area to be explored, with either fear or fascination, it would symbolize the unconscious. A small pool may have similar connotations, particularly when enclosed in a house or basement. The question to ask is whether the dreamer is drawn to it or afraid of it.

The bathtub may relate to cleansing, but it can also be a symbol of the womb, especially if it is filled with warm water. Does the dreamer wish to stay interminably? Or is there a fear of drowning in it?

Inasmuch as a ship is traditionally considered female, the hold of a ship is often a symbol of the womb.

When in a dream one encounters a long corridor or hallway, particularly when there is some sense of urgency or wish to escape at the other end, and even more frequently when the passageway is a tunnel with a glimpse of light at the end, the dreamer's psyche may be going through the emotional constriction that can precede self-understanding, and that is analogous to the passage through the birth canal.

There may be several stimuli for the dream of drowning. One has to do with birth symbology. It is recognized that sometimes what we fear most is a subconscious wish. If the hidden wish is to return to the dreamer's source, by regressing to the prenatal state, the dreamer might awaken in a panic over the fear of submersion.

Here is an example. The dreamer is a middle-aged woman who had lived her whole life with and for her mother. She could not imagine existing otherwise, so when she received the sad news that her mother had a degenerative disease and might not live long, she had the following dream. The child here symbolized the child within her, as revealed in her own statement that the little girl was "just like me at that age."

> The dream centered around a warm swimming pool. My little three-year-old niece was circling around and around the pool. I was so afraid she would fall in that I watched her carefully. She just kept getting closer and closer to the edge almost as though she wanted to fall in. I knew if she did she would go right on down to the bottom and drown and I felt I'd have to keep my eye on her every minute to keep her from it.

In other words, it was taking all the concentration of her conscious mind not to yield to her unconscious and infantile wish to "return to her source" before her mother did.

Intrauterine Trauma

Dr. Helen Flanders Dunbar, the late eminent psychiatrist, in the first chapter of her book *Psychosomatic Diagnosis and Treatment*, reported in detail the movements of the fetus in the womb during the last few months of pregnancy. She observed that when it was experiencing stress, there were movements that indicated emotional response to the stress. "The human fetus may on occasion be subject to certain stress situations which are perhaps not greatly different from those experienced after birth. . . . In this period it consists of convulsive movements of the arms and legs and arching of the back. There is also an instantaneous acceleration of the heart beat. . . . Pregnant women often complain of marked increase in fetal activities from the vibration of the washing machine, a piano, a violin." Dr. Dunbar further described how a number of digestive, skin, nervous, and other psychosomatic disorders can result from a prenatal trauma.

If the baby's nervous system is recording experiences, particularly frightening ones, in the last days or weeks before birth, one may wonder how much the baby is threatened by intercourse between the parents. Since there can be no proof, the interpretation of the following two dreams is purely speculative. The symbology is nonetheless impressively corroborating. Here is one man's dream:

> I was in a dark, rather tight place. I was being chased by what seemed like a big something—somehow I thought of an earth-mover and I couldn't get out of its way. I was afraid it would run over me. Once it seemed like it did.

And a woman's dream:

> I was in a small hot, steamy room and a big something, kind of like a huge fist, almost filling the room, was coming toward me. I kept moving back as far as I could but it filled the room and I couldn't get away from it. I woke up wet with perspiration and with my heart pounding.

On being asked if there was any color in the dream she replied, "It was all dark, but somehow dark red comes to my mind."

Carl Jung himself experienced a similar dream in very early childhood. In the dream he came upon an enthroned phallus inside an inner room or chamber with an arched roof. This huge phallus was "made of skin and naked flesh, and on top there was something like a rounded head with no face and no hair. On the very top of the head was a single eye, gazing motionlessly upward . . ." After describing the terror he felt in the dream, thinking the phallus was probably a "man-eater," he added: "I do not know where the anatomically correct phallus can have come from." We know the infant cannot see through the membrane enclosing it, but such dream content must come from somewhere. Overwhelming emotions or reactions of the infant are often replicated in later life by huge animals or objects in dreams. Certainly the arched roof of Jung's "phallus chamber" is symbolic of the female genitalia.

Death Symbols

Many people have dreams that they fear are omens of death, their own or someone else's. As already pointed out, almost never do such dreams have anything to do with actual death. They usually relate to the death of an attachment, a neurosis, or a relationship. The symbol of death, when it does occur in a dream, is rarely direct or obvious. It may be going west, starting on a long journey, going home (wish), or joining a loved one who is gone (wish). Some dream examples follow in which death represents the termination not of a life but of an experience.

The first dreamer was an attractive young married woman with a bad habit of constantly criticizing and nagging at her husband:

> In the dream it was as though I woke up and found my husband missing from the bed. I went into the bathroom and found him lying prone on the floor, apparently dead. In a panic, I called to him, rubbed him, tried to bring him back to life, but there was no stirring of life. When I woke up after the dream I was so relieved to see my husband in bed beside me—but I had to check immediately to be sure he was still alive.

In answer to questions she said that their love life was almost nonexistent, and that the previous night when he had attempted lovemaking, he was totally impotent. No matter how she attempted to stimulate him sexually ("rubbed him, tried to bring him back to life") her efforts proved hopeless. Only after the interpretation of her dream did she realize the true meaning of the "prone" man and what had truly died in their marriage.

Many doctors are aware of the need to carefully observe relatives of a deceased person, particularly children, to see that they don't develop a debilitating illness or even have an accident to fulfill an unconscious wish to join the lost relative. There was, for instance, the case of a young woman in her early thirties, apparently in good health, but convinced because of some tightness in her chest that she was on the verge of a heart attack. The doctor, a heart specialist, was unable to detect any symptoms that supported her fear and urged her to see an analyst, which she did reluctantly. Her first dream:

> I dreamed that I went to a new doctor and after he examined me, he told me that my heart was in a very bad condition. When I asked him what did that mean, he sighed and said, "I don't like to give you the bad news, but it looks like by the time you are thirty-four you may have a serious heart attack."

In the process of free association, she said she was relieved because the doctor in the dream confirmed what she already knew about the condition of her heart (love nature). And what did "thirty-four years old" mean to her? She replied that her father, whom she loved more than anyone in the world, had died at thirty-four. When her very evident wish to join her father was carefully and gently explained to her she refused to accept it, stating emphatically that her first doctor (who had given her a clean bill of health) and the analyst were unable to recognize the truth. She accepted her dream as an omen, and that was that. (The doctor reported sometime later that, despite his patient's determined wish, her heart continued to function in a strong and healthy manner.)

How many parents have said to a recalcitrant child, "You'll be sorry when I'm gone," and how many unhappy children have said to themselves, "I wish I were dead." Although remaining healthy, one can get such revenge at night by seeing oneself as a corpse in a dream.

When someone dreams a healthy, loved pet dies, whether a dog, cat, or bird, it frequently indicates that the dreamer, usually a woman, is feeling sorry for herself and fears her love nature is dying from lack of attention. An illustration is the following short dream of a middle-aged woman, an alcoholic with personality problems and a resultant conflict with men in her life:

> I was just going home from work, looking forward to seeing my cute little dog (a female) who is always glad to see me, but just as I drove up to the yard I saw two big vicious dogs taking out after her, snapping and snarling at her. The poor little thing was running as fast as she could, whimpering in fear. I tried to chase the big dogs away, and then I woke up terribly upset and had to go and check on my little dog to be sure she was all right.

Later she complained that the men in the office had been picking on her.

Warning Dreams

Some dreams might be compared to a flashing yellow traffic light that warns of danger on the road ahead. The purpose of discussing such dreams is not to frighten the dreamer, but to help him—or his analyst—to read the signs, to become aware of approaching hazards.

Because the dreamer's house generally represents his body as well as the structure of his life, we must recognize that some psychic repair is necessary when, in a dream, his home is crumbling. A young man had this dream:

> It was like the whole house was sort of falling apart. The walls slanted in, parts of the ceiling were coming down, and what worried me the most was that all the electric wiring was frayed, hanging down and disconnected.

Slanting walls, insecurity; ceiling, fear of mental collapse; frayed wires, frayed nervous system becoming disconnected from reality. (When in such dreams the floor is seriously slanted, the dreamer's understanding or beliefs may be on such a "slant" that he is losing equilibrium, his sense of balance.) This was a man in serious need of psychiatric help.

Here is another example of imbalance with the added symbology of the object in the dream assuming human characteristics:

> I was trying to cross over a deep chasm on a slender swinging bridge. It kept swaying back and forth. Then it seemed like my coat just floated off my back and as it drifted away it started laughing back at me.

One has only to read the dream to sense the extreme emotional and mental imbalance within the dreamer.

A little history is necessary to understand why this next dreamer was over-reaching herself. Because of an unfulfilled emotional life as well as a disappointing marriage, she had for some time been studying intently and trying to expand her consciousness along metaphysical and spiritual lines. From her dream, it is apparent that she had done this not wisely but perhaps too well:

> I had started climbing up some stairs in a house. They went on up to the top floor and then it seemed the stairs extended right on up through the roof. I kept on climbing and climbing. By now it was like a staircase going right on up and up into the sky. Somehow I had the feeling Jesus was there and I must reach him. After I had climbed a little longer I could see it was getting misty, and the stairs started sort of weaving. By now I was getting scared, and when I looked down, I couldn't believe how far off the ground I was. My greatest fear was how will I ever get back down there?

This dreamer, while too far off the ground, at least knew she was and wanted to get her feet on the earth again. Far more serious is the dream in which the dreamer feels his rightful place is above, looking down on others, an attitude that not only implies delusions of grandeur, but is sometimes the forerunner of paranoia.

The following dream, that of a very disturbed and rather weak young man, is a clear statement of the law of compensation—superiority to balance a deep inferiority:

> I felt like I was a minister. I was standing on a sort of pulpit several stories up on the face of a building, trying to teach or preach to the people down below. But they seemed to ignore me. I felt they were stupid.

Another similar dream is the one in which lurking sadism and no regard for the feelings of others appear. This dreamer was also a young man:

> There was a great group of people gathered together, waiting to be judged as to who was intelligent and worthwhile enough to be allowed to live. I was in the small group judging them. We were the superior ones. The purpose of the plan was to select those who would be able to create a better world. There were just a few good enough. All of the others, who had nothing to contribute, were to be put to death.

When asked how he felt about the poor unfortunates in his dream not being allowed to live he replied, "I had no feeling at all; it should happen. That way we'd have a superior civilization much more quickly. When people are inferior why should anybody feel bad about getting rid of them?" The suggestion that the dreamer seek psychiatric help naturally fell on deaf ears. From his ego's lofty perch such an idea was inconceivable. After all, who could improve on perfection?

The following dreams are not in the usual category of nightmares in which the dreamer is threatened. More serious is the scenario of the dreamer trying to kill someone, particularly by choking them or attacking them with a knife, not in self-defense, but in a cool detached manner. This is illustrated by the dream below. The dreamer was an intelligent young man with an attractive manner but who had been known to have sudden frightening flashes of rage.

> There is an older man whom my mom has been dating. In the dream I was sitting across from him. I took a sharp pointed knife and threw it at him. It struck him in the knee. Blood started spurting out of his knee, and I couldn't keep from laughing. To me, it was funny.

His potential sadism was serious enough, but the amusement he felt indicated emotional, even mental imbalance. It was suggested to his mother that her son needed psychiatric care, and the dreamer's later actions verified the wisdom of the decision.

Occasionally there will be a dream relating to an actual physical problem. Regardless of how clear the message seems to be, it is first essential to emphasize that never, *never* should a person rely on his dreams for diagnosis of a physical problem. Both Freud and Jung, however, believed that occasionally the unconscious will send up a dream in which there is a sign of the beginning of some physical trouble. Even though the dreamer may not understand the dream, he is invariably deeply impressed by it. And Jung added that such a dream could be oracular or prophetic. Sometimes the dream indicates symbolically the organ of the body where trouble might be brewing. These, it must be added, are rare dreams. Here is an example, the dream of a middle-aged woman:

> I was standing looking at a high bulging dam. As I watched, I could see a little trickle of water seeping out of the wall of the dam. I was very frightened that the whole dam would break loose.

Rather direct symbology. The dreamer was developing bladder trouble.

After the next dream, that of an older woman, had been related and discussed she could understand its psychosomatic implications. First, it should be explained that she had for some time been studying art and doing oil painting.

> I walked into a room which seemed like a school room. There was a flat-topped desk similar to the ones used by art students to hold their paints and art supplies. I went over to the one I felt was mine and found the drawer was locked. "Never mind," I said to myself, "I have the key." I took it out of my pocket and started to insert it in the keyhole. Much to my distress I found that the keyhole was covered by a round, white, film-like substance, making it impossible for me to unlock the drawer.
>
> Alone and somewhat disturbed I started to leave, but as I went out the door a mood of optimism came over me with the thought that, anyway, I still had the key and I was sure I'd find somebody to help me uncover that lock.

A short time later this woman was told by an ophthalmologist that she had an advanced cataract over one eye and the beginning of one on the other. She remembered the optimism of her dream, she said, and remained undiscouraged.

10

Emotional Growth Dreams

It is natural, of course, that we would expect the healing process to start in the conscious mind and end up in the subconscious. The reverse is usually true. The idea may enter through the logical conscious mind, but when healing begins the change takes place first in the unconscious, on the deeper emotional level, and then moves upward. Consider for a moment what happens with a physical injury, such as a deep cut. The best doctor in the world can do little more than cleanse the wound, sew it up, cover it with a bandage, apply medicine, and wait for results. Does the healing start at the top? No, it starts at the very bottom of the cut, and when it has reached the top, the scab falls off and the patient then knows his wound is healed. Because of this healing process, it is frequently possible to read hopeful and encouraging signs in a person's dreams before he consciously recognizes them. Frequently an individual will say, "I don't seem to be getting anywhere; things seem just as bad as ever," and then relate a dream that is, in effect, saying, "Don't give up hope; it's starting!" These are dreams in which whatever part of the body was ill is recovering, in which the ugly grows more beautiful, rejection dissolves into acceptance, and coldness thaws and dislike turns to love.

Some dream examples might be helpful. A young woman in her early thirties, who had always been sexually frigid, came for counseling. She learned that her problem was rooted in bad childhood conditioning. At the time of her dream, her marriage was about to dissolve and she said she had almost despaired of ever enjoying lovemaking. Then she dreamed:

> I was looking at a thin sickly young girl about twelve years of age. She looked very pale, but she smiled and said to me: "Don't worry. I am getting well. You will see."

The night following this dream she experienced her first orgasm, complete and fulfilling. She called her counselor and with joy in her voice said, "For the first time I feel whole and complete." But her dream had already told her health was on the way.

The next dream is that of a young woman with a very warped and unattractive animus image. Early rejection by her father had created a poor relationship with men and she had ended up living, unhappily, with a sadistic man. Her first dream:

> I was sitting on a couch, as far at one end as I could, because at the other end was an ugly man I was a little afraid of. Not anybody I knew, just a man. And I didn't want him to come close to me.

Those who are familiar with Jung's concept of the animus can readily understand the meaning of her image of men. Sometime later, after clearing up her early conditioning by her father and recognizing the source of her negative relationship with men, she dreamed:

> I was sitting on the same couch as in my previous dream. But this time the man on the couch was very attractive, warm and kind; he was sitting near me and I hoped he'd put his arm around me.

Within a week after that dream she left the apartment of her sadistic lover and not long afterward was dating an attractive man who treated her well. Again, her subconscious self was aware before her logical mind was.

This is the dream of a young woman who had been deeply involved in the seamy side of the hippie movement, including not only heavy use of drugs but a number of unsavory sexual experiences. She ultimately reached out for help and was responding well when her subconscious sent up this beautifully simple dream:

> There was a garbage pail full of junk, and I was taking some trash off the top. After I had taken quite a bit of stuff off, I saw something gleaming and was thrilled to find a beautiful string of pearls. I realized it had been lying there all the time hidden by the trash.

Here is a boy's dream showing the progress of analysis. The dreamer was a thirteen-year-old boy from a broken home who had been failing in school, was in trouble with the law over a stolen bicycle, and had a very poor self-image. After a few weeks of counseling he brought in this dream:

> It was real nice, made me feel real happy. It was about this boy, Gregg—I only knew him a little while, just up to seventh grade; didn't know him very much. He and I were in school together and we were the most popular people. There weren't any teachers there. There weren't any fights. We walked around and visited old friends, like a class reunion.

Here is his free association:

> Gregg is now in ninth grade, but even back in my grade he always acted mature all of the time. He was real fun to be around and popular. Never got in any trouble of any kind.

Gregg obviously is Bobby's alter ego that, at the time of the dream, was coming to the fore, a side of himself he "had not seen for a long time" but with whom he was very happy.

It is sometimes revealing to read a series of dreams through in chronological order, as one would read a story. This can be particularly helpful if the dreamer happens to be under analysis. With this in mind, here is a series of four dreams, all occurring within a period of approximately four weeks. The dreamer, Karen, was a very disturbed young lady with serious emotional problems. Fortunately, however, she had an open mind that could not only grasp the meaning of her dreams but use them for self-guidance. Her parents had divorced when she was quite young. She had been reared by a gentle and patient mother who did the best she could for her daughter. None of that gentleness rubbed off on Karen, however; on the contrary, she rebelled against any guidance, often skipped school, had violent temper tantrums, and in general was concerned only with herself and what she wanted to do. At one time she had attempted suicide by cutting her wrist and ended up in the hospital. She ran away from home and became involved with a ne'er-do-well young man who got her pregnant. Within a year after her son was born, she had the good fortune to live next door to a hard-working, kind young man who, first out of pity and later love, took care of her and her baby. They were subsequently married and had a little baby girl, who was less than a year old at the time the mother sought counseling. Meanwhile, the security of marriage and the affection of her husband had helped somewhat, but not enough; there were times when her domineering temperament and tantrums were more than the most loving husband could take. Difficult as her disposition was, she was far from stupid. Reading the handwriting on the wall, she turned to counseling before it was too late.

Never having assumed responsibility for anything, including her own actions, it was natural that the responsibilities of motherhood weighed heavily on her, something very apparent in her first dream. She confessed that she realized she had never really loved anybody in her life, but now sincerely wanted to become a kinder and more loving person. When she brought in her dream, she reported that on the whole she had been feeling better, but the day before, while taking care of the children, she had for no apparent reason suddenly been overcome with an attack of anxiety. It was so severe she was rather shaken by it. It is helpful to remember that, when one is gripped by anxiety with no logical conscious cause, it is usually a warning of some problem in the unconscious, a signal that an unacceptable and possibly threatening impulse is being "triggered" by an outer stimulus. The tension is caused by the instinctive fear that this taboo urge might break through into expression in some way.

When the young woman was asked at what time her anxiety had gripped her and what she thought had caused it, she replied: "It's not really depression; it's anxiety. I was feeding the baby and all of a sudden it came over me and I got panicky; was I going to be able to deal with life every day? . . . I think it's the kids. I was afraid I wasn't going to do right with them. My son is getting rebellious and doesn't mind me, and I have to spank him nearly every day. And of course I have to give constant attention to the baby." Asked then if she had had a dream, she related the one she had had the night before. Here another reminder is necessary: the wild animal in a dream symbolizes untamed, even dangerous instincts in the unconscious of the dreamer. In her dream, as often happens, scene one outlines the beginning of her problem.

> When the dream started I wasn't in the dream, but kind of looking on. It started out when a girl came to a boy's room and they went in and shut the door and I knew they were having sex. I wasn't watching that, but when it was done, then it seemed I knew the guy was standing next to the bed and the girl he was with was asleep, and he pulled the blanket up over her and said quietly to himself, "Now she will be pregnant," as though he knew it was going to happen. Then I was in the dream. I looked out the

window and there was a volleyball net in the yard. Caught in the net was a very large wolf. He was really cut up as though he had been struggling to get out of the net, but he wasn't moving. Then somebody made a noise to see if he was still alive and he was, started moving again to get free of the net. I called the animal shelter to tell them there was a wolf there and they should come and get him. When I hung up the phone, the wolf was coming into the room and another girl and I got him in the bathroom and shut the door and trapped him in there. Then the people from the animal shelter came in, calmed the wolf down, cleaned up his wounds. As he came out of the bathroom, he didn't seem vicious; he was really frightened at that point, like he was afraid of what we were going to do to him after that. But when he was in the net, he was really vicious.

The sequence of her dream was that, after her pregnancy, she got a glimpse of the wolf, of her unbridled selfishness and rage. She had played volleyball a lot while under her mother's care but had violently rebelled against her mother's restrictions, as the creature in the dream struggled against its bondage. At this point she, the dreamer, put in a call to the "animal shelter" (the analyst) to come and tame this wild animal (her instincts). Before that, however, she and her girlfriend (her alter ego) were able to capture and lock it up. And it is significant that after the "animal tamer" calmed the "wolf" down, it then feared the result of its own actions.

Why did she have this dream and what was it trying to tell her? We must go back to the fact that her anxiety struck her at the moment when she was feeding the baby and to her concern for the quality of her motherhood. That was the point at which she felt the coming to life of the "wolf" in her unconscious, her primitive, instinctive wish to be free of her children, by whatever means, and of all responsibility for their care. This was the message from her unconscious and she was honest and courageous enough to face it and want to change.

Not long afterward she brought in another significant dream in which the progress she was making in her attempt to tame her shadow self became apparent. This time it does not appear as a wild animal, but is, at first, nonetheless threatening. Here is dream number two:

I am at a family reunion and I have forgotten a gift I am supposed to buy for someone. [The recipient could be her mother; she had often stated a wish to make up to her mother for the pain she had caused her.] My husband, Jim, and I go to the store. We stop at a gas station to get some gas. There are three guys in there. Everybody starts fighting with each other; I don't know why. One of the guys, a tall black man, goes to the cash register and starts to take all of the money. I run over and grab all of the money from it so he can't take it. He chases me over fences, but I'm running and he can't catch me. Then he trips and falls. I walk over to him then and start to rub his temples to calm him down. He settles down and I tell him he should talk to someone because of his problems. He says he drinks a lot of alcohol and has had a lot of other problems that bother him. As I talk to him he seems to be getting smaller and suddenly he is a little black dog. Everybody in the garage is watching and they are amazed that I was able to do this—and I am amazed, too!

I tell his friends to take him to a mental hospital where they can help him. I go back into the garage and the little black dog is there again, the one who had been the black man, so I say that I will take him to the hospital myself.

The wolf in the first dream now becomes a black man (her shadow animus) who finally falls, giving her an opportunity to tame him through gentleness, whereupon he, like all problems when properly approached, diminished until he was a little dog. But all was not yet well, as evidenced by her free association on the dog: "We have a little black dog, got it right after we married. She doesn't get along with the children, snaps at them." By now the dreamer had reached the point of not calling for an "animal tamer" but for the "mental hospital" with the final decision to take the problem there herself.

Sooner than one might expect, in fact in exactly two weeks, she had another dream whose entire meaning she could not grasp. She reported nevertheless that it was a pleasant dream and that she felt good after it. She had moved into an entirely different realm—and how different were the creatures she now encountered:

My husband and son and I are at a little swimming pool like a pond. I am swimming underwater and I see some very small dolphins. Jim and I go in and are petting and holding them. They only like for me and Jim to hold them, nobody else. We let them go and they swim away. We all three swim to the other side and are talking to some people, and then I swim back to the first side. I notice the water is now draining out of the pond; it all drains away and then everybody gets out. The bottom is clean and grassy and I walk across the bottom thinking I will find things that have been dropped to the bottom over the years. I don't find anything like that, so I start looking for sea shells. I find one oyster, a lot of sea snails, and some coral. A woman comes up to me and asks if she can talk to me, and I'm glad to see her and she starts talking about psychology, etc.

Here is her free association:

> The woman I associate with a woman in the soap opera "One Life to Live." She's a newspaper editor, mature. I have always respected this fig-ure, she's strong. At one point some time ago she went through a person-ality disorder, was two different people, and was cured of it and is now strong and capable.

While maturity in her dream appears in the guise of the woman from the soap opera, her dream is telling her about herself, about how the two sides of her own nature are blending and she is becoming a whole person.

Many people under analysis have dreams about water as the emotional unconscious. Not only is her pond clear, but in it she encounters delightful, friendly creatures. About the dolphins she had this to say: "When I think of dolphins, I think of their freedom. And they are so friendly and gentle. We were at the beach several weeks ago and saw a school out there swimming and playing; it thrilled me." Because everything in a dream has some mean-ing, we must note that, despite the fact that she had searched on the bottom of her pond for any debris from the past, she found none, only natural sea shells. And the oyster can be interpreted as a female symbol; perhaps she is finding lovemaking more attractive.

This next dream followed within about a week. In a dream, a girl's sister frequently personifies her own alter ego. Before relating the dream, Karen said: "I have been thinking a lot about my sister Louise lately. She is four years older than I am, and she was really very cruel to me when I was little. I was afraid of her. My other sister Mary, who is eight years older than I am, was always kind. The other day I went to visit Mary, and I told her I kind of blame Louise a lot for my emotional problems. The night after my visit I had a dream":

> I was living with Louise and her two kids, but living in the house where I live now. And we were the ages we are now. I was very angry with her and wanted to get away, so I was trying to call Mom to come and take me home. But the phone wasn't working, and I kept getting the busy signal at Mom's, and I couldn't get through. Louise came in and said, "Don't call Mom," and we had an argument and she left.

There were other people in the living room, and they all started look-ing for Louise. They knew she was upset, and they were afraid she would go out and do something foolish, maybe harm herself. I didn't care; I just wanted to get away from her.

I went into my bedroom, looked up, and there was something drip-ping from the ceiling into a small puddle on the floor. It was red. I asked somebody what it was, and a man said it was blood.

I got very upset, and thought that Louise had gone up on the roof and cut her wrist to kill herself. I blamed myself, that I had made her upset like this and went to help find her. I went into the backyard and saw Louise sitting on the patio roof; she was trying to get everybody's atten-tion. I kept trying to get a look at her wrists, but couldn't see anything, felt she had done something. But looking at her on the roof, I realized she was doing this to make everybody sorry for her—and then I didn't feel sorry for her any longer.

While this dream makes very clear statements, we must keep in mind that every dream has many levels: the past and the present, the self and other aspects of the self. The stimulus of the dream, as she states, was her conver-sation with her "good" sister about her "bad" sister who was, as she be-lieved, in her childhood the cause of her problems in the present. Yet in the dream they are both adults and, further, in the dreamer's present home. That places the content of the dream squarely in her own present life and home.

That her sister Louise is her shadow self is evident in the fact that both young women have two children, a boy and a girl; also, each has a kind and patient husband who puts up with their outbursts of ill temper. And it must be noted that right in the middle of all this Karen not only wants to get away from her shadow self but wants "Mom to come and take me home." But her mother is too busy for the message to reach her.

Karen could recognize, when discussing the dream, that she had pro-jected her own negative side onto her sister (whom it fitted well enough) and hated it in her. She added: "When I was in my teens, I tried twice to cut *my* wrists, and also took some pills. Even then I knew I did it for attention. 'Everybody, look at me, I have problems!'" She related that she was in her bedroom when she cut her wrist. Then she was asked what she thought it meant in her dream when the girl slashed her wrist on top of the roof. "That was so everybody could see her and feel sorry for her. Anyway, she was showing off; she hadn't cut her wrist too badly." Then she laughed at herself—and nothing could be healthier!

There is one more dream that followed in a week's time. She had been very troubled and wanted to talk about it. "I had awakened that morning a little bothered. I have a real dread of getting old; I know I am young, but when I think about some day getting old, it sort of scares me. I think I have a pretty good idea as to why we are here, to learn and to grow, and then in the next life, we learn and grow more, and I thought I had accepted it. But when I woke up, I was a little bothered by the thought that I am going to have to grow older before I can be reincarnated. I was looking at an old lady the other day, all of her wrinkles—I don't want to be like that. Getting older bothers me, and I was asking what is it all about? Then the next night I had this dream":

> I am panning for gold, another woman with me. We were scooping dirt from a flower bed I had recently planted. We were in a very small room and the other woman noticed that one of the walls had a very hollow sound to it. She pulled the boards off the wall and there was a short tunnel that led outside. At the time, I was watching myself in the dream. I slowly walked through the tunnel and there was a bright light at the end, real bright light coming from above. I walked into the light and started to turn around slowly, going around and around. It reminded me that I had been in this situation before, being in a tunnel and walking through the bright light and then standing in the light. It also reminded me of an experience in a movie I saw once called *Resurrection* where people have died and come back to life and are alive. At first I was lifting my arms slowly; it was like I had electricity in my hair and it was standing out real far. I was turning around in my dream, and I remembered that it had all happened before. I remember coming back through the tunnel and then I was lying on the bed resting and the woman who had been helping me pan for gold was making sure I was okay.

No special knowledge of dream analysis is necessary to appreciate the meaning of this last dream, which is archetypal. Here is beautiful proof that as we try to grow, our psyche leads us to the light. In symbology, the tunnel frequently symbolizes the birth canal, so that when we are struggling to attain rebirth spiritually, our unconscious puts us in the same symbolic passageway. The stimulus of the dream was her concern about old age and death, and the beginning of the dream was her panning for "gold," her true worth, interestingly enough, from the soil in which she herself had planted flowers! While one robin does not a spring make, a dream like this is a harbinger of the beginning of a new life for the dreamer.

Examination Dreams

Examination dreams can be of two kinds, one in which the dreamer is preparing for an examination, and another in which the dreamer is putting someone or something else to a test. The first sort, usually accompanied by a sense of anxiety, may be stimulated by the challenge of an anticipated new experience. It can be a business problem, a social meeting, or even a sexual challenge. Also, people who are under analysis may project onto their analyst the threatening figure of the teacher whom they fear will discover that they haven't "learned their lessons" in life.

The other kind of examination dream places the dreamer in the role of examiner. Perhaps he's studying something under a magnifying glass or even a microscope. Such a dream might occur when the individual is undergoing a great deal of self-scrutiny. Somewhat similar is the dream in which a blueprint is scrutinized in an attempt to understand the underlying structure of the dreamer's experiences.

11

Animals in Dreams

After people, animals are the next most important symbols in dreams. In contrast to human beings, who operate with free will, memory, and imagination, animals are directed more by their instincts. So the animal in a dream symbolizes the instinctual nature or the unexpressed primitive drives of the dreamer.

Animal symbology may be divided into three main groups: the ferocious, carnivorous beasts, the gentle, herbaceous creatures, and the beloved pets. In a descending scale of importance and frequency are the reptiles, birds, fish, and finally the insects. All of these, in dreams as in real life, have their own unique characteristics and, therefore, symbolic meaning.

Ferocious Wild Animals

In general, the wild animals that pursue us with claw and fang in our dreams are personifications of a destructive impulse, usually our own, that we fear will overcome our higher self. Anything that attacks with the teeth can represent oral sadism and aggression. "But," one might argue, "if I am angry at someone else, why is that tiger threatening *me*?" Because our inner negativity, in the final analysis, is directed against ourselves.

Human beings, as creatures of greater intelligence and awareness, are threatened, morally and spiritually, by their hidden aggressive drives. Turning our backs on such impulses does not make them disappear. Once the dreamer has brought his hidden antagonisms to the surface, acknowledged and faced them, he has then taken the first step toward overcoming and outgrowing them. Proof? Rarely, almost never, does the dreamer again feel on his neck the hot breath of his previous tormentor. Once faced (that is, the problem it represents) and cleared up, the symbolic animal loses its mystery and its strength. Here are some examples of animal symbols in dreams.

The lion is the king of the jungle, hence he is the ruler of the dreamer's untamed nature, or id. The examples of lion dreams given below scarcely call for interpretation, so clearly do they illustrate the dreamer's primitive drives. A virile young man who had been experiencing difficulty suppressing his irritation at problems on the job had this dream:

> I was looking at this big lion pacing back and forth in his cage. He was so big and looked so fierce I said to myself that I was certainly glad that he was locked up in that cage.

> Q. Was there anything that made you angry in the last few days?
> A. I'll say so. I wanted to hit a guy so bad but I managed to control my temper and walk away.

The following week he came in with this:

> In my dream I was inside a cage, looking out. And prowling around outside the cage was a big roaring lion.

> Q. Now that you know what a lion symbolizes, what do you think your dream means?
> A. I know what it means all right. My temper got away from me and I was about to get violent. But the strange part of it was that all the time one part of me knew what I was doing, sort of watching me make a fool of myself.

A young woman who lived unhappily alone with her mother had this dream:

> I looked out our front window and saw several lions prowling back and forth. In a panic I called to my mother to quickly lock all the doors and windows. Then after we did, I turned around and saw one of the biggest lions inside the house, right behind me. I woke up very frightened.

It is impossible to lock our problems out; sooner or later they must be faced inside.

The woman who had this dream was more successful in controlling her aggressive drive:

> This lion was up on the drainboard. I am showing it to someone. I know I have to get it back in its cage. So I keep trying to get this lion to go back in the cage—which in the dream seemed to be a cooler—where it belonged. I am being very careful because I respect his power. While I am doing this, he gets hold of my hand very lightly and softly and I say to myself, "See, he won't hurt; he's not so mean."

Not only did she "cool down" but realized that her temper wasn't so bad, after all!

Here is one more lion dream, ending on a more positive note. The dreamer was again a young woman, who had been sincerely trying to outgrow irritation and sarcasm directed toward her frustrating husband:

> It seemed I walked out the front door down a winding path to go to work. Standing across the path and blocking my way was a huge tawny lion. In fear, my first impulse was retreat. But instead I said quietly to myself, "No, I know everything responds to love." So I approached the lion and started gently stroking it, saying, "I don't hate you and I know you don't hate me." While this was taking place the lion started shrinking in size, getting smaller and smaller until it became a little yellow kitten and wandered away and disappeared. I woke up with a feeling of peace and happiness, which stayed with me all day.

One might interpret the lion as her husband but that would be a mistake, for he remained the same. All that changed was her own aggression, which disappeared. But she had to face it first. Had she run away, the lion symbol would have doubtless not only remained but grown larger.

Being swift, subtle, and ferocious, the tiger symbolically implies those same hidden characteristics within the dreamer. The tiger can bear a more female connotation than the lion. The following dream of a career woman, a "loner," reveals much of her personality and her pride:

> I walked into my living room and saw, standing in the middle of the room, a great beautiful tiger. We just stood and looked at each other; he was gorgeous. I wasn't really afraid because I admired him so much. As we looked at each other I had a strong feeling we respected each other.

One can understand from the content of this dream why her co-workers said they were reluctant to cross her in any way!

In a man's dream, a wolf embodies hidden aggression and always represents a masculine threat of some kind. In a woman's dream, the wolf is a sexual prowler. The appellation "lone wolf" is a familiar term for the man who prefers to go after what he wants in life unencumbered by friends or relatives. The following dream in which the wolf appears is an example of a young man's fear of releasing his hidden antagonism. At the time of the dream he was in love with a young woman who had two small children to care for. He had pretended to accept the children; his dream, however, shows his true feelings:

> In my dream the two children were in the back seat of my girl friend's car. I was on the outside. Then I saw a vicious looking wolf circling and circling the car. I called to the children to be sure and keep the door locked and I knew it was up to me to protect the children from being attacked by that wolf.

Threatening as the "wolf" was, his stronger wish was to protect the children from that antagonism. How different it would have been if he had dreamed the wolf attacked the children.

This is the dream of a married woman, outwardly passive and submissive, but increasingly frustrated over her husband's unwillingness to communicate with her:

> I don't know exactly what was going on, but I was in a house with a very flimsy door and outside there was a big pregnant wolf trying to get in. It never got in, but I was very worried for fear that any minute it would break through the door.

Her defenses against her suppressed rage were very flimsy. And pregnancy in this dream does not imply physical pregnancy, but that the "wolf" was "pregnant" with unexpressed smaller irritations, potential aggressive words or actions.

A bear connotes grumpiness, grouchiness, and the wish to socially hibernate, be left alone.

Crocodiles or alligators usually represent oral aggression. The next dream clearly illustrates the dichotomy within the dreamer. He was a young married man with strong mood swings, sometimes aggressive and sarcastic, even violent, then passively dependent, even parasitical.

> I woke up terrified from this dream. There was this big crocodile and two long baby seals, wrapped in something like cocoons, were attached

to the crocodile, one on the back and one on the underside. The crocodile was struggling to free himself. I was terrified; apparently I identified with the crocodile. They were attached like leeches and if he couldn't have gotten free they would have drained the life and blood out of him.

One wonders if the dreamer was afraid that his gentler side (still a baby) would in some way devitalize his orally aggressive side, which apparently he wishes at all cost to keep alive.

Before we leave the subject of the carnivorous animal and all it symbolizes in primary instinct, let us consider the ultimate. Almost always the dreamer, the higher self, is the observer and the prowling animal the observed. However, one could go no farther than this recurring dream of a young woman:

> I dream I am a panther, walking through my hometown in Italy. It is so real I can feel my paws on the cobblestones as I move silently through the dark.

Gentle Wild Animals

These are herbaceous creatures, nonviolent by nature. And they mean in a dream just about what they mean in nature.

Ponderous and huge, the elephant often symbolizes a large, overwhelming presence or experience in the dreamer's life. Adults and their actions sometimes loom awesomely large to an infant or small child. The following dream illustrates such a feeling by an infant, appearing much later in an adult dream. The dreamer was a young woman who as a baby had slept in the same bed with her parents the first year or so of life and was therefore subjected to what is called the primal scene, the sexual activity of the parents.

> I have had a recurring dream that I am on a rocky hillside. Two huge elephants are near me and they are hooked together in some strange fashion that I cannot understand. I am afraid they will crush me and I feel very helpless and frightened.

One young woman, very obese, dreamed of a fat ugly elephant that was repulsive to her, representing as it did her own obesity. In some other context the elephant might symbolize patience and wisdom or "the memory of an elephant."

Gentle, graceful, and appealing, deer rarely appear in dreams because we tend to dream more of our negative drives than of our more attractive characteristics.

Like the deer, the rabbit symbolizes gentleness, but also timidity, fear, and fecundity in a dream. The following dreamer's unconscious used the rabbit as a symbol of her own emotional nature. The dreamer was a mature woman under analysis who had been outgrowing her rather aggressive manner, defensiveness, and constant need to "be right."

> The dream centered around a white rabbit. It was kind of a geometric thing: a bunch of people lined up in a kind of square. They were to work out answers to questions put to them and the solution was always to come from a white rabbit that was sort of at the head of it all. I guess the stimulus of this dream was a fantasy movie on TV about white rabbits. They had these rabbits and had taken them to another planet. Then when they went back the rabbits had multiplied until they had become the power figures; they were in charge. But the rabbit in my dream was not a power figure as much as it just knew the answers. In answer to the questions everybody would say what they thought the answer would be, and the rabbit presided over them like an arbitrator. When the answers got back around the square, then if nobody had given the right answer, the white rabbit would tell them so and then explain to them what was really right.

The white rabbit was associated by the dreamer with innocence, gentleness, and kindness.

> Oh, I know what my dream is saying—to let the gentle and peaceful side of our nature rule our lives. We don't need antagonism, that isn't the answer. I've been learning that that is the answer and it is so relaxing not to always need to prove I'm right and to control everybody.

Domestic Animals

Domestic animals represent the dreamer's gentler nature and disciplined emotions, which are obedient to mental control.

The horse almost always represents masculine strength and intelligence. Given that all animals symbolize instinctual drives, it is easy to see the hidden meaning of the following dream of a schoolteacher, rather pedantic, who had always resented having been born a female:

> In the dream I was riding a horse across desert land. The horse was
> strong and healthy and as I rode it I wasn't sure whether I was a man or a
> woman.

The sterility of the "desert land" is understandable in view of her sexual
ambiguity.

The symbology of the next dream casts the horse in both male and female
roles. The dreamer was a young man, recently married, who had just spent
part of his honeymoon trip in the home of his parents in the East. It helps
to know that the young man was devoted to his family, particularly his
mother.

> My dream was about horses. It seemed to take place in New York, back
> in Syracuse where I used to live. In the dream I had a mare; there were
> several medical people—veterinarians—around. I remember feeling grief
> because they told me my mare had gotten kind of old and sick and they
> would have to shoot her. In fact, it seemed that they had already shot her.
> There was grief, I remember that.
> But then that day it seemed I had a new stallion. There was something
> about getting rid of the old and getting something new. I now had a stal-
> lion and was much happier. It was winter outside. I remember taking the
> stallion outside.
> The mare that was shot was brown, and the stallion was also brown.
> When I went outside, there was a young white mare standing in the
> snow, sort of breathtaking, beautiful! I felt a lot of joy that the old mare
> had been replaced—that somehow my loss had been more than replaced
> and I had been awarded with the beautiful young white mare.
>
> Q. Just why did they have to destroy the old mare?
> A. It was a sickness connected with age, she had finally succumbed to it.
>   I felt grief; I felt it was a horse that had been there for a long while
>   that had served its purpose and I had developed an affinity for it. I
>   have had animals and it's sad when old age takes them. But I know it is
>   inevitable; you know they will have to go in time. That was the kind
>   of grief I felt about the old brown mare; I loved her but knew it was
>   time for her to go.

The acceptance, albeit with sadness, of the passing of the old mother attachment is obvious. The healthy young stallion, the same color as the
mare, doubtless symbolizes the dreamer's newly recognized masculine viril-

ity and strength. His delight with his young wife is graphically illustrated by his joy over the young white mare that had come to replace the old. The meaning (and his attitude) would have been very different had he wept in the dream over the passing of the old and rejected the new. Sometimes it sharpens the meaning of a dream to try reversing its order and meaning.

In most women's dreams their animal instincts or inner emotional selves will appear as a kitten, cat, or female dog. However, the examples below are interesting because this woman's subconscious uses the horse to represent her inner self. She was undergoing counseling and new developments were stirring:

> It seemed I had a house full of ponies. Lively, cute little ponies. The house reminded me of the one I lived in as a little girl. The ponies didn't make any droppings in the house. I was wondering how I could get some fresh grass for them to eat. I couldn't get over what nice sweet little animals they were.

Before the next dream she was feeling some irritation with her husband, Tom.

> The place had vines on the walls, reminded me of a college [probably the analysis itself]. The ponies were there, but now they had changed to centaurs, half-human and half-horse, and they were no longer young; they were like high-strung college boys of twenty-one or twenty-two. But this time I noticed their droppings across the pathway where unsuspecting people might step in them. They were laughing and one said, "Tom has stepped in them."

While on the positive side one can see growth taking place, it is apparent her displeasure with her husband, Tom, produced the anal aggression symbolized by the droppings in which he stepped.

A winged horse embodies fantasy and soaring imagination. A white horse represents purity and sometimes death, while a black horse connotes negative strength and power. A gelding in a man's dream implies castration fear.

A mule can represent stubbornness or "mulishness." Also a neuter animal, it may in a man's dream imply the fear of sterility. The stubborn jackass rarely appears in dreams but when it does it carries the implication of foolishness.

The unicorn is a mythical figure of purity and Christianity.

Goats are tough and self-reliant; sheep are gentle and easily led. And the lamb always symbolizes gentle helplessness and, if white, purity.

The pig symbolizes gluttony, selfishness. The sow is an embodiment of the "devouring mother." The boar represents an elemental phallic drive.

The bull symbolizes "bull-headedness," stubbornness, and aggression, as shown in the following dream. The dreamer was an elderly woman who felt dominated by her unmarried daughter, who lived with her and had a very stubborn disposition.

> I dreamed I was backed into a corner by a bull. I wasn't exactly afraid, but I was certainly frustrated, because I couldn't seem to get around him.

The bull in a dream is most often related to the unconscious image of the father. It survives as a phallic image from the ancient worship of the bull in the spring as the giver of life (later replaced by worship of the phallus itself). Therefore in most dreams it will be the personification of the dreamer's feeling about the father, and frequently appears in women's dreams as an expression of the Oedipus attachment. A cow, on the other hand, is the giver of milk and so usually represents the mother image or attachment.

Pet Animals

Loved pets nearly always symbolize the dreamer's own emotional nature, the dependent inner self that needs love and understanding and perhaps the care of others.

The dog almost always embodies loyalty and a sense of protection. But, just as there are many sizes, types, and dispositions of dogs, there may be many meanings of the dog in a dream. Free association is essential. Is it big and vicious, gentle and loyal, small and helpless? The vicious dog would personify aggression, possibly verbal in nature; the gentle, loyal dog would represent friendship. The small pet dog needing protection epitomizes the dreamer's inner emotional self, which he feels must be protected from the vicissitudes of life. The dreams given below illustrate widely divergent meanings of the dog in dreams.

This dream was that of a young woman working for a man whose tenacity and belligerence were becoming increasingly annoying to her. Adding to the imagery was the fact that he was stocky and had a broad head:

> In the dream there was a bulldog. He had hold of my ankle. He wasn't really hurting me but no matter how hard I tried I couldn't shake him loose.

Often dreams involving pets contain evidence of self-pity; certainly there is some aspect of narcissism. Here is the dream of a woman much too dependent upon alcohol and feeling neglected by all her friends:

> I was going home from work when all of a sudden I started worrying about my little dog at home. It came over me that I hadn't been taking care of her properly. When I went in the house I found her weak and emaciated, so starved I was afraid she was going to die.

In reality her poodle was overfed. Her anxiety was that her own love nature was dying from neglect.

The cat almost always bears feminine connotations—except the occasional prowling tomcat. Again, like the dog, it can be vicious or gentle. By nature a predator, a vicious cat, whether domestic or wild, always implies some sadistic impulse. The two dreams below are clear statements of the dreamer's fear of her own hidden "cattiness" or sadism. The first woman was the owner of a female cat that she adored. She herself was inclined to subtle sharpness and sarcasm.

> I dreamed that when I came home after work I found my little cat blocking my doorway. She had grown to be bigger than I was, and she was arching her back and glaring at me. I just couldn't believe my nice cat had grown so mean, and I was really scared.

The second woman, head of her own business, confessed she had become a nag with her husband and was afraid it would ruin her marriage.

> My husband and I went into our living room. Perched on the mantel over the fireplace was a vicious cat, yowling and spitting. I was afraid it would attack my husband, so I called to him, "Look out, it's going to hurt you!" Just then the cat sprang at me instead, right at my throat, scratching and clawing, and I woke up in a cold sweat.

This is another case of the dreamer being attacked by her own problem. First fearing for her husband, she then had to face what her constant sharpness was doing to herself. It is significant that it attacked her throat, from which her sharp words came.

On the pleasanter side of cat symbology, there is the kitten. Kittens, like puppies, generally represent children or attractive childlike qualities. The soft kitten in a dream always symbolizes young femininity. The soft fur of the kitten can also symbolize pubic hair.

Other Animals

Either a nuisance or a threat, rodents symbolize something disturbing, repulsive, or frightening to the unconscious of the dreamer. And because they live in holes or underground and creep out mostly at night, and also because all creatures long and round have phallic meaning, they are generally associated with some fear or guilt relative to the male sex organ. A rat may also represent someone conniving and deceitful or embody guilt, perhaps a repressed sexual impulse. A mouse scurrying about in our dreams can indicate that we need to set a trap for a subconscious problem that is probably not too large in the first place! Mice also may be associated with pubic hair.

Anything that moves through the air is related to the world of thoughts and fantasies. Bats, however, always symbolize dark, frightening fears. Vampire legends have added to this concept. Bats swooping around the head in a dream may indicate a fear of insanity. We should remember that they do not indicate insanity itself, only a fear—"If I don't stop thinking these dark thoughts I might lose my mind."

While not strictly in the animal category, "monsters" often represent repressed and threatening instincts. Neither human nor beast, male nor female, this symbol is reserved for some hyperbolically "monstrous" feeling emerging from the depth of the subconscious. Rage, wishes for revenge, death wishes against someone—all these are emanations from the id, and their energy is so intense that it is forced to emerge from the darkness of the subconscious while in slumber. As mentioned in a previous chapter, the child who secretly yearns for the elimination of a sibling may awaken screaming for fear of the monster that he fears will come out of his own closet and kill him. If the dreamer is about to be swallowed by some animal or huge bird it may indicate his unconscious fear of being devoured by some overwhelming oral or nursing demands or needs.

The following dream illustrates symbolically the magnitude of the unconscious problem. The dreamer was a young mother trying to handle her rage
at her young daughter, whom she had rarely physically punished but deeply
resented.

> I was standing on the shore looking at the ocean [her subconscious]. I
> was horrified, as I stood there, to see a horrendous monster slowly
> emerge from the depths of the ocean. It was huge. Then, as it slowly sank
> beneath the waves, I said to myself, "I don't think it is really necessary for
> me to tell my counselor about this."

But she did, and felt better for it.

Prehistoric animals represent deeply buried, racial, even primordial memories and instincts.

The dragon is an archetypal symbol of ancient origin representing great
power. It stands for the yang in eastern philosophy, as opposed to the yin,
or feminine principle. It is universal in meaning because it incorporates the
four elements: earth, water, air, and fire. It walks on the earth, swims in the
ocean, flies through the air, and breathes fire. It rarely appears in dreams
today, but as a creature of myth and fable one must assume that it emerges
from the profound archetypal memory of the dreamer when it does appear.

Birds

The bird in the element of air relates to the dreamer's wishes and fantasies in
the realms of thought and imagination. But, in an entirely different context,
the bird can also be a phallic symbol.

White birds connote innocent, pure thoughts. Sometimes they represent
the soul in flight. Black birds symbolize negative thoughts or fears.

The eagle soars the highest and is considered the "king of the birds"; it
represents lofty ambition and accomplishment. Since it is, along with its
nobility, a predator, a potential for ruthlessness is implied in the drive for
power.

The dove symbolizes the soul, purity, peace, gentleness, spirituality. The
owl represents wisdom. The peacock, spreading its beautiful tail, embodies
exhibitionism and narcissism.

The raven is a shadow figure, representing sinister thoughts and dark fate.

This sort of symbol appears in Edgar Allan Poe's poem "The Raven" and in Vincent van Gogh's last painting, in which a great flock of dark birds swoops down from a leaden sky onto a barren field, signifying his despair and hopelessness.

All pet birds, caged or free, symbolize aspects of our own nature that we love and wish to protect. A simple illustration is the dream of a young woman whose gentleman friend had given her a pair of love birds in a beautiful cage. At the time of the dream she was dating no one and felt a little sorry for herself.

> I dreamed I came downstairs one morning into the living room where I keep my birds, and when I removed the cloth I put over the cage at night, I was shocked to see both of them lying dead at the bottom of the cage. A wave of self-reproach went over me—I had neglected them, allowed them to starve to death.

A canary, particularly if it sings, symbolizes a spontaneous expression of happiness and well-being. A chicken represents weakness, cowardice.

Fish and Other Water Creatures

To interpret the meaning of fish in a dream we must remember that their natural element is water and that water represents the world of the unconscious emotions and, in a deeper and broader sense, the source of all life forms.

The form of the fish generally gives it a masculine, phallic connotation. That is why to "go fishing" in a dream often means to pursue a sexual experience; but there are so many different kinds of fish that one must remain open to other interpretations.

With its double row of vicious teeth and its voracious appetite, the shark can only be interpreted as verbal aggression and expressed or unexpressed sadism. The following dream clearly illustrates this. The dreamer was a young married woman with a habit of constantly nagging at her husband about everything he did or did not do. She had been warned that she was mentally and even sexually castrating her husband. Then she dreamed:

> It was as though I could see underwater. I could see a big shark and then I could see a man on top of the water. The shark was slashing

and slashing at the man as he struggled on the surface. I was horrified at what was happening and woke up in a cold sweat.

Her husband, who had become impotent, left her a few days after she had this dream.

The octopus does not appear too frequently in dreams but when it does it seems to represent bisexuality—round (female) and yet with long tentacles (male). A young woman, not too well adjusted in her relations to the opposite sex, dreamed:

> It seemed I had, of all things, a pet octopus. In some ways it seemed unattractive, but I knew it wouldn't hurt anybody, and it was my friend. I was stroking it in the dream.

The octopus may also symbolize clingingly passive tendencies.

Shellfish, oysters, and clams, whether closed or open, represent female genitalia.

A crab symbolizes the threat of a hidden neurosis. It can indicate homosexuality lurking in the depths of the unconscious.

Anything huge in a dream, like a whale, represents a memory of someone or something relatively immense, a "whale of an experience." The story of Jonah and the whale contains much meaningful symbology. Jonah, instead of doing as the Lord instructed, which was to go to Nineveh and preach the gospel, decided to go in another direction. He boarded a ship (a female or mother symbol), only to be cast in the water (deeper regression) and finally ended up in the belly of the whale, a symbolic enactment of the return to the womb. When he discovered his plight, the ultimate in regression, he cried aloud to God to save him. He was luckier than most regressive people; by the whale's throwing him up on the beach he had a chance for a new start!

On the positive side, sometimes the fish that surfaces in a dream is beautiful, for example, iridescent goldfish, which would signify something of great beauty and value heretofore only latent within the dreamer. Here is the example of a woman's dream:

> I was in an Oriental country and was somehow involved with the people there. First I was on a ferry boat, and fish were everywhere in the water. This Japanese woman stepped down into the water, which came to her waist, and lovely goldfish swam into her hands. At first I was afraid

for her but she seemed safe and happy and the beautiful fish kept swimming up to her.

Here is her free association:

> To me the Oriental symbolizes humility and kindness. I always thought if I am ever reincarnated I want to be a Japanese woman, very humble and beautiful. And the fish in the dream seem to mean that good things come to you freely when you are that kind of person.

Insects

In general insects represent annoying, unhealthy, and sometimes stinging ideas or problems. Those that fly are worrisome thoughts, like a swarm of gnats buzzing around the head that one would like to brush aside. Dirty creeping bugs such as cockroaches, on the other hand, symbolize hidden "dirty" little guilts that crawl out of the recesses of the subconscious—things that need to be cleaned out. The same applies to ants, although they are not quite so unwholesome. A long beetle or bug, by its shape, must be considered a phallic symbol.

The spider is an ancient symbol of the racial unconscious. The spinning of the web implies subtle entrapment. The spider then is often related to a clutching or conniving woman. The black widow spider would be the most sinister example. People who have never heard of the proclivity of the female black widow spider to destroy her mate still have dreams in which this dark symbol appears. The following dream is that of a young girl, whose mother had divorced her father years before and had ever since spoken disparagingly of all males. She had since given all of her very considerable devotion to her daughter. The girl had recently, against her mother's wishes, gotten married. Her mother insisted the marriage would fail (it did finally) and that she was the daughter's only security. Here the black widow appears as the all-devouring possessive mother. The girl's dream:

> I was standing on the porch of my mother's home. Before me, clear across the porch, was a veil, a curtain of spider webs. In the center of each web sat a black widow spider. As I looked through and beyond the web I could see my husband walking away toward the horizon. He was going further and further from me and I became panicked and desperately tried

to call to him or even wave farewell, but I could not break through the web of spiders.

With its long hairy legs, the tarantula is a masculine sex symbol. It is not too difficult to interpret when it appears as a threatening figure in a woman's dream. But in a man's dream the tarantula appears usually as the threat of homosexuality. An anxious young man whose marriage was failing because of his sexual inadequacy had this dream:

> I found myself going through a winding tunnel underground [his sub-conscious]. It was a sort of labyrinth and just light enough for me to see. I felt very apprehensive. As I turned a corner I came face to face with a frightening apparition: It was a huge tarantula with my uncle's face on it! It completely blocked my way and I woke up in a cold sweat.

Later he recalled sexual advances his uncle had made to him as a boy.

This next dream is that of a lonely young soldier who had been unsuc-cessful in his relationships with girls. He had become closely involved, much to the disturbance of his family, with a stocky, swarthy male compan-ion. The implication is obvious in his dream:

> I was walking along a road and a huge tarantula was going along beside me. He was dark and hairy and almost as tall as I was. At first I was self-conscious and somewhat embarrassed about it. But when we came to some people and they acted shocked and upset about my friend—be-cause I felt somehow we were friends—I got angry and said to them, "There's nothing wrong. I have a right to have some companionship, don't I?"

The butterfly is a delightful symbol with which to end the discussion of insects. It represents the most ethereally beautiful aspects of the psyche. Be-cause it emerges from a confining chrysalis, it can be a symbol of the soul itself.

Reptiles, Toads, and Frogs

Reptiles, poisonous or not, represent a subtle, often hidden emotional problem that is anathema to our moral and emotional health. In nearly all dreams, a reptile, particularly a snake, is a displacement of a penis symbol. If a man has a disturbing dream about a snake, he may be ill at ease over some lurking sexual fear or guilt. If the snake is poisonous, there is an implication of the threat of homosexuality.

The threatening snake in a woman's dream symbolizes her fear or dread of the male sex organ, whether from a trauma or some early negative conditioning. It may represent guilt instilled in the child by parents or religious teachings for some innocent sex play; it may be a hangover from some reproach for adolescent masturbation; or she may have experienced molestation as a child.

The size of the snake—as the size of all dream symbols—is significant. Size is relative to the importance or intensity of an experience. A huge snake, such as a python, may symbolize the adult phallus as seen by the child; a small snake or large worm would relate to some early experience with a smaller, more youthful sex organ, involving less fear.

Crocodiles, alligators, and lizards are also phallic symbols, varying in size and threat. Naturally the huge and vicious crocodile would be the most menacing, and its huge mouth would indicate some form of oral aggression or sadism. The lizard, in contrast, would symbolize a much less threatening fear or guilt.

The turtle has an androgynous connotation, inasmuch as it can withdraw into a round enclosure (female), or by protruding its head and neck assume a phallic form (male). Its dichotomy is also symbolized by its ability to live either in the water or on land. The following dreamer was a man with powerful sexual compulsions. It was his first dream of analysis.

> I went fishing in my dream. [Fishing usually represents sexual activity.] Soon after I dropped my hook in the water I became aware that it was snagged on something solid and immovable. The water was dark and murky so that I could not see what was beneath. I wanted to free my hook and when I thrust my hand deep in the water to loosen the hook, a huge turtle grabbed my wrist in its mouth. I was horrified, and found that no matter how I struggled to get free, he hung on. I awoke in a panic of fear.

Later he brought up memories of early sex play with a boy friend and admitted a fear of homosexuality. He was finally able to pull free of his problem.

Inasmuch as the evolvement of the frog, from tadpole to adult, might be compared to the evolvement of a human being from sperm to fetus to infant to adult, and because the frog lives in both water and air, often in a dream it implies duality—infant/adult, male/female—and sometimes transition. The old fairy story of the ugly frog who became a prince illustrates this idea. We might say that the ugly frog represents the unattractive, undeveloped masculine animus that, upon the kiss of the lovely "princess" anima, springs forth as the handsome prince he was always meant to be!

12

Structures, Places, and Natural Elements in Dreams

Structures and Places

In a dream the house symbolizes the dreamer's life, his emotional patterns and experience. An old house in a dream, therefore, is an old way of living, the framework of memories and experiences; a new house represents a change of consciousness, new beginnings. A bigger house implies expansion within the dreamer. There are temporary as well as permanent abodes: apartments and hotel rooms imply impermanence; a motel room may even represent "one night stands," or sexual escapades. These residential symbols are, however, much less common than that of the dreamer's home, past or present.

The condition of the house in a dream also relates to the emotional state of the dreamer's life. A dirty house, cluttered with junk, connotes emotional confusion; an abode devoid of furniture implies a barren emotional life; locked doors indicate areas of the dreamer's life he has been either afraid or unable to open up (sometimes buried traumas); unstable or slanting floors represent shaky, unstable convictions or attachments that give the dreamer no support.

The front of a house is usually the persona, the facade that the dreamer presents to the world, while the back of the house represents some aspect of the dreamer's shadow self. The roof symbolizes reason, the "uppermost" intellectual faculties. A roof that is leaking or caving in implies a fear of loss of reason.

The upstairs represents the conscious mind, while the basement is always the unconscious mind, the hidden emotional nature. The following basement dream is so rich in symbology it needs no interpretation. The dreamer is a religious, middle-aged woman living a comfortable life in a lovely apartment:

> It seemed that I discovered, much to my surprise, a trap door in the middle of the carpeting of my living room floor. I decided to lift it up, and I went down some steps. When I got down there I was amazed to see only rough earth. Then I saw over in a corner a group of aborigines. They had dark stringy hair and wore only loin cloths, and squatted around a little fire. I wasn't too frightened, but I was astonished, and I said to myself, "I never dreamed all this was down here!"

Each component of the home, whether castle or cottage, has its own meaning in the interpretation of dreams. The rooms in general represent chapters or sections of the dreamer's emotional experience. The living room embodies social relations with family and friends. The kitchen, where food is prepared, is always associated with motherhood, love, and nurturing. This includes the stove, which should be warm and glowing; if empty and cold, a lack of maternal love is implied. Also important in the kitchen is the refrigerator. It is generally female in symbology, since it contains food; and because it is also closed, it can relate to an area of the unconscious. Most important, however, is that it is a container for food that is kept "on ice" until used. Food, of course, represents emotional nourishment. The implication of this young woman's dream is clear:

> In reality I have a new apartment, with a brand new refrigerator. But I dreamed I had instead an old ice box with a heavy lid, just like the one my mother had, but not quite as big. It was filled with ice.

The dining room, where food is served, has to do with emotional fulfillment. If the table is bare, emotional starvation is indicated.

The bedroom is very significant in a dream, though the specific meaning may vary. Is someone asleep or ill in the bed? Most dreams about bedrooms are in some way related to sex. The message is this young woman's dream, a few days before she was to be married, is very evident:

> I dreamed the marriage ceremony was over and we had gone to our hotel room. There was only one single bed in the room and I wondered where my husband was going to sleep.

The bathroom usually connotes an urge to eliminate or wash away something for which the dreamer feels guilty, even "dirty." Brushing the teeth implies an attempt to "clean up" some oral activity. Profuse defecation and urination symbolize attempts to eliminate a subconscious problem; they represent a form of physical catharsis. Frequent dreams of this nature may imply that the dreamer has some memory of guilt surviving from the potty training period.

All passageways, or hallways, in a dream connote transition. It is important to notice what is at the end of the hall, or what rooms it connects. Remembering that a series of rooms might mean a series of experiences, the meaning of this young woman's dream is easier to comprehend:

> I was walking slowly down a long hall. There were rows of bedrooms on each side and the doors were open. I looked in each room as I passed by and in each of them there were a man and woman in bed.

Asked what the dream meant to her she stated: "I've been reviewing my life and all the men I've been to bed with."

If a stairway appears, it is important to ask where it leads. Is the dreamer climbing up or going down? The upper stories often represent the intellect; the basement of course represents the subconscious. Just as frequently, we find that climbing stairs indoors is a displacement of the attempt to reach a sexual climax. Here is the dream of a middle-aged woman, very involved in metaphysics and the study of the "higher mind." The stairs here have an unusual inflection.

> It took place in my home, which is a bungalow, but in the dream it was two-storied. It was a nice house but I discovered there was no connecting stairway between the lower and the upper floors.

This dream revealed to her that there was really no connection between her metaphysical and philosophical concepts (top floor) and her everyday existence. She needed some psychological carpentry!

An elevator, again depending on its direction or destination, may represent the dreamer's emotional mood swings.

The attic, by contrast with the basement (the subconscious), in which dark and obscure things are hidden away, symbolizes the "top of the memory," old attachments that we consider too precious to throw away.

Windows symbolize the dreamer's attitude toward the outside world. To wash the windows or move into a place with larger windows indicates a new, clearer, and more expansive point of view. On the contrary, closed shutters or draperies symbolize shutting out the world. This is the dream of a young woman under analysis who believed she was open to help. Her dream told her otherwise:

> I looked out the window and saw this lady coming to the door whom I had invited in but decided I didn't want to see her after all. I quickly closed my draperies hoping she'd go away. But on turning around I found she was inside after all and I said to myself, "How did she do that?"

There are few symbols in dreams more fraught with meaning than the door. Just as in reality a door connects one room with another, a door in a dream may represent a symbolic passage from one experience to another, from one stage of consciousness to another. It is important, therefore, to recognize whether the dreamer is locked in or locked out, or perhaps attempting to lock someone or something out. The front door is our face on the world; the back door is the more secret, inner self. The front door can occasionally have a sexual implication, as in the following husband's dream:

> I came home and found the front door locked. I tried my key and found it would not work. I knocked on the door but my wife wouldn't open it, and I felt very irritated and frustrated.

Here we have two symbols, the locked door and his inadequate key. As illustrated above, to leave the door unlocked or ajar is to invite entry, as in the case of this young man's dream:

> While making love in bed with my girl friend, I noticed I had somehow left the door to the hallway ajar. I could see a man walking back and forth outside, looking in the door as he passed by.

It would seem that while heterosexually involved, he had left the door ajar for the possible approach of homosexuality.

If in the dream the person hears a knocking on the door, his subconscious is usually trying to deliver a message or impulse, good or bad, and is "knocking" on his conscious awareness to that end. If something threatening tries to enter and it takes all of one's strength to hold it out, something negative that the higher self refuses to admit is trying to force its way into consciousness.

Here are some dreams that show some of the different meanings a door may have. The first dream is that of a young woman who had been striving diligently, but with intermittent lapses, to reach what she called a higher plane of spirituality, or "God's mind." Assisting her in her search was her religious teacher, a woman. The pupil dreamed:

> My teacher and I were both locked in a small narrow room. There was only one window, too high for us to see out of. There was only one door and it was locked. My teacher had a whole bunch of keys and she tried them all, but none would unlock the door. I woke up with a feeling of panic. How would we ever get out?

Her teacher turned out to be emotionally locked up in the same problem that the dreamer had—they both disliked and distrusted men. How could she release her pupil from a problem for which she herself had no key? The dreamer accepted that while her well-meaning teacher had opened many doors of awareness in the past, she was not suited to offer much help in the present circumstances.

The eternally closed door in a dream is unhealthy and sad. A gentle woman with a terminal illness confided that all of her life she had had this recurring dream:

> I go all through a house, an old house, and I always come to a closed door. I look at it, but I never open it. Over and over I come to that door.

She died with the door still closed.

If the house represents the emotional and philosophical structure of our lives, then the furniture symbolizes specific concepts within that structure. A well-to-do woman, for instance, with an elegantly furnished home, had a dream in which she walked through her front door and was surprised and depressed to see that her home was almost completely bare. What furniture she did see was old and drab. She was ready for a complete emotional renovation. There is also the case of a young woman who had been reared by her aunt, whose old-fashioned teachings she had never outgrown. A short time after starting analysis she dreamed:

> It seemed that I had moved out of my aunt's home into a brand-new apartment. I liked it very much but I noticed on looking around that I had brought all of the old furniture with me to the new place.

The bed in a dream usually has to do with sex. Whether it is a single or a double bed is significant. If a married person dreams of being in a single bed, the message is loud and clear that there is no room for the spouse!

The significance of a chair depends on what kind it is. A highchair may indicate infantilism; a soft overstuffed chair, the wish to take life easy. A young businessman revealed more than he thought when he had this dream:

> I was at work in my office. It seemed that I was sitting in a big soft overstuffed chair and it had rollers under it so that I could easily move from desk to desk without getting out of my chair. I must admit it was rather pleasant.

The dreamer had been the favorite son, denied nothing by his mother, and at the time of the dream had found himself incapable of denying himself rich food. In fact he himself was rather "overstuffed," tipping the scales at around three hundred pounds.

The closet is another storage area, usually filled with belongings collected over a period of time. The case of this dreamer, a young woman who had been enduring a difficult marriage for some time and felt it her wifely duty not to complain, illustrates. After hearing at a lecture that it is essential to bring repressed negative feelings to the surface and discharge them, the unconscious of this young lady went right to work. A few days later she related, with some relish, the following dream:

> In the dream I was cleaning out my closet. I'm really a rather neat person but in the dream my closet was a mess, filled with a lot of old dark heavy clothes. I just waded in and started throwing things out as fast as I could, stuff that apparently had been in there a long time.

When asked what she planned to do after cleaning out her closet, she added cheerfully, "Why, get some bright new things, of course."

A castle often symbolizes the fantasy life of childhood. Fairy stories, like parables, draw on universal symbols. The castle portrayed in the lovely fairy stories that start, "Once upon a time there was a little prince (or princess) who lived with the king and queen in a castle on a hill" reflects the childhood memory of being Mommy's and Daddy's little "prince" or "princess" and living in the great fortress of their love and security.

A school in a dream is generally related to one of two meanings: frequently it is a specific memory of a childhood frustration or rejection, or it is the "school of life" with its experiences and challenges from which the dreamer must learn a lesson. Many people under analysis dream of being back in a classroom. Often the dreamer will feel he is "late for class"; he wishes he had been able to deal with his emotional problems sooner. Occasionally the dreamer will feel frustrated because he cannot find the classroom to which he belongs. This would mean that he is seeking to learn and grow but has not yet found the right guidance.

A church represents the dreamer's religious background and spiritual beliefs. All churches are rich in symbolic meaning, the Catholic church particularly so: the "mother church"; Latin, the "mother language"; the Virgin Mary, the pure mother image; the priest with his title of "Father"; the acolytes called "brothers" and nuns "sisters." In the following dreams religious structures appear clearly. The first dreamer was a young man whose parents had been of widely divergent faith. He had grown up with almost no religious teaching of any kind. After reaching out for some analysis he dreamed:

> I was going through a dense forest, thick with trees and tangled vines. There was no path. I was climbing a hill, and I didn't know where I was going but knew I had to keep on. Then I came to an ancient structure, falling into decay. I pushed the vines aside and pushed open the door and suddenly realized I had discovered an old temple, long neglected. I felt good that I had found it, and awoke with a feeling of peace and happiness.

Nobody led this young man on his search; he reached his destination on his own, within himself.

The next dream is that of another young man, but one exposed in early childhood to a great deal of strict religious teachings. His attitude toward all of this at the time of his dream is quite apparent:

> In my dream it seemed I went back to look in on the orthodox church I attended as a child. But it was the strangest thing: The minister was up in his pulpit preaching, but I saw that all of the church pews were turned backward, so that while he talked everyone was facing the other way.

A temple is significant in the same way as a church but with a more eastern and even archetypal inflection. The minister, rabbi, or priest in either case symbolizes the dreamer's higher consciousness, his spiritual superego. The nun in a woman's dream would indicate virginity or a retreat from masculine contacts. In a man's dream the nun may also appear, through the process of displacement, in the place of some female in his life who he realizes is "untouchable." For example, a young man, living alone, had this dream after his attractive younger sister had come for a visit with him.

> I don't know why I'd dream of a nun, since I am not a Catholic. But I dreamed I was talking to a young pretty nun and she smiled at me and I kept wishing she weren't a nun.

This young man was totally innocent of conscious awareness of any incestuous impulse.

Almost never does the dream of a prison relate to any real experience of incarceration. To be in jail (or for that matter any enclosure) means that the dreamer feels helplessly locked in a set of circumstances or relationships. This prison is made of memories, attitudes, and emotions such as guilt and self-pity. The jailer, therefore, personifies the dreamer's own conscience or superego. The following dream illustrates. The dreamer is an intelligent, sensitive young man who, since childhood, had been criticized and rejected by his father, resulting in a sense of inferiority:

> This has been a recurring dream, over and over. I am always locked up in a jail, which is down in a basement. Nobody ever knows I am there. I feel completely forgotten. People are passing by up above, going about their lives, but no matter how I call out, no one ever hears me.

This man reached out for counseling. What developed is shown in his later dream:

> I was in the same cell as before. I looked through the bars and a man I had never seen before [his true self] came down from outside and unlocked the prison door. I walked out into the sunlight with a great sense of freedom and joy.

Sometimes the ego has become so immersed in self-pity, persecution, or martyrdom that the individual may feel a sense of virtue in his emotional confinement. As Lord Byron put it in his poem "The Prisoner of Chillon," "My very cell and I grew friends, and I regained my freedom with a sigh."

The hospital, like the jail, seldom relates to an actual confinement; instead, as a place of healing it usually symbolizes analysis or emotional help. Free association is important. Is the dreamer undergoing surgery or being treated for a long-term illness? The doctor may represent the analyst; the nurse, the mother. It is of course promising if the dreamer feels he is getting well.

Since any store represents a source of supply, the kind of store in a dream is of course significant. Whatever it is the dreamer is selecting and buying symbolizes what he at the time is emotionally choosing, for which he is willing to pay the price of attention and energy. The department store, with its many sections, selling everything from baby shoes, men's suits, and ladies' lingerie to pots and pans, may be interpreted as representing the wide variety of life's choices. Each item of purchase, of course, has its own symbolic significance.

Since almost all food in a dream is in some way related to emotional, not physical, nourishment, the kind of food the dreamer buys is meaningful when interpreting the symbolic significance of a grocery store. Everyone is at times "hungry for love and affection," so he goes shopping in his dream. But he must be sure to pay the cashier—to steal ripe sweet fruit in the dream, for instance, might indicate indulging himself in an illicit sexual affair!

Office buildings by their very nature imply concern about business and office work and the dreamer's feelings about it. Coworkers in the dream generally symbolize sides of the dreamer's own nature, animus or anima, and how he likes or dislikes that facet of himself.

A trailer appears in the following dream, which illustrates how emotional expansion and growth can take place without the dreamer's conscious awareness. It is the dream of a middle-aged man, a bachelor, who lived by choice alone in a small house trailer. He said he liked the snugness and coziness of living alone in such a small place. After undergoing analysis for some time he surprised himself with this dream:

> I came home from work and as I approached what had been my snug little home I saw with great consternation that a lot of changes were being made. Workmen were everywhere making alterations. The roof had been raised higher, the walls expanded. Everything was wider and longer. The two tiny windows were gone; in their place were large expansive windows, letting in a lot of light. I was angry that all this had been done behind my back, so to speak. I demanded of one of the workmen: "Who told you to do all this?" He smiled, shrugged his shoulders, and, pointing heavenward with his thumb, replied, "The Man Upstairs," and went on about his work.

After the dreamer understood the meaning of his dream, that growth was taking place in spite of himself, he grinned and admitted, "I must say, after all, it was a great improvement."

A tower may be phallic, but on the other hand it could be a "lookout" tower.

Bridges symbolize a period of change, or passage, in the dreamer's life. Very frequently there is a sense of peril, a fear of falling off the bridge. The bridge may break, or the dreamer may tumble into the water below. This indicates a sense of anxiety about emotional changes. The bridge is suspended over water and water always symbolizes the dreamer's unconscious emotions. Here is the dream of a young man experiencing a great deal of rage and frustration over a divorce:

> I was trying to cross a bridge. It broke and I fell into the water. It was like a kind of gluey mud and I could hardly move. What frightened me the most was that there was a big ugly hairy monster down there with me. I was trying to get away from him when I woke up.

The monster might be an ugly aspect of his id, in this case, rage.

The meaning of a wall in the dream depends on whether the dreamer feels blocked or protected by it. If it inhibits his freedom then, like the symbol of the jail, it represents some fixed idea that the dreamer has not learned to transcend. Here is an example. The dreamer was a middle-aged man with a rather tragic childhood history of poverty and what he had always believed was rejection by his overworked and half-starved mother. She had been unable to nurse him and he had always believed he was an unwanted baby. Financial success as an adult had failed to alleviate his deep sense of rejection and depression. This was his first dream in analysis:

> In my dream I was traveling a path across a barren land. I came to a high, dark, and apparently endless wall. There was no way to go over it and it seemed to stretch endlessly on both sides. I felt hopeless and overcome with sadness.

He responded well to counseling and later had the following dream.

> I was walking along the same path that I traveled in my previous dream. But this time instead of barrenness, there was a touch of green everywhere and I saw little blades of grass showing beside the path. And when I came to the place where the wall had been, it was completely gone! There was no sign of a wall. Then on looking beyond where the wall had been I saw a beautiful sight: Sitting in a pool of light was a young mother, nursing her baby. A warm feeling swept over me and I had a rush of joy—that my mother did love me after all.

He added that since that dream he had felt better physically and emotionally than he had for years.

A gate is an opening from the psyche to the conscious mind. The gate that swings open is an invitation to spiritual awareness.

A foreign country or city may generally be interpreted in one of two ways: either as a wish to escape from the humdrum to something new and exciting, or foreign to the present life, or it may mean that the dreamer is involved in some experience or relationship "foreign" to his everyday life. Sometimes involvement with something the dreamer feels is dishonest or immoral may appear in a dream as dealing with a foreigner or being in a foreign country. Free association is essential in interpreting such a dream.

The mountain is a universal symbol of attainment and growth. The ease or difficulty with which the dreamer climbs his mountain symbolizes how he feels about his progress in life. To get a glimpse in a dream of a beautiful, lofty mountain might have metaphysical or spiritual meaning, a glimpse, one might say, of a higher level of consciousness. The Bible, like most sacred texts, contains many references to "going up the mountain." Negatively, of course, falling off the mountain, or falling generally, implies a sense of failure, and from a religious standpoint, it sometimes means "falling from grace."

A deep valley can, under certain circumstances, symbolize the female genital area or it could signify some emotional rift in the dreamer's life.

Nearly always a gently rounded hill in a dream represents the female breast. Looking lovingly and admiringly at a beautiful landscape with soft rolling contours may mean the dreamer is remembering what he felt as a child when viewing his mother's body. On the other hand, if the hill is rough and rocky, another meaning is implied. Again, free association is necessary.

The cemetery or grave represents the dead past, moribund memories and attachments.

A garden represents the dreamer's emotional life. If it is neat and tidy, in orderly rows, the dreamer's emotional life is disciplined and scheduled— spontaneity, like weeds, is not allowed. If, on the other hand, the flowers and vines have been allowed to grow naturally, one might assume that the dreamer's libido is allowed to express itself spontaneously and naturally. Weeds in the garden represent unattended problems.

A jungle signifies confusion, a lack of direction. But if there are wild animals in the jungle, then the dreamer is touching his id, the source of his primitive instincts. The animals (instincts) prowling there are usually dangerous.

A desert symbolizes barrenness, a lifeless emotional nature. Crossing a desert in a dream implies that the dreamer is going through an arid time in life.

An island represents emotional isolation, a lack of communication with others. If there is a wall around it, the dreamer may feel beleaguered as well as lonely. Instead of waiting for those on the mainland to discover and rescue him, perhaps his psyche is telling him that he needs to start building his own bridge to them!

The beach and shore might be classified as the borderline between the logical, conscious mind and the fluid, emotional unconscious. Of course, beach and shore may also, through association, symbolize seashore experiences in the past.

Natural Elements

In our dream world, as in our waking moments, we move, breathe, and have our being in all of the natural elements of the conscious world. We try to keep our feet on the ground of reality, we swim (or drown) in the ocean of our emotions, we wish to take flight in the air of our imagination, and sometimes we are "burned" by the fire of our own rage.

The earth represents reality, the foundation of our life and beliefs. To "come down to earth" implies the dreamer is returning to the realm of logic and reason. To go below the earth, as in a cave or tunnel, is to enter the realm of the unconscious. To dream of an earthquake indicates that the individual is undergoing some jolting revelation or change, a dislocation of what he had previously believed was unshakeable. It may be a religious belief or some sense of security, or even a long-standing attachment. An interesting illustration is contained in the two dreams below, one of a mother and the other of her son, both dreams occurring the same night. A very intense attachment existed between the two of them, an attachment of which they were rather proud. The night before their dreams they had attended a lecture in which the Oedipus complex was outlined and emphasized. The next morning the mother related this dream:

> Last night I dreamed there was a big earthquake, everything was being shaken up. It really scared me.

Then her son came down to breakfast and he also related a dream:

> I had a vivid dream last night. It seemed I was in my mother's bedroom—it had the same pretty flowered wallpaper. But somehow it was in the basement of the house [the subconscious]. All at once an earthquake jolted me and I was horrified to see the walls of my mother's bedroom starting to crack. I woke up very shaken.

Their dreams revealed that they had both had the same psychic jolt.

Mud represents some clinging, cloying problem that makes it difficult for the dreamer to make progress, and because it is dirty mud implies guilt.

Quicksand symbolizes the relentless pull of a neurotic attachment that the dreamer instinctively feels will destroy him unless it is broken. Because the earth is related to the mother, the individual can fear mother-love pulling him back to the womb. This can result in a nightmare. The next dream may make the point clear. The dreamer was a mature woman, divorced, living alone with her daughter. While she was definitely heterosexual, her relations with men had been very frustrating.

> In my dream I was just walking along when suddenly I found my left foot was caught in wet sand that seemed to be sucking it down. As I tried to pull it loose my right foot got caught, too. I was being sucked down, deeper and deeper. By the time it was up to my waist I was screaming and screaming for somebody to rescue me. When I woke up I was shaking with fear.

Asked what she feared the most, this devoutly religious lady replied, "I would hate more than anything to discover that I have some hidden homosexuality." It was explained to her that everyone has a touch of latency. Her background had certainly confused her feelings about men: she had been reared by a devoted mother, without a father present; her own marriage had failed, causing her to turn to her only child, a daughter, for love and understanding so that their companionship was the most meaningful part of her life. She realized that she was becoming trapped in a rather unhealthy attachment. Quicksand is a trap in *mother* earth, and can symbolize a pull back toward the womb. With an understanding of what her dream was trying to tell her, that she was really heterosexual, she was able to pull herself out of her panic.

In a dream the ocean can signify the womb of the world, the source of all life, the racial unconscious. On a more personal level the ocean can represent the hidden depths of the dreamer's subconscious from which emerge strange and sometimes frightening creatures; it can be clear water across which the dreamer sails cheerfully, or dark depths into which he falls, screaming for help. Many people who have never seen the ocean dream they are standing on a shore, gazing in fear at a great dark tidal wave sweeping toward them, generally awakening just before it sweeps over them. The dream of a tidal wave almost invariably means the dreamer is going through a deep sense of anxiety about some impending problem. Occasionally people dream of walking on water. This does not necessarily mean that they feel glorified to the point of emulating Christ; instead it implies that the dreamer, instead of looking down at all the pitfalls into which he could sink, has learned to overcome them.

A gentle rain may mean that the dreamer has achieved some new awareness that will bring growth. If a heavy downpour occurs, the dreamer is overwhelmed, flooded with disturbing emotions. One mature woman, after being helped to find some answers to her troubled life, dreamed:

> It seemed it was raining, but the raindrops were not like regular drops of water. They were like large beautiful drops of crystal. They were like water and yet they were not water. It was a lovely dream.

Fire can be beneficial and warming, or consuming and destructive. A warm glowing fire connotes enthusiasm, vitality, even love. Sexual passion can also appear in a dream as a fire, for instance in this dream of a woman who was leading a single life because her husband had been confined for quite some time in a hospital.

> I have a mailbox out in front of my house, and in my dream it seemed there was a fire inside of the mailbox. I was yelling, "There's a fire in the mailbox. Hurry, somebody, and come and put it out quick!"

When asked who she thought would have to put it out, she replied, "The mailman, of course." After the symbology of the mailbox and the implication that she was more than anxious for her husband's return had been explained to her, she laughed and agreed heartily with the interpretation. She was concerned that it should be the "mailman" who quenched the fire, but was relieved that no doubt "mailman" stood for "male man."

A destructive fire symbolizes a consuming rage within the dreamer. Children who are filled with resentment and frustration over a home situation frequently dream that their home is burning up—with everybody in it— only to have their conscience take over at the last minute and call the fire department or make some other desperate attempt to rescue the trapped family members. They wake up with a great sense of relief that everybody is all right, that they didn't burn them up after all—proof that their love outweighed their resentment.

A cool white flame symbolizes light more than heat, is more mental and even spiritual than emotional in meaning. The dream of a flame flickering out implies the waning of hope, or even of life force.

The sun symbolizes God, the father, the source of life and energy, or even the animus. It is always masculine. Sunrise connotes the beginning of a new experience or positive awareness; sunset implies the winding down of certain aspects of the dreamer's life, the ebbing of energy, old age. When in a dream (or in a painting) the sun appears as black, there is the implication of a dark, even hopeless image of the father and/or God.

The moon is always feminine and often associated with a sense of mystery. In Egyptian symbology, it represents Osiris, the giver of fertility. While there is a constancy about the sun, the moon is cyclical.

A dream of the end of the world means the dreamer is undergoing an emotional experience so shattering he feels it is the end of his own personal world. Mountains tumble down, cracks appear in the earth, and sometimes fire flares over the horizon. In a way such dreams symbolize the death of the dreamer's ego, a death of hopes and wishes. It is as though the unconscious were saying, "All that I believed in is coming to an end, so it is the end of me, too."

Light in any form is a beautiful and hopeful symbol. The halo around someone's head, the dawn of a new day, sunlight breaking through dark clouds, all symbolize awareness, hope, and promise. This is the dream of a confused and troubled young woman:

> I was in a dark room. I was aware that there was a light bulb above my head and I kept reaching and reaching to turn it on, but never could quite reach it. I even jumped up to reach it, but couldn't.

This was a simple statement from her subconscious that understanding and awareness were still beyond her grasp. But she was trying!

A spotlight implies attention focused on something or someone. It may mean a narcissistic wish to be the center of attention. The dreamer's attention may be being directed to an organ of the body, or a message. Hiding from the spotlight would of course have another meaning, as in the dream below, that of a young woman under analysis:

> My boy friend and I were hiding in a ditch behind some bushes. Up above on a hill there was a detective or somebody who had a searchlight and they were beaming it all around trying to locate us—or at least I thought that was what they were doing.

Reassured that her analyst was not playing the role of a detective and would not be critical of any thing or person in her life, she confessed that there was something very unacceptable about the man with whom she was involved and that she had been trying to hide it from the counselor.

Darkness scarcely needs interpretation. It always has some negative or depressing connotation. To be in the dark in a dream implies not only ignorance but frequently confusion, loneliness, or fear. The dark figure personifies some hidden problem or aspect of the dreamer's nature not yet brought to light.

13

Children's Dreams

Children, because they are closer to their unconscious, their instinctual nature, not yet having developed a superego to censor and screen out their emotions, dream in almost pure symbology. Their dreams are usually graphic and uncomplicated. Their dream content generally expresses some wish, either to annihilate an "enemy" (frequently a member of the family or the bully next door), or some more positive fulfillment of need. Poor children dream of comfort and gifts; the unloved child often dreams of someone who gives him loving care. (Many people have related the memory of night and daydreams in which they learned that their own rejecting parents were not really their parents after all, and that somewhere they had a real mother or father who loved them very much and whom they hoped to find someday.)

From research in the field it has been learned that the child, up until age five, is the center of his own dream, rarely the observer, and does not separate dream from reality. After seven, his dreams come to involve his relations with his family, and he becomes aware of the difference between his dream life and his real life. Ralph L. Woods learned in his research on dreams that the figures in children's dreams that caused the greatest fear in both sexes were generally, first, a mean old man, and second, large animals such as lions and tigers. Later girls feared dogs, rats, and snakes. As girls entered adolescence and became aware of religion they frequently peopled their dreams with angels or other benevolent figures who appeared to guide and help them.

Frequently, after seeing a movie or reading a book, the child will have a dream in which he identifies with one of the characters in that movie or book. Insight into the child's own character and qualities may be gained by noticing the over-emphasis the child puts on the qualities of the hero or heroine, these being of course the ones with which he identifies.

If the parent wishes to understand the child better through dream content, it is best to approach the subject quietly and casually, because the child may instinctively be on guard—the "bad" dream may be about the parent and, without knowing its meaning, the child may still be reluctant to relate it. At the breakfast table, for instance, the mother might casually mention that she had a dream the night before and while she realizes dreams are not really true, they are still interesting to talk about. She might even mention that dreams are "like fairy stories in the night" and relate briefly something that happened in her dream. This often makes it easier for the child to discuss his dreams.

The dreams below were all related within a half-hour and represent two weeks of dreaming. The dreamer was an intelligent, sensitive little girl whose parents quarreled constantly. In all the disharmony she had grown to fear her father the most because he had physically hurt her as well as her mother.

> Lots of times I dream I am falling off a cliff into the ocean.

Insecurity, nothing to hold onto.

> Last night I dreamed I was walking to school and a guy came and he kidnapped me. Long hair, beard and mustache, a mean-looking person. He took me to an old shack. Then I woke up.

Captured and imprisoned by her image and fear of men.

> The other night I had a scary dream. Me and my sister were at the beach and my Daddy was out swimming in the ocean. Me and my sister were just wading in the shallow part, and a shark came and ate my Daddy.

That took care of him! The ocean is her unconscious; the shark is her hidden aggression.

> Two weeks ago I dreamed that me and my sister were in the den and a man came to the door and when my Daddy answered it, the man came in and me and my sister came in to see who it was and he got his gun out and shot Mommy and Daddy.

She'd had it with her mother, too!

> I was reading one of my *Little House on the Prairie* books and in one of those books this lady was mad at her husband. She had a butcher knife and was going to kill him, but didn't.

The day before this dream the child had witnessed a violent quarrel between the parents. It is easy to recognize which side the child was on.

> My Daddy had a pet snake and the snake had babies. Then the big snake died and one of the baby snakes grew up to be a big long snake and wrapped himself around my Daddy's neck and choked him. It was a cobra.

In this, this father's own offspring destroys him. The choking probably was her wish to choke off his verbal abuse. From the above dreams, one can recognize the dichotomy developing in this child: seething, almost destructive rage and resentment beneath a gentle, sweet-natured exterior.

Very often a fire appears in children's dreams, indicating rage. Who and what is being consumed by fire is of course the key to the child's dream. But it is also very significant to observe that after the conflagration has started and the enemy (usually a member of the family) is about to be consumed, the child's better nature comes to the fore and at the last minute he attempts to rescue the victim. For example, here is the dream of a six-year-old girl whose over-strict parents not only punished her for the slightest mistake, but also blatantly favored her younger brother:

> I was playing outside when I saw our house on fire. My Mommy and Daddy and brother were inside and the fire was spreading fast. I couldn't call the fire department because the phone was inside. I was real scared that they would all get burned up before somebody could save them. I woke up real scared.

Apparently her remorse didn't arrive in time to rescue them.

While the above dreams are examples of negative wishes, we must remember that far more of the child's wish dreams are of escape or fulfilling some fantasy. An imaginative child can come up with a dream right out of Grimm's fairy tales. The next dreamer was a young boy who, as the result of a divorce, had been taken by his mother to a foreign country to live, with little hope of ever seeing his father. He had this dream night after night:

> I dreamed I had wings and I could fly. I would fly and fly over mountains and oceans. I always felt I was going back to my home and my Dad, but I always woke up before I got there.

As a rather pitiful sidelight, this child developed a habit in school that disturbed his teacher so that she insisted he see the school counselor. He would stare out the window during class and move his elbows up and down at his side like the flapping of a bird's wings. He did finally get home to see his father.

The next dream is an interesting one, in which a seven-year-old girl worked out her own inner conflict. In her dream experience she confronted her "bad" side, protected her "good" side, and managed to give herself a lesson. The day before the dream, the little girl had had a stormy confrontation with her mother, ending in her running out the front door and then falling and skinning her knee. Her dream:

> In the backyard there was a big old mean gorilla. Curled up on the grass was a cute little baby lamb. I was very afraid the gorilla would hurt the little lamb, so I started yelling at it to go away. The gorilla jumped over the back fence, and then it fell and skinned its knee.

When her mother asked what she thought it meant, she said that she guessed the mean old gorilla was the bad side of herself that had been ugly to her mother. When asked, "Then what was the baby lamb?" the child became self-conscious and said she didn't know. Her mother explained to her daughter that the lamb was the sweeter side of her nature that she had wanted to protect from her own temper, whereupon the little girl gravely replied, "The gorilla knew it was naughty; that is why it skinned itself." Then after thinking it over, she added, "And I guess that is why I skinned my knee." Would that more adults could be as honest!

Sibling rivalry is behind many frightening dreams. The child is nearly always relieved to awaken and find that his or her negative wish did not come true after all!

In this dream the young dreamer neatly disposed of an annoying baby-sitter:

> Me and my sister were in bed and my baby-sitter was asleep on the couch and Mom and Dad were out to dinner. A fire started in our house and no one could get out, and my baby-sitter died in the fire. My sister and I got out, but we got burned a little on the legs and had to go to the hospital.

She dispatched the irritating baby-sitter, but not without some atonement for her guilt by getting "burned a little" on the legs!

Giants and witches frequently pursue or capture little dreamers. These are archetypal personifications of the dominating or threatening parent. The unconscious always exaggerates for emphasis, drawing on the archetypal imagery of the racial subconscious to express fear, dread, or resentment.

In the eyes of the child, all adults appear huge, particularly if in a threatening mood. An example is this dream of a young boy who, after picking an apple hanging over the fence from his neighbor's yard, was warned by the neighbor, somewhat jokingly, about what he would do to the boy if it happened again. That night the child awoke frightened by this dream:

> I was in the backyard when I saw a great big giant coming after me. He was so big he stepped right over the fence and I ran as hard as I could but I was very scared he'd catch me.

Just as the giant is a negative symbol of the overpowering male, the witch often appears as the negative personification of the female, usually some threatening female figure of authority: mother, teacher, aunt, grandmother, or neighbor. And despite the fact that the child has never even seen a picture of a witch, she appears in the dream in the usual clothes and peaked hat, with hooked nose and scraggly hair. This, it must be understood, does not represent the woman herself but how the child feels about the woman, the projection, so to speak, of the child's own "witchy" feelings upon the person who threatens him.

Here is another archetypal symbol, this time the dragon, in the dream of a seven-year-old girl. It helps to understand the dream when we learn that her father, a very big man, had frequent bursts of temper.

> It was in our house. A great big dragon came in and we were scared. He had bombs in him and they kept exploding all over the place. Mommy came in with a hose and held it pointing up so that the water came down like rain. It sort of cooled off the dragon, so he went away. But he came back.

At least mother tried!

When the child has some form of sexual concern or anxiety his subconscious will employ the usual phallic symbols: snakes, worms, long bugs, etc. If in the dream the child is frightened by a large snake or lizard, it may be that there has been some exposure or molestation by an adult male. Smaller symbols such as snakes, worms, or bugs generally imply some exploration or play with a small boy. Not only, in this case, is the symbol smaller, but the guilt or fear is not so great. One boy dreamed:

> I was looking at this big dog, a male dog, lying down on a sort of bench in front of me. Its tongue was hanging out and it was a long red tongue. I kept looking at it, but at the same time I was kind of scared.

His mother learned, soon after the dream, that he had been approached by a neighbor who exposed his genitals to the child.

The next dream, a boy's, scarcely needs interpretation.

> I used to dream this all the time. It was when my Mom was getting a divorce. I dreamed they were in court and we kids were in court, too. [In reality, they were not present.] My sister and I wanted to leave, so we did. It was dark outside and we got lost. We saw this big house and thought it was ours, but it wasn't. We knocked on the door and it opened. It was pitch dark in there. Then the door slammed shut behind us. We didn't know what to do.

After putting his head down and wiping away some tears, he added, "We were real scared. Then I woke up."

A child who has known no love may even dream that he is dead. Another dream of a child with serious implications was one about a mechanical boy, made all of metal parts; no blood, no heart, no mind—and no feeling, therefore unable to suffer.

It is well known that children are reluctant to tell their parents or other adults when they have been approached sexually. There are several reasons: fear of punishment, fear of doubt on the part of the parents, threats by the molester of what he might do to them if they tell, and sometimes a secret guilt for having enjoyed the stimulation. Nevertheless, every child experiences some deep disturbance at the excitement and the strangeness of the experience. This reaction, if not expressed verbally, will generally appear in dream symbology. This is another important reason for parents, particularly the mother, to become knowledgeable about dream symbols, particularly phallic symbols, since most child molesters are male. In children's dreams they appear particularly as something longish that is proffered to the child or threatens him. They may be a candy bar, a bottled drink, a nozzle or spray, a stick, red hands (being molested), or games the child is afraid to play. One little girl dreamed that two bigger boys were chasing her and her girl friend with sticks, telling them that "it's just a game; don't be afraid." An eight-year-old girl had this dream:

There was a dog, a big dog, and he seemed friendly to me, but he stuck out his long red tongue and came toward me and I was real scared.

A young boy who lived on a ranch and on rainy days spent time in the cabin with one of the ranch hands later dreamed:

It seemed I was on a little engine on a narrow-gauge railroad and as we moved forward we passed yellow flashing lights on the side that I knew were danger signals and right after that I saw coming toward me down the track a huge engine; the front of the engine was big and rounded and it was coming right at my face. I woke up scared.

We have established in previous chapters that most vivid dreams, either of adults or children, usually result in part from a stimulus the day before, whether a book, movie, or incident. The content of the dream that follows is always to some degree related to that stimulus. With this in mind it might be well to consider the effect that so-called horror movies have upon the psyche of the child. Many children can view such a movie in the afternoon and after being deliciously scared by all the monsters and mayhem, go to bed and sleep peacefully that night. But there are other children who, having experienced the same excitement, toss and turn in their beds, and then awaken screaming with a nightmare. Why? It is not the stimulus but what it *arouses* in us that forms the dream content. We are well acquainted with the id of the adult, that elemental source of all drives, the will to survive, to destroy that which stands in our way, to take what we want. It has been said that a child is pure id until it becomes aware of and develops its higher self. For instance, the unconscious (and sometimes conscious) wish of the small child is to eliminate by whatever means a sibling that he believes has robbed him of the parents' love and attention, a "monstrous" wish that is suppressed as quickly as possible, and then in turn converted into an excessive show of devotion for the hated rival. (A child soon learns to hide from his parents that which, as an adult, he learns to hide from himself.) Hidden though the impulse may be, it lies dormant, to be stimulated by the sadism in the movie and, later, while the child sleeps, to break through in the frightening images of a nightmare. The child who has emotional problems, who feels rejected, dominated, and abused or has strong cause for jealousy, is the one most likely to be over-stimulated by the sadism and masochism of the horror movie, and then, in turn, to be most frightened by the "monsters" lurking in his own closet or emerging from under his own bed.

14

Archetypal and Guidance Dreams

Generally we think of the unconscious side of our nature as only a repository or source of that which is immature and, if not expressing a wish, then something negative or troubling. While this is often true, we need to become aware of another level of consciousness, another level of the psyche that is rather wonderful, a far deeper, wiser, and more spiritual self that has been called the superconscious, the psyche or the soul. It is the center of which the conscious rational mind is too often unaware—or too busy to listen to. But sometimes when we have become disheartened and hopeless and have suffered enough that we are ready to surrender our ego wish and in humility pray for guidance, then behold! an answer will come, we will have a dream in which a wise and kindly figure appears with a message of hope or sheds some light on our path. These dreams are rare and of great value and they do not occur unless the person is in deep travail—spiritually, one might say, on his knees.

Because we cannot dream in abstractions, such messages appear in symbolic form, usually in what is called archetypal imagery. It may be in the person of a teacher, a minister, or other religious leader. Sometimes the Wise Old Man, with his flowing white beard, appears, ancient wisdom personified. If the bearer of the message is a religious figure it will assume the form of the religious belief of the dreamer: the Christian sees the white-robed Christ, the Catholic sees the patron saint to whom he prays during his waking moments, while to the student of eastern philosophy Buddha may appear. Actually this may be interpreted as the archetypal personification or projection of the dreamer's own inner wisdom emerging from his own psyche or soul, clothed in the visage and garments he can recognize and understand. One might almost say it is the God voice within us projecting its own image for our conscious recognition and awareness, which we could not or would not receive were it not for the dream world.

"The psyche spontaneously produces images with a religious content; it is by nature religious," said Dr. Stephen Hoeller in his lecture on the waking and sleeping dream. By whatever name we call it, the essence is of the spiritual: there have been those, such as Emerson, who called it the "over-soul"; others claim it is a "guiding spirit." If one believes that it is the voice of God "out there," then we can be grateful for the dream that becomes the door that lets Him "in here."

The Archetypes

Let us start with Webster's definition of the word. "To the Platonists the archetypal world is the world as it exists as an idea of God, and the pattern of creation. . . . One of the ideas, or transcendent essences, of which existent things are imitations." (One might well spend hours meditating on the meaning of those words.)

Now let us turn to that profoundly metaphysical man, Carl Jung, for his definition. He termed the archetypes self-portraits of the instincts. They are to be found in all religions, myths, legends, fables, and fairy stories. He mentioned also that astrology, in which he was a believer, "uses the archetypes by projecting them into the constellation of heaven."

In the collective unconscious then are to be found all of the suprapersonal psychic elements that are common to everyone, part of our inheritance and part of our congenital psychic background. They appear in various forms: human, animal, or natural elements. They appear in religious literature and art in the form of the angels, the saints, the madonna, and the devil. (In this connection it is interesting to note that the term Virgin Mary symbolically means pure water, since the word Mary stems from *mare*, the sea. And the sea is of profound meaning among the archetypal symbols.)

Archetypal symbols include Greek gods, goddesses, and heroes; religious figures such as saints, the madonna, Lucifer the devil, and the highest, Jesus as well as Buddha; the Wise Old Man, or the Ancient One; the Wise Inspiring Woman; the Mother (positive); the Witch (negative). Animals, fish, birds, and insects that can appear as archetypal symbols include the dragon, unicorn, bull, cow, horse, snake, whale, seaserpent, mermaid (half human), turtle, phoenix, owl, raven, dove, egg, scarab, and butterfly. Natural elements and forces include the sun, moon, star, wind, rain, lightning, and fire. Landscapes include the earth, ocean, seashore, mountain, river, and oak tree. Abstract and geometric figures include the circle or mandala, square, or triangle. Fairy story figures include the witch, fairy godmother, frog, prince, and princess. Each of the above is the embodiment of an idea, a force or energy, or an essence, and appears in the dream in the form acceptable to the experience and background of the dreamer. It is recognized that in mythology and Christian parables both positive and negative images appear: female figures representing the beautiful and inspiring aspects of womanhood, starkly contrasted with the seductive wiles of the mermaid and the deadly visage of the Medusa, while in Christianity behind the inspiring figures of Jesus and the saints lurks the dark shadow figure of Lucifer, the devil.

Meaningful dreams seem to contain the human archetypal images more than any other, perhaps because their forms are most readily understood by the dreamer. A figure that appears most frequently is that of the Wise Old Man, the embodiment of ancient wisdom, usually with white hair and beard and always with an air of compassion and wisdom. The female embodiment of wisdom or reassurance and guidance also appears, and, while not so old, she is never young either. She is usually quite tall, clothed in flowing garments, with a visage illumined with profound knowledge and compassion. Dr. Stephen Hoeller, philosopher and professor of comparative religion, mentioned in one of his lectures on dreams that when the Wise Old Man appears in a dream that means the dreamer is seeking wisdom within himself.

The figure of the teacher often manifests itself in the dreams of those who are seriously trying to find what their own problems are and how to become a better person; in other words seeking the path of spiritual growth. In answer to their need they may have a dream in which a minister, a philosopher, or a lecturer appears who brought forth an idea that lit a spark of awareness in their psyche. Even the counselor (if they are under analysis) may take the role of the teacher. When this happens it is well for the dreamer to remind himself that it is not the person per se in the dream, wise as he might at the moment have appeared to be; instead the image is the archetypal projection of the dreamer's own seeking, the embodiment, one might say, of his own forgotten knowledge presenting itself to his consciousness. The archetypal image is both the seeker and the sought; the psyche of the dreamer contains the question and the answer.

How do we know this is so? Because no teacher, religious or philosophical, can arouse within the listener more than that which already lies inherent and unrecognized within his own psyche. The seed of awareness may be implanted by what seems to be an outside figure but only the truth within can recognize the truth without. (This theory proves itself in the way a dreamer responds to the interpretation of his dream: if valid, the light of recognition; if incorrect, no reaction, period.)

Jung added to the human archetypes the animus and anima, although he did not consider them to be on as high a plane of meaning as most of the other images. But they are, nevertheless, deep within the unconscious nature of us all, each man with his "woman-soul" and each woman with her "man-soul," or contrasexual side. As previously discussed the inner images may be noble, inspiring, alluring, loving, or, when distorted, rejecting, threatening, even evil.

It is scarcely necessary to define the characteristics of the many animal archetypal forms; anyone who has read the myths and legends of long ago is already fairly cognizant of their symbolic meaning. However, discussion of a few of those most frequently appearing in dreams might be in order. For instance, the horse as an animal represents the subhuman side; it also represents the lower part of the body and the animal drives that rise from there. It symbolizes dynamic power, and in some connotations masculine logic and reason (witness the horsehair wigs judges in England wear). Webster's dictionary points out that the astrological sign of Sagittarius symbolizes the human characteristics growing up and out of the animal nature. The horse can also be female in connotation, as the Trojan horse containing the Greek soldiers. And then there is the nightmare with its frightening implications.

The bull is an archetypal symbol of primeval masculine force and propagation. The cow, placid, milk-giving, and almost immovable, is a classic earth-mother symbol. While the unicorn rarely appears in modern dreams, in mythology it was recognized as a wild creature tamed only by the virgin in whose lap it lay its single horn.

The mermaid is a composite creature, half-human, half-fish. According to legend, she used her feminine charm, beauty, and music to lure hapless sailors to a watery grave.

The symbology of the whale has previously been discussed, but it does belong among the archetypes, the mammoth mother symbol in whose belly Jonah took refuge. Because its habitat is the ocean, in dreams it represents some huge emotional experience taking place in the depth of the dreamer's unconscious self.

The turtle, an ancient symbol of eternal life, living half in the water and half on the land and burying its eggs in the sand, is somewhat androgynous in connotation. The head and neck protrude in a phallic form from its round enclosing shell. The frog, a symbol of change and evolvement, has been likened to that of the human from conception.

The symbology of the archetypal bird images is fairly evident and recognized by most people: the black raven with its doomlike, foreboding aspect; the wisdom of the ancient figure of the owl; the spiritual message of that gentle bird of peace and love, the dove. And then there is the phoenix. As it rose out of the ashes of the fire of its own death it gave us one of our most vivid symbols of regeneration, even ever-lasting life.

The scarab is another legendary symbol of regeneration, this time a very earthy one. Rolling a bit of dung into an earth-shaped ball, it lays an egg in it; later the egg hatches and draws its sustenance off the material in which it was immersed.

Of course in considering archetypal images we must not overlook the ubiquitous snake with its dual meaning: the seductive temptor of evil (the most widely accepted image, as Eve would testify) and the metaphysical picture of the snake swallowing its own tail, interpreted as the eternal cycle of life without beginning and end.

The meaning and implication of the above images cover many aspects, both positive and negative, but now let us consider an archetypal symbol that is always and under all circumstances an image of beauty and transcendence, the ephemeral jewel-toned butterfly. Emerging from the constriction of its ugly cocoon, it spreads its wings in lovely flight, and from then on relates only to the flowers. Could there be any more perfect symbol of the soul?

The archetypal symbols of nature, the great mother of us all, are more cosmic in their imagery and meaning. The sun, always masculine, is the source of life; the moon is a feminine symbol with mysterious and sometimes disturbing influence; the shining star ever guides us onward. The earth itself, the cosmic mother, is our home and our security, and the boundless fathomless sea, from which all life emerged, is the symbol of the universal unconscious with its restless moods and boundless depths. Then there is the mountain, the celestial peak, which the soul of each yearns to reach; and the ever-shifting wind, the invisible breath of nature with its flow of life's energy.

Since dream content is not of the conscious or physical mind, it must by its nature be called metaphysical. Although most people today are familiar with the term metaphysics it might be interesting to consider how others have defined it. Albertus Magnus (as quoted in Webster's dictionary) long ago called it "the trans-physical science," and Saint Thomas Aquinas considered it "to be concerned with the cognition of God." Few dreams are as metaphysical in essence as the so-called guidance or superconscious dreams. Superconscious means transcending human consciousness, pertaining to the highest consciousness or to a margin of consciousness (Webster's dictionary).

Carl Jung has probably contributed to the fields of psychology and parapsychology deeper and wider concepts of the theory of archetypes than has anyone else. For years while he was the student and associate of Sigmund Freud he was exposed to the theory of the unconscious as an area where the residue of personal experiences, unfulfilled wishes and desires, and frustrations and repressed conflicting emotions reside. Later, however, Jung, after much research into his own psyche and his dreams and the dreams and yearnings of others, came to the conclusion that somehow beyond all this there exists a much deeper region of the unconscious, and he likened this depth to the fathomless depths of the ocean. And from these depths arise the forms or beings that are centers of psychic energy, and he gave these images or forms the name "archetype," which means "ancient image."

Through various means these archetypes come to our attention, whether through the images in our dreams or by some outside encounter, religious or mythical. Its imagery and meaning go within and as it makes contact with the archetypal self within something profound happens; the dreamer will be deeply stirred, will feel he has received a revelation and a new understanding, and perhaps even a new self will emerge.

Jung emphasized that the origin of archetypal symbols resides within the self, that the symbols of transformation, such as the mandala, originate within the individual. This is contrary to the ancient belief that the symbols came from outside and entered and changed the dreamer. In other words, the archetype responds to or recognizes its own image in the self. Jung did not believe that the archetype and the dream image were the same thing; the image is the form through which the archetype chooses to manifest itself. When we recognize these archetypal presences within ourselves, not outside ourselves, we begin to be transformed.

Guidance Dreams

Greek literature and the Old Testament of the Christian Bible are filled with visions and dreams of divine intervention. Why, we may ask, do we have so few, comparatively speaking, such dreams today? Is it that in those days people lived with a constant awareness of their spiritual source, as did the American Indians and other peoples of primitive cultures? Have we grown too far from our own spiritual source, is our faith today not so pure, our humility not so deep, and our goals not so noble? You may go to sleep praying that you will get a promotion or a raise in salary, that you will win in the lottery or be able to float a loan to buy that Cadillac, but maybe the higher forces are not inclined to become concerned with such needs. It is scarcely feasible to believe that God will send a messenger with guidance as to how to close that real estate deal!

All facetiousness aside, there are still today many, many despairing people humbly and sincerely praying for guidance along spiritual lines who do have comforting and helpful dreams; in other words, it seems that God (or the God within) does not extend His hand in comfort or guidance until we are about to drown in our problems, and then only when we sincerely call for help.

And how do dream messages appear? In archetypal symbols, images that are related to the soul consciousness of everyone in the world, from a source of wisdom long forgotten. In all parapsychology and also in the teaching of Carl Jung it is recognized that while most of our dreams and images come from the level that we call the unconscious, there is a far deeper, more mysterious and wiser level or source, whether called the psyche, the soul, or God, whence come our most meaningful dreams. Such dreams do not come *from* us but *through* us, and we instinctively know that they are from some limitless wellspring, profound and awesome in its depth and power.

All students of the Bible are of course aware of the many dreams in which God or one of his angels brought warnings, prophecies, or guidance to some of His mortal children in need of them. It was while Jacob slept with his head upon a stone that in a dream God appeared at the top of the ladder (symbol of ascension) and, after prophesying the blessings that were coming to Jacob, said: "And behold, I am with thee, and will keep thee in all places whither thou goest, and will bring thee again into this land; for I will not leave thee, until I have done that which I have spoken to thee of." And when Jacob awakened he said, "Surely the Lord is in this place and I knew it not." There are many more biblical examples, to say nothing of the myriad Greek myths in which a god or goddess intervened in the affairs of mortals to extricate them from horrendous predicaments.

But now let us consider some more modern dreams of archetypal figures that were harbingers of hope and faith. The first dream is that of a young man who at the time was in deep depression over the breakup of his marriage plus financial anxiety brought on by the loss of his job. His dream:

> I was standing on the shore of the ocean. It was pitch dark, the wind blowing and the rain pouring down, and the waves seemed to be rushing toward me. I felt utterly hopeless. Suddenly I felt a hand on my left shoulder. I turned to see a kindly old man in a raincoat and cap; he had a white beard and looked like a wise old sea captain. "Don't worry, son," he said. "This storm will pass." I woke up feeling better than I have for a long, long time.

It is interesting that in this dream the Wise Old Man appeared in the clothing suitable to weather any storm.

The next is also the dream of a man, of middle age, and also trying to cope with almost insurmountable problems. He was the sole support, nurse, and caretaker of his mother during a terminal illness, and he, too, was in financial straits because he could not make a living at the time. Although coming from a background of limited education and religious training, in his mature years he had become an eager student of metaphysics and eastern philosophies. When it seemed that his future was the most clouded this dream came to him:

> I was standing in the semidarkness feeling confused and rather lonely. Then it seemed like I could see a path stretching out before me. While I

stood there I saw far down on the path a figure, at first dimly, then when I drew nearer I could see clearly it was a figure of Buddha. He paused, looked back, and then raised his hand as if to beckon me onward.

The next dream is that of a woman who had undergone major surgery for a very serious condition and at the time of her dream was courageously and apparently successfully overcoming her illness.

> In my dream St. Luke came and stood right in front of me. I saw details of his clothes down to his sandals and he had close-cropped hair and a pointed beard. He spoke to me strongly, then he went away. I couldn't remember what he said but I felt it was very important and encouraging. I woke up and then I dreamed again. This time my counselor was interpreting my dream for me and said, "This is so wonderful."

When asked her association with the name St. Luke she replied that he was the saint of healing.

In this dream the archetypal star appears. The dreamer was an emotionally insecure college boy who during his vacation period was torn between the desire to spend the summer in his lovely home with his ever-loving parents or take temporary work in another town where it would be possible for him to undergo some much-needed counseling. In his ambivalence he had this dream:

> It seemed I was standing on the edge of a town. It was dusk and I felt remote and confused. Then a star appeared in the evening sky, with one ray pointing downward. It was pointing toward the place I was considering working and having counseling. My indecision was gone and I felt better.

The next dream is a very simple one from a disturbed young woman who was both mentally and emotionally immature, but, as is often the case, she dreamed in simple archetypal imagery:

> I was going to explore a deep cave, but I wasn't worried, because in my hand I had a golden thread which I knew if I got lost would lead me back out into the light.

Two strong universal symbols appear in the following dream. The dreamer was a lonely sensitive middle-aged man whose mother on the East Coast had recently died under rather tragic circumstances. Although he lived on the West Coast he had always been very close to her emotionally and his grief was hard to bear. His dream:

It was about water. I was with my mother but I couldn't see her, just knew she was there. It seemed I swam out to this island in the middle of the ocean. Mother called to me, "Hold on tight to those rocks, because a big wave is coming." All of a sudden I looked up and there was this tidal wave a hundred feet tall coming in. I said, "Oh, my God!" and Mother said, "Hold on, Son. . . ." Then the wave broke and I could just feel the water splash. It broke before it reached us and we felt the mist. And that was it.

Here again the ocean is the archetypal symbol of the universal unconscious, and the island to which he swam would probably represent his feeling of isolation and loneliness. The tremendous tidal wave symbolizes the over-whelming wave of depression under which he feared he would drown, and the warning and yet encouraging voice of his mother is symbolic of her love and concern for his welfare—and how do we know, for that matter, that his mother from wherever she might be after her death was not trying to reach him in his sleep with her love and encouragement? The fact that he did not succumb to the wave but felt only its mist (and, it might be added, felt stronger after the dream) is proof of the rightness of an admonition by Dr. Stephen Hoeller that we should not try to escape depression, but instead let ourselves "hit bottom," go through it, and by finishing that test of life emerge a stronger, wiser person.

Here is the dream of a troubled young man with a poor sense of self-worth, for which he had sought help. He had been struggling with a homosexual relationship, and while in reality he was a very personable young man, he was undergoing a lot of self-criticism. And no encouragement from someone else could have meant half as much to him as the message from his own dream did:

I was in a long dark cave. I couldn't see very well but I felt I was there for a purpose. A little light was coming through the crack from above and as I went further I discovered gleaming little veins of gold running all through the earth around me. Suddenly I felt rich and happy that this treasure was there—and I woke up with a feeling my life was going to be much more worthwhile.

The background of the next dreamer, a twenty-year-old man, had created in him a feeling of aloneness and great self-doubt. His parents divorced when he was four years old, and his mother, who really preferred his sister and constantly reminded him of it, moved with the two children back to

Europe where she had been born. Infrequent short visits to the United States had not been enough for the boy to establish any meaningful relationship with his father. Just prior to the following dream, however, he and his father had been together for about a month, during which time they visited Hearst's castle (mentioned in the dream). It is evident from his dream that a real transformation was taking place within him.

> About a ship at sea. It was a big old-fashioned ship. I think I was captain of the ship, and somehow I dropped a drinking glass into the water and I didn't want to lose it—it reminded me of the glass my father had been giving me milk and water out of, so I jumped in after it. I didn't think I was going to find it but I did find it lying on the bottom. But the wonderful part of it was that it was so beautiful down there, like a rug or floor with antique beautiful patterns. Reminded me of Hearst's castle, gorgeous! And there were treasures down there, jewelry, gold coins. And I found the glass.
>
> I think I stayed down there, or perhaps I went up to show the other crew members what it was like. I remember there was a dolphin there and I played with it and we had a lot of fun. What I remember most is that it was very beautiful down there and I had a lot of fun. It was all set up on purpose, organized beautifully but still wasn't apart from nature. Nature was there, too, with coral reefs and dolphins and fish.

Not only did he dive into the depths of his unconscious to recover the glass, a symbol of the concern his father had shown for him, but he found in the depths of his own nature beauty and joy. The mother symbol of the dolphin is particularly significant in view of his sense of rejection from his own mother. The relationship between the beauty of what he found and what he remembered of Hearst's castle is clear evidence of how much the trip (like the glass) as evidence of his father's love had meant to him. He had remembered many dreams earlier in his life, mostly troubled, but he said this was the happiest one he ever had. It is a rather Jungian dream in its use of archetypal symbols.

The next dream will be found to contain symbols of guidance and the resultant transformation. The dreamer was an intelligent and ethical young man who at the time was caught in emotional cross-currents. He had recently failed in his attempt to pass the bar, his last job had terminated through no fault of his own, he felt he really should be studying for the examination again and/or looking for another job, but meanwhile he was most comfortably ensconced in a lovely home with a devoted wife who earned an excellent salary. He vehemently stated he didn't want to be "a kept man," but he was really enjoying cooking and taking care of household duties. His logical mind had been urging him to get going; the sybaritic side of his nature was enjoying the status quo. After he firmly decided to return to his law studies he had this dream:

> It was taking place inside of a cathedral-like building, something like that, but all shiny-white tile, reminded me of an old-fashioned swimming pool. The gist of the dream was that a voice on a large PA system said that everyone was in danger and had to leave. All of a sudden there was water rising up in this cathedral or whatever. I calmly led everyone out, as the water was approaching the top. Then the people said, "You will never make it; you saved us but you will never make it." I calmly swam across the rising water as it was approaching the ceiling. Then I got out of a tiny opening. And when I got out there was a blinding white light.

During his free association he said the cathedral was like a sanctuary, very peaceful and tranquil and safe, even holy.

> Q. What do you think the cathedral symbolizes?
> A. Probably the womb. The reason I say the womb is that it was totally enclosed. I knew I was safe in there, relaxed and by myself. Maybe it was the way I felt before I left home and in a way now in our comfortable place.
> Q. How many people were in there with you?
> A. Many, many.

This dream lends itself to interpretation on two levels, both rather clearly stated. Logically he realized he was physically relaxed and safe in his comfortable protected atmosphere; metaphysically he sensed the rising of the water of his emotional anxiety in which he knew he would drown unless he made an effort to get out. (We get a modern touch here: the voice of warning does not emanate from God but comes over the PA system!) And what might the other people signify? Probably the advice and concern of his friends and relatives whom he feels he must care for before he takes care of himself. The cathedral-like structure in which his trial and resolution take place represents his truly spiritual yearning to grow into a finer person, while the way he calmly swam across the rising water is evidence of his inner strength and guidance. Finally there is his rebirth experience of emergence out of the tiny opening into the blinding white light.

He reported that the morning after the dream he felt much calmer and happier. But this question comes to mind: Was the dream the result of a conscious decision to get up and out of his problems; or, on the other hand, did his psyche respond to his confusion by coming through in a dream and, like a guardian angel, giving him the direction and strength to move out into the light? Either way, it was right and good.

There must come a time in life (and in dream interpretation) when we move from concern only with our emotional problems into a desire to see our relation to life itself, where we are and where our soul is going. It is at that time that our dreams begin to take on a larger, more universal aspect. Then we are no longer drawing from the shallower layers of the personal unconscious but from the deeper collective layers. Then we are in touch with our spiritual self, which is uniquely ours yet universal as well. Dr. Hoeller described it as "a transcendental element, a creative element, an element of ultimate wisdom that resides in the psyche and toward which we are all moving. . . ."

Rebirth and Transmutation

Just as our dreams give us symbolic information of our emotional and psychological problems, they will just as clearly later tell us when we are emerging into the light of understanding and therefore becoming a new person. Dr. Stephen Hoeller in a talk on sleeping and waking dreams clearly and beautifully described this urge of the soul for growth: "Because the human psyche contains the dynamic principle of death and resurrection, it therefore can only find growth and satisfaction by yielding to these eternal cycles. Whenever anyone is at war with this principle of nature by clinging to outlived concepts, it is inevitable that he will suffer for he is in reality at war with himself."

And what, one might ask, brings about growth or for that matter rebirth? It would seem that it never happens until the individual has met some great challenge, resolved a conflict, learned a hard lesson. When two opposing forces come together the result may be conflict but it may also be creative because with the resolution something, or the person himself, may emerge as though reborn. The opposing forces may reside within the individual as polarities, as the animus and anima, the yin and yang, or, on a more basic level, the primary instincts versus the higher instincts, self-indulgence versus self-discipline, or the wish to hurt instead of healing. When confrontation has taken place and the battle is won, the person is not just better, he is a new person.

Many people have felt that after they had met and resolved a deep conflict within themselves transmutation has taken place. Even without their conscious awareness their psyche will tell them in a dream. Some symbols of transmutation or entering a new stage of consciousness include crossing a stream or bridge, climbing a mountain, searching through caves, emerging from the ocean, finding gold or jewelry, slaying a dragon, the mandala, giving birth, or something beautiful you thought was dead coming to life. Carl Jung said he had found that when an individual seeks wholeness the circle or mandala may appear in his dream. In fact, he explained the "flying saucers" observed by many as the release of spiritual energy by nations of people as they are seeking to grow; as we reach for higher consciousness the energy manifests itself in the heavens in the form of mandalas or whirling circles of light.

The dream experience given below was a complete puzzle to the dreamer until Dr. Jung's theory was brought into the interpretation. The dreamer was a middle-aged man who sought through counseling to find some meaning to his life, a life that had started with complete rejection from his father, which robbed him of any sense of self-worth, and had seemed to be a series of disappointments and heartaches. Because of the quality of his nature (humility of spirit, sensitivity to music and beauty—he had tried his hand at poetry and as a youngster had played the mouth organ beautifully) he was a receptive subject for analysis. After the release of pent-up resentment and rage he eagerly sought some metaphysical answer as to why his soul had been so tested and what he could do to transcend it. And then he had this dream:

> It was night and I was alone. I noticed some light and as I looked up at the sky I saw many circles of light moving and whirling through the sky. As they moved they gave off rays of light. I stood and watched them for some time; there were many of them and they were very beautiful.

Sometime later he had another dream that is archetypal in symbology also:

> It was daytime, and up in the sky I saw a sort of platform and on it was a great box, all in white, and as I watched out of the box flew a great white bird that rose higher and higher into the sky.

15

Reincarnation

There are people to whom the concept of reincarnation is reasonable and there are just as many to whom it is not. However, with no attempt to prove anything, it is still interesting to study dreams that seem totally unrelated to the dreamer's present life experience.

Occasionally there will be a recurring dream repeating the same theme that seems to have no association with anything in the dreamer's memory. Usually in such dreams the setting, the clothing, and the people themselves seem to belong to another place, another time, an earlier historical era. In relating such a dream the individual will nearly always remark, "I felt I was really there" or "I just knew this was a place I had really been at some time."

Just as important experiences, particularly traumas, in this life often leave such an impression upon the psyche that one keeps reliving them both awake and asleep, one wonders if it is also possible that the vividness of some trauma or the strength of some attachment in a prior lifetime might have left its impression so deep in the unconscious memory that it can carry over to the next life and float to the surface in a strange and meaningful dream. Regardless of the validity of this concept of *déjà vu* dreams (which we must admit it is impossible to prove), it is still an interesting, even exciting theory to contemplate.

It seemed almost impossible to interpret the dreams given below as having any relation whatsoever to the dreamer's present life pattern. The first is the dream, almost a visitation (which Jung interprets as one and the same) of an eighty-year-old woman, healthy and mentally alert:

I lay down in the afternoon for a nap. Then it seemed I saw a long scroll unrolling before me. It seemed to be starting at the present time and unrolling backward. I knew it was showing me something about myself. Faces appeared on the scroll, one face after another: women's faces, men's faces, some English, some French, different nationalities. Their hairstyle and their costumes went further and further back in time. As I watched I had the feeling that they were people I had known, or perhaps had once been myself. [Then, as a gentle afterthought] They were good faces!

From whatever source, the next dream certainly contained tragic implications. It is the recurring dream of a thin, quiet young woman, the wife of a minister. In seeking the stimulus of the dream no memory or experience such as abuse or persecution in this lifetime was uncovered that could explain why she had the dream.

I am always standing in the middle of a cobblestone courtyard. I feel it is in Europe somewhere. I am surrounded by a circle of people who are taunting me and throwing stones at me. Because I am tied to a post I cannot move, so there is nothing to do but stand there. I feel the stones hit me, one by one—I really feel them and they hurt terribly. Then I just don't know anything any more. I guess I died.

The next is a pleasanter example of a memory, if it is a memory, and again nothing in the dreamer's life was in any way related. She was a small, very feminine girl of Jewish background, born and reared in New York City, and, incidentally, not at all athletic, with no desire to be anything but an attractive girl.

I have had many dreams with always the same theme. I am always in the West and always a man. Often I am on horseback, wearing heavy clothes, chaps, and boots. It seems long ago, like in pioneer days. And there's always a feeling of pleasure as I ride across the plains.

Then she had another one:

I was in a wagon train going West. It was daylight, mountains all around. We weren't quite to California but I knew that was where we were going. We were all dressed in clothes of the 1800s.

The next dream is that of a young woman born in Germany, orphaned as a baby, adopted very young by an American couple, and reared in the United States.

My dream was very real and very frightening. I was in a city that I knew was in Europe. A war was going on, bombs falling and tanks rolling through the streets. My mother and sister and I were refugees and we were pushing a cart with an old man in it, and all of our personal belongings. The shooting was getting closer to us and we ran and hid in a doorway.

Right after that everything became very strange. I was wandering alone through the streets. I could not find my mother and sister and didn't know what had happened to them. I would go up to people on the street and when I asked them to help me they acted as though they did not see or hear me, as though I didn't exist. I felt frightened and totally lost.

In free association she said she had the feeling the city was Berlin although she had never been there. When asked what did she think the dream meant, she replied, "I feel I was really there, and that once I died there."

Here is another unhappy dream (after all, aren't the traumatic memories the hardest to forget?) that the dreamer, a young woman, had had several times, each time so real she would wake up gasping for breath:

I am in deep water, and drowning. I can't swim, I keep struggling to stay on top and can't. And as I go down deeper and deeper the water turns from pale green to dark blue. And then it all turns dark and sort of peaceful. I guess I just died.

A mature woman reported the next dream, fortunately much less dramatic than the preceding ones, but nevertheless meaningful to her. She is single, of Swedish descent, and she herself has never been out of the United States.

I keep dreaming I am in England. I see the same house each time, an English type, and as I stand out on the neat front lawn my husband emerges from the house. He's a rather stocky man, with a ruddy complexion, and he's always smoking a pipe. That is all there is to the dream—I am there, he is there, and I know we are in England. And it is very real.

The next dream is that of a twenty-three-year-old man who had never been out of the United States and who said he had read almost nothing about Egypt. He said the dream was more than a dream, it was an "experience":

This has happened over and over. It always takes place in a hot sandy desert. I am one of a long line of men, we are all naked to the waist and are struggling to drag very heavy stones across the sand. We are taking them to a pyramid being built. It seems endless. The sun is boiling down.

I am always very hot and exhausted. What a relief to wake up from that dream!

The next dreamer, a man, had also never been out of the United States:

> I am in this underground passageway, like a thousand years ago, and there is a stairway at the far end. A man is behind me, but it seems like he has no face. Along one side it was full of cobwebs, a dusty, dank place. Dead bodies were stored in little apartment-like places, all in wooden caskets or wrapped in cloth. There were creaky noises. Oil lanterns. I took my little lantern and looked in these little dark crevices, trying to understand what made the noise. I knew it couldn't be the dead bodies. It was a scary dream.

Not only had this man never seen, he said he had never heard of the catacombs in Italy.

The young woman who related the following dream said at the beginning she was confident she had been shown glimpses of her past lives.

> Someone took me by the hand and said, "Come with me." They led me to a stairway, one that seemed to go up and up a long way. A woman was on the first step and my guide told me her name, then I was told the name of the girl on the next step, and then step by step I was introduced to other people, some young, some old, and given their names. When I woke up I remembered some of their names but the only one I can remember now is Celeste. As we progressed their clothes were more and more of other eras and I knew we were going backward in time. Each, I felt, was a life I had lived, personalities I had once been.

The next two dreams are those of a twelve-year-old girl who had lived all of her life in Malibu in southern California and never been more than fifty miles from home. She is a rather solemn dark-eyed girl, with braided hair. Her name, instead of Brenda, could be Minnehaha. She has one much younger brother.

> In the dream I felt I was maybe in northern California or some place like that. There were brown leaves on the ground and my brother, a little older than me, and I were running through the woods. We were barefoot and had simple clothes on. We saw a young deer and my brother, who was brown-skinned and very strong, told me he was going to see if he could creep up on the deer and kill it with a stone. That was all I remember.

A short time later she had this dream:

> My mother gave me some money to buy myself some new sandals. As I
> started across the street, it turned into a dusty path. On the other side of
> the path was an old lean-to kind of shed with a slanting roof and in front
> there were some boards laid across a wood sawhorse that made a kind of
> counter. On it were some beaded moccasins and other Indian things. An
> old Indian man showed them to me and I bought a pair of moccasins
> from him. As I started to leave I saw a pretty flat pink stone with a hole in
> it and a leather thong to put around the neck. I liked it so much the old
> Indian gave it to me.

On being asked if she had any feeling she had lived before this life she replied immediately, "I know I was once an American Indian. I feel so close to
them that whenever I see them in a movie I want to walk into the picture
and put my arms around them and hug them. Sometimes when I think of
them I want to cry."

Incidentally, this little girl had a predilection, which brought much concern and consternation to the fire department, of running off into the
wooded hills above the town and with another little girl building small fires
out of a pile of sticks.

The girl who had the next dream was a young married woman, quite
metaphysically inclined. She believed in reincarnation and had several
dreams that might be interpreted with that meaning. When she related
the dream given below she said it had been so vivid she felt she was really
experiencing it, had really been there. Interestingly in the dream she moves
back and forth in time.

> It was like back in the goldrush mining days. I was riding through
> the hills with a man who was a stranger; I had just met up with him and
> I didn't know him or he me. We were looking for a town, any kind
> of town. We saw smoke coming from a chimney and we followed it into
> this town and kept on riding until we came to this little house; it was as
> though we were meant to head toward this house. We opened the door
> and there were this very old man and woman lying on two single mat-
> tresses placed together in the middle of the room. It was like they were
> waiting for us.
>   The man rolled over to one side and the man I was with lay down in his
> place, then he beckoned for me to come over and lie down in the woman's
> place, which I did. I felt like we and the old people were somehow the
> same, but we were back when they were young.

Pretty soon the door opened and another man walked in and I knew he was looking for me and was there to hurt me. But something else comes into it at this time, the fact that I had had a baby; at this time I was not pregnant and didn't have a baby but I knew that I had been pregnant.

I got up when this man came in. He had a gun and somehow I wrestled it away from him and headed him out the door and made him go to the sheriff's office. I told the sheriff this man had tried to hurt me and he took the gun away from him and locked him up. Two men were there talking and I knew they were talking about the fact that I had been pregnant. I turned around to them and said, "Women can handle a great deal more than men think they can."

If the content of these dreams did not arise from unconscious memories of this life, whence did they come? Many wise and sincere people have totally accepted the theory that we have lived many lives and that, through the law of cause and effect, each of us in this incarnation is reaping the results, good or bad, of past actions. The most logical and hopeful aspect of this belief, which is called the law of karma, is that we can believe that we are given another chance, an opportunity in this life to learn what we didn't learn before, to atone for previous mistakes and to proceed further on the path of growth. None other than the wise and profound Carl Jung believed in reincarnation, as evidenced in his book *Memories, Dreams, Reflections*, in which he describes how he felt an instant strong identity with a man who had lived two generations before, including recognizing the elegant carriage in which he "remembered" having ridden, and feeling that he had worn exactly the same shoes.

# 16

Conclusion

While the purpose of this book has been to give the reader as simple and yet as broad an understanding as possible of the symbology and techniques necessary for the interpretation of dreams, it must not be forgotten that dream analysis is a subtle and complex procedure—there are no simple answers or cut-and-dried interpretations. Not only is the free association of the dreamer essential, but also of major importance are the experience and subjectivity of the interpreter. The understanding of dreams is a highly creative process, requiring not only knowledge and understanding but, most important, intuition.

The dream is a great humanizer. In the instincts and impulses of our dreams we are all kin. The egotist, confronted with his darker shadow self, can only accept humility; the timid person, troubled by inferiority, may by decoding the messages of his dreams gain a feeling of much greater worth.

If one wants to improve, it is not essential to give more attention to the development of one's outstanding virtues—they are already developed or they wouldn't be "outstanding"—but to focus instead on discovering and transmuting the "devils" in the basement. Except for the experience of hypnosis, there seems to be no way but dreams by which hidden pressures and attitudes can be revealed. Once the pressure required to contain unacceptable, hidden drives has been removed—once the "lid" is off—individuals find that the energy spent in repression can now be released into other and much happier channels. They become more loving, often full of creative ideas, and even their sex lives become more fulfilling.

No one could have expressed all this more beautifully than Carl Jung:

The dream is the small hidden secret door in the deepest and most intimate sanctum of the soul, which opens into the primeval cosmic night, that was so, long before a conscious ego, and will be so far beyond what the conscious ego can ever reach. . . . In dreams we pass into the deeper and more universal truth and more eternal man, who still stands in the dusk of original night in which he himself was still the whole and the whole was in him in bright undifferentiated pure nature free from the shackles of the ego. From these all-uniting depths rises the dream, however childish, grotesque or immoral.

It is the author's hope that this book has helped to open that "small hidden door" for the reader.

Bibliography

Allen, Mary Wood. *What a Young Woman Ought to Know*. Philadelphia: Vir Publishing Company, 1898.

Dunbar, Helen Flanders. *Mind and Body: Psychosomatic Medicine*. New York: Random House, 1947.

Fenichel, Otto. *The Psychoanalytic Theory of Neurosis*. New York: Norton, 1945.

Freud, Sigmund. *Basic Writings of Sigmund Freud*. New York: Random House, 1935.

Guethel, Emile A. *The Handbook of Dream Analysis*. New York: Liveright Publishing Co., 1951.

Harding, Esther. *Woman's Mysteries*. New York: Pantheon, 1955.

Horney, Karen. *Collected Works of Karen Horney*. New York: M. W. Norton and Co., 1942.

―――. *Our Inner Conflicts*. New York: Norton, 1945.

―――. *Self-Analysis*. New York: Norton, 1942.

Jastrow, Joseph. *Freud, His Dream and Sex Theories*. New York: Pocket Books, 1932.

Jung, Carl G. *Flying Saucers*. New York: Harcourt, Brace and Co., 1959.

―――. *Man and His Symbols*. New York: Doubleday, 1969.

―――. *Memories, Dreams, Reflections*. Edited by Aniela Jaffe. New York: Random House, 1965.

―――. *Modern Man in Search of a Soul*. New York: Harcourt Brace Jovanovich, 1955.

―――. *Psychology and Alchemy*. New York: Pantheon, 1953.

Maltz, Maxwell. *Psychocybernetics*. New York: Prentice-Hall, 1960.

Menninger, Karl A. *The Human Mind*. 3rd edition. New York: Alfred A. Knopf, 1951.

Mullahy, Patrick. *Oedipus Myth and Complex*. New York: Hermitage Press, 1948.

Schaer, Hans. *Religion and the Cure of Souls in Jung's Psychology*. New York: Pantheon, 1950.

Seabury, David S. *Growing into Life*. New York: Blue Ribbon Publishing, 1928.

———. *High Hopes for Low Spirits*. New York: Little, Brown and Co., 1955.

———. *Why We Love and Hate*. Los Angeles: The Commonwealth Press, 1955.

Toksvig, Signe. *Emanuel Swedenborg, Scientist and Mystic*. Biography Index Reprint Series. New York: Ayer Company, 1972.

Woods, Ralph L., and Herbert B. Greenhouse. *The New World of Dreams*. New York: Macmillan, 1974.

Index

Adler, Alfred, 4
Africa: dreams in cultures of, 4
Age: significance of, in dreams, 66
Aggression: dream images of, 3, 109,
    113–14, 165, 166, 167, 172, 199; anal, 171;
    oral, 62, 95–96, 164, 165, 167–68, 180;
    verbal, 176–77
Albertus Magnus, 210
Allen, Mrs. Mary Wood: *What a Young
    Woman Ought to Know*, 136–37
Alter ego in dreams, 84, 109, 116, 122, 128,
    139, 141, 156, 158, 160, 161
Anal stage of child development, 12
Analyst, 10, 35, 109, 155
—role of, in interpretation of dreams, 17,
    18, 19, 20, 22, 27, 43, 44, 142, 225
—dream images of, 43, 44, 79, 89, 91–92,
    101, 110, 121, 127, 158, 163, 175, 189, 197,
    207–208, 213
Animals as dream symbols, 9, 164–81 *pas-
    sim*, 207, 208–209; bats, 175; bear, 167;
    birds, 175–76, 209; bull, 207, 208; but-
    terfly, 4, 179, 207, 209; cat, 173–74; cow,
    172, 207, 208; crocodile, 167, 180; dog,
    159, 172–73; dolphin, 159–60; dragon,
    175, 202, 207; elephant, 168; fish, 176–
    78; goat, 172; horse, 169–71, 208; in-
    sects, 178–79; lamb, 172; lion, 165–66,
    198; mule, 171; pig, 172; rabbit, 169; rep-
    tiles, 179–81; rodents, 174; sheep, 172;
    snakes, 180, 207, 209; tiger, 166, 198;
    unicorn, 172, 207, 208; wolf, 158, 167
Animus/anima, 12, 58, 60, 61–68 *passim*,
    73, 78, 84, 86, 87, 90, 102, 116, 155, 159,
181, 190, 196, 217; as archetypes, 208; de-
    fined, 58–59, 145; in female dreams, 84,
    85, 92, 124, 127, 130; in male dreams, 136
Anxiety in dreams, 106; sexual, 5, 42, 120–
    22, 124–26, 135–36, 202
Aquinas, Saint Thomas, 210
Archetypes in dreams, 3, 7, 11, 13, 14, 60,
    81, 83, 162, 175, 187, 188, 202, 205, 206–18
    passim
Artemidorus Daldianus, 4
Astrology, 206

Bible, 3, 4, 11, 39, 56, 81, 82, 93, 100, 177,
    192, 207, 211, 212
Birth: giving of, in dreams, 145–46. *See
    also* Pregnancy; Traumas, during birth
Bisexuality and dreams, 129–30, 177
Blindness: significance of, in dreams, 99
Blockage, psychic: and dreams, 20–21, 25,
    98, 121
Body, parts of: and dreams, 93, 95–97

Castration: fear of, 42, 93, 96, 98, 110, 117,
    122, 123–24, 171; female urge to commit,
    128–29
Catharsis, dreams of, 10, 104, 112, 113, 146,
    184. *See also* Wish fulfillment
Censor: role of, in dreams, 5, 6, 7, 15, 34,
    45, 105, 117, 198. *See also* Conscience
Chiang Tzu, 4
Children: dreams of, 198–204; images of,
    in dreams, 2, 84, 85, 86, 87–88, 103,
    145–46
Climbing: dream images of, 107

Clowns: dream images of, 90
Collective unconscious. *See* Racial unconscious
Community: dream images of, 92–93
Compensation, mechanism of, 39–40
Condensation, mechanism of, 41–42
Conditioning, childhood, 72
Conscience, dream images of, 89–90. *See also* Censor

David Seabury School of Psychology, 4. *See also* Seabury, David
Daydreams, 35, 198, 217
Deafness: significance of, in dreams, 99–100
Death: significance of, in dreams, 11, 47, 102, 103–104, 148–50
Death wish, 146, 149, 150, 174
Depression, 5
Diary: role of, in recording dreams, 16
Displacement, mechanism of, 7, 42, 46, 79, 91, 96, 112, 117, 118, 121, 122, 124, 128, 133, 179, 184, 188
Distortion, mechanism of, 45–48
Diving: significance of, in dreams, 108–109
Doubling, 46
Dreams: analysis of, 4–5, 7, 12, 15, 16, 17–19, 26–33 *passim*, 34, 36, 56, 74, 103, 128–29, 225
—books on, 1
—frequency of, 6
—patterns of, 17
—recording of, 15–17, 18
—relationship of, to life style, 34
—settings of, 30. *See also* Location
—stimuli of, 19–20, 45–46, 146–47, 157, 161, 162, 169, 204, 220
—types of, 7–8
—universality of, 15
Dreamer: roles of, in dreams, 18–19
Drinking: significance of, in dreams, 112–13
Drunkenness: significance of, in dreams, 99
Drowning: significance of, in dreams, 109, 146–47
Dunbar, Dr. Helen Flanders: *Psychosomatic Diagnosis and Treatment*, 147
Dwarf: significance of, in dreams, 90

Eating: significance of, in dreams, 112
Ego, 6, 7, 14, 16, 22, 34, 38, 46, 48, 49, 52–54, 55, 57, 58, 74, 75, 93, 95, 101, 103, 105, 108, 117, 121, 122, 152, 189, 196, 205
Ejaculation: dream images of, 112, 113, 120
Elden, Dr. Frederick cam, 35
Elimination, function of: significance of, in dreams, 113, 184
Emerson, Ralph Waldo, 206
Enemy: role of, in dreams, 31, 33, 90, 102, 103, 116, 198, 200
Entrapment: significance of, in dreams, 101
Escapism: dream images of, 7–8, 98, 99, 100, 104, 192
Exaggeration, mechanism of, 54
Examination: significance of, in dreams, 163
Exhibitionism, 100, 175

Falling: significance of, in dreams, 108, 192
Father: dream images of, 82–83, 85, 92
Fenichel, Dr. Otto: *The Psychoanalytic Theory of Neurosis*, 137
Fire: significance of, in dreams, 200
Flying: significance of, in dreams, 104–106, 200–201
Food: significance of, in dreams, 183, 190
Foreigners: significance of, in dreams, 90, 192
Free association, 11, 13, 14, 21, 45, 78, 84, 91, 93, 96, 100, 107, 112, 114–15, 116, 189
—examples of, 21–22, 23–24, 30, 31–32, 41–42, 44, 47–48, 99, 102–103, 119, 138, 141, 149–50, 156, 159, 160, 178, 216, 221
—role of, in interpretation of dreams, 8, 20, 21, 22–25, 27, 29, 33, 35, 36, 40, 70, 80, 90, 172, 192, 225
Freud, Sigmund, 1, 4, 10, 12, 13–14, 15, 17, 18, 19, 21, 28, 34, 35, 42, 43, 48, 50, 52–53, 60, 76, 78, 85, 100, 106–107, 109, 115, 117, 118, 126, 129, 153, 210
Frigidity, sexual: images of, in dreams, 88, 99, 117, 118, 119, 123, 124–25, 139, 142, 154–55

Growth, emotional: dream images of, 72, 154–63 *passim*, 190, 192, 195, 217
Gutheil, Emil, 4
Guidance, dreams of, 2, 8, 11, 81–82, 83, 91, 198, 205, 207, 210, 211–18
Guilt: effect of, on dreams, 3, 5, 22, 29, 32, 42, 48, 80, 87, 94, 95, 96, 97–98, 110, 112, 113, 116, 117, 122, 123, 131, 135, 136, 137,

142, 174, 178, 180, 184, 189, 194, 201, 202, 203

Hall, Manley, 56, 104
Hiding: significance of, in dreams, 110
Hoeller, Dr. Stephen A., 16, 35, 36, 53–54, 206, 207, 214, 217
Homosexuality and dreams, 69, 92, 93–94, 97, 98, 102, 110–11, 112, 116, 117, 122–23, 129, 130–33, 177, 179, 180, 185, 194, 214
Horney, Karen, 4
Hypnosis, 5–6, 225

Id, 9, 10, 49–50, 51, 56, 57, 58, 165, 174, 191, 193, 204
Illness: symbolic meaning of, in dreams, 20, 93, 97, 153; mental, 93, 174; psychosomatic, 70
Imbalance, psychic: and dreams, 151, 152
Immorality in dreams, 10, 35–36. *See also* Taboos
Impotency, male: and dreams, 99, 115, 120, 121, 123, 139
Incest and dreams, 51, 76, 77, 81, 91, 92, 93, 97, 98, 110, 117, 120, 121, 125, 142–43, 189. *See also* Oedipal attachment
Indians, American, 4, 90, 211
Introjection, mechanism of, 72
Intruder: significance of, in dreams, 88–89, 92
Inversion, 40–41, 59, 62, 63, 65. *See also* Animus/anima; Homosexuality; Lesbianism

Jastrow, Joseph: *Freud, His Dream and Sex Theories*, 10, 34
Jung, Carl, 1, 4, 12–14, 15, 18, 19, 25, 34, 35, 43, 50, 58, 59, 60, 68, 74, 90, 145, 148, 153, 155, 206, 208, 210–11, 215, 218, 219, 225–26; *Memories, Dreams, Reflections*, 224; *Modern Man in Search of a Soul*, 51

Karma, law of, 224
Kant, Immanuel, 36
Killing: dream images of, 110

Landscape: significance of, in dreams, 192–93, 207
Laughter: significance of, in dreams, 104
Lesbianism, dream symbols of, 133–35. *See also* Homosexuality; Inversion
Libido, 49, 50–52, 53, 66, 192

Light: significance of, in dreams, 196–97
Location: significance of, in dreams, 100. *See also* Position

Madonna/prostitute complex, 138, 141–42
Mandala, 207, 218
Marriage, dream images of, 91
Masochism, dream images of, 97, 204
Masturbation, dream images of, 96, 98, 107, 114, 117, 123, 135–37, 180
Meditation, 25
Metaphysics, 210
Mirrors, dream images of, 37, 71
Monsters, dream images of, 174, 204
Moral judgment, as revealed in dreams, 19
Mother, dream images of, 80–81, 83, 215
Motion: significance of, in dreams, 114–15
Mythology, 15, 36, 207, 208; Greek, 4, 11, 12, 14, 21, 41, 56, 59–60, 75–76, 81, 82, 211, 212

Nakedness, dream images of, 100
Narcissism, 12, 100, 173, 175
Natural elements: significance of, in dreams, 193–97, 207; as archetypes, 209–10
New World of Dreams, The, 35
Nightmares, 8–9, 14, 36, 37, 61, 69, 90, 92, 101–102, 108, 131, 152, 194, 204, 208. *See also* Problem dreams

Ocean. *See* Water
Oedipal attachment, 12, 75, 76, 77–79, 81, 102, 143, 170–71, 172, 193–94. *See also* Incest
Oedipus, legend of, 75–76. *See also* Mythology, Greek
Oral stage of child development, 12

Pandora, myth of, 21, 41
Paralysis, dream images of, 98, 101
Paranoia, 151
Parapsychology, 211
Parents and dreams, 55, 80. *See also* Incest; Oedipal attachment
Penis envy, 126–28, 129. *See also* Phallus
People: significance of, in dreams, 2
Persona, 12–13, 58, 68, 69, 70, 71, 73, 74, 75, 85, 95, 97, 99, 182, 185. *See also* Shadow self
Pets, dream images of, 164, 172–74, 176. *See also* Animals
Phallus, dream images of, 24, 40, 95, 96,

97, 102, 110, 118, 119, 126, 132, 133, 148, 172, 174, 175, 178, 179, 180, 191, 202, 203, 209. *See also* Penis envy
Philosophical Research Society, 16
Plato, 10
Position: significance of, in dreams, 81, 116
Pregnancy, dreams of, 87, 100, 145, 167. *See also* Birth
Problem dreams, 8
Projection, mechanism of, 38–39, 42, 59, 72, 84, 202
Prophetic dreams, 11. *See also* Guidance dreams
Psyche, 3, 6, 13, 18, 22, 39, 45, 53, 59, 60, 64, 68, 70, 93, 105, 106, 109, 145, 146, 162, 179, 192, 193, 205, 206, 207, 208, 209, 211, 217, 218, 219
Psychoanalysis: dream analysis during, 10, 17, 18, 53, 155–56
Pubic hair, dream images of, 137–38, 174
Purchasing: significance of, in dreams, 190
Pygmalian, myth of, 59–60. *See also* Mythology, Greek

Racial unconscious, 12, 13, 60, 178, 195, 202, 206, 211, 214. *See also* Archetypes
Rage and dreams, 3, 5, 77, 80, 96, 97, 101, 110, 112, 113, 117, 126, 174, 191, 195–96, 200
Rank, Otto, 146
Rape and dreams, 98, 102, 123, 124
Rebirth, psychic: dream images of, 86, 87, 88, 145, 162, 216, 217–18. *See also* Reincarnation and dreams
Reincarnation and dreams, 219–24
Religion and dreams, 15, 94, 198, 205, 206
Revenge, dream images of, 52, 174
Role models, 91
Running: significance of, in dreams, 107

Sadism, dream images of, 69, 97, 152, 164, 173, 176, 180, 204
Sadomasochism, dream images of, 110, 123
Saint/satyr complex, 138, 139–41
Schaer, Hans, *Religion and the Cure of Souls in Jung's Psychology*, 59
Seabury, Dr. David, 50, 55, 112, 146
Self, dream images of, 83
Sexual instinct, 50
Sexual intercourse, dream symbols of, 120
Sexual molestation, dream symbols of, 202, 203, 204

Sexual themes in dreams, 51, 90, 92, 96, 97, 101, 107–108, 110–11, 112, 113, 114, 115, 117–43 *passim*, 163, 170, 174, 176, 180, 182, 184, 186–87, 190, 195
Shadow self, 12–13, 39, 58, 68–69, 70, 71–75 *passim*, 84–85, 89, 93, 94, 158, 159, 161, 182, 185, 225. *See also* Persona
Shame, 100
Sibling rivalry, dream images of, 85–86, 89, 112, 174, 201, 204
Size: significance of, in dreams, 44–45, 177, 180
Sleepwalking, 115
Soul. *See* Psyche
Spiritual dreams. *See* Guidance dreams
Status quo dreams, 8, 10
Stekel, Wilhelm, 4
Sterility, fear of, 171
Structures: significance of, in dreams, 182–88
Subversion, mechanism of, 104
Superconscious, 8, 56, 57–58, 101, 205
Superego, 36, 54–56, 57, 92, 94, 98, 110, 188, 189, 198
Swedenborg, Emanuel, 59, 78
Swimming: significance of, in dreams, 106–107
Symbology, 3, 5, 6, 11, 14, 15, 16, 17, 18, 29, 30, 35, 36, 66, 67, 69, 78, 79, 82, 111, 117, 118, 122, 148, 151, 153, 162, 170, 174, 183, 195, 198, 203; classifications of, 7; Egyptian, 196; female, 30, 183; personal, 7, 8; sexual, 118

Taboos, 5, 10, 93, 117, 157
Talking in one's sleep, 115
Talmud, 5, 11, 36
Teachers, dream images of, 91, 207, 208
Temperature: significance of, in dreams, 99
Transference, mechanism of, 42, 43, 44
Transposition, mechanism of, 42–43, 48
Traumas, 5, 8, 34, 45, 87, 180, 182, 219, 221
—during birth, 101, 106, 144–45
—prenatal, 147–48
Twinning. *See* Doubling

Unconscious, 13, 16, 17, 18, 21, 34, 36, 51, 89, 121, 136, 146, 154, 157, 158, 162, 169, 171, 175, 183, 184, 185, 191, 195, 196, 215
—areas of, 49–79 *passim*
—and dreams, 6, 14, 15, 25
—and conscious, 6, 39

—mechanisms of, 38
—study of, 12
—symbols of, 108–109, 160, 194
—theory of, 210

Villain in dreams, 91. *See also* Enemy

Walls: significance of, in dreams, 191
Warning, dreams of, 150–53
Water: significance of, in dreams, 108–109,
   160, 175, 176, 191, 195, 206, 209, 214
Wise Old Man: as dream symbol, 3, 205,
   206, 207, 212

Wish fulfillment, dreams of, 8, 9, 10, 13, 35,
   46, 47, 99, 114, 115, 198, 200
Woman: archetypes of, in dreams, 81–82,
   83
Womb, dream images of, 48, 79, 109,
   146–47, 177, 194, 216
Woods, Ralph L., 198
Words: as elements in dreams, 42

Yin/yang, 12, 59, 175, 217. *See also* Animus/
   anima